SPRINGTOWN 1967

VICTORIA HIGH SCHOOL 1877

ST LURACH'S 1900

DUNCREGGAN 1928

FOYLE COLLEGE 1814

The first boys' school was the Free School founded by Springham in Schoolhouse Lane (Society St.) in 1617. This later became known as the Diocesan School of Derry and moved in 1814 to Strand Road where the name Foyle College was later adopted.

In 1868 a rival school – the Academical Institution was set up, moving to Academy Road in 1877.

In 1896 the two merged as Foyle College which later moved to Springtown in 1967 and amalgamated with the High School in 1976

STRAND HOUSE SCHOOL 1860

VICTORIA HIGH SCHOOL 1877

LONDONDERRY HIGH SCHOOL 1928

ST LURACH'S 1900

ollege 1617-1994

M.H.Gillespie '93-'94

A View the Foyle Commanding

A Portrait of Foyle College

A View the Foyle Commanding

A Portrait of Foyle College

General Editor: Sean McMahon

THIRD MILLENNIUM
PUBLISHING, LONDON

She left the walls and occupied
A grove the Foyle commanding…

The song of Foyle College.

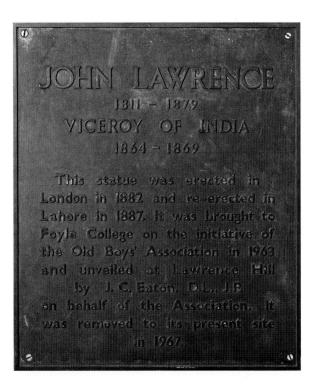

JOHN LAWRENCE
1811 – 1879
VICEROY OF INDIA
1864 – 1869

This statue was erected in
London in 1882 and re-erected in
Lahore in 1887. It was brought to
Foyle College on the initiative of
the Old Boys' Association in 1963
and unveiled at Lawrence Hill
by J. C. Eaton, D.L. J.P.
on behalf of the Association. It
was removed to its present site
in 1967

Contents

LONDONDERRY.

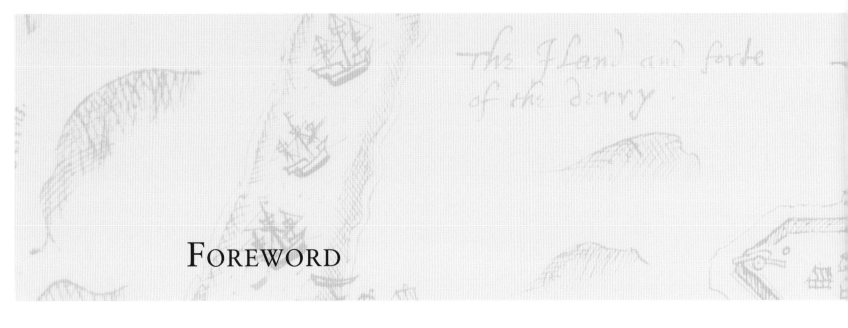

FOREWORD

I am delighted to accept the invitation to write the foreword to *A View the Foyle Commanding*. As one who has lived in Londonderry for over 30 years and who has been diocesan bishop and a school governor I have the utmost admiration for Foyle.

Foyle has a well-deserved reputation of being an outstanding, inclusive school in which young people from different traditions and backgrounds are made welcome and learn and work together. This diversity creates a unique enrichment which few schools can emulate. Foyle can rightly claim that it has made a major contribution in helping young people to respect diversity and to appreciate that the things we have in common are far more significant than those that divide us.

The story of Foyle has evolved over four centuries. Founded by Matthew Springham in 1617 as the Free Grammar School, it became Foyle College, Derry in 1814 and later merged with Londonderry Academical Institution (LAI) in 1896. Further mergers took place among schools in the city until in 1976 an amalgamation took place between Foyle and Londonderry High School creating the first co-educational grammar school in the city.

Londonderry High School, a product of many strands, like Foyle has a long tradition going back over many years. In 1860 a girls' school was established in Hawkin Street. Later it moved to larger premises on Strand Road and became known as Strand House School. The founding of Londonderry Ladies Collegiate School in 1877 and St Lurach's in 1900 were significant historical developments. When Foyle and Londonderry High School were amalgamated each brought the richness of their historical past into the new situation.

Foyle has had several important links with the Church of Ireland diocese of Derry, and two names stand out. William King, appointed Bishop of Derry in 1691, was a major influence in the rebuilding of the city severely damaged during the siege and in providing financial support for education. The other name was William Knox, who became bishop in 1803. He provided a site for the school on diocesan land in Strand Road, as well as financial support. He also used his office to obtain the financial backing of the Irish Society, the London Livery Companies and several civic and private benefactors.

In many respects the history of Foyle mirrors the history of the city. The school has helped to shape the city and in turn it has been shaped by momentous local events. The 17th-century siege, the 19th-century emigration from Ireland through the port and the civil unrest and violence of the 20th and 21st centuries have left a unique historical legacy. In understanding communities and institutions while we look back and reflect on our roots in history it is important to look to the future. The story of a school such as Foyle is essentially about people – principally young people – and their future in education and in society.

You can celebrate the past and you can learn from the past but you cannot live in the past. May the past be an inspiration and give hope that the best years of Foyle are yet to come.

Rt Revd Dr James Mehaffey – Retd Bishop of Derry and Raphoe

OPPOSITE: *View of Londonderry c.1900, from a hand-coloured postcard.*

HEADMASTERS' PREFACES

I believe that the essence of a school comprises the community the school serves, the parents who entrust their children to it, the pupils and teachers themselves and their experiences during their school years in determining their futures. All of these are represented in this book which attempts to capture the essence of Foyle College 400 years after its foundation.

I hope it is of wider interest than merely to former pupils. The school has been a fundamental part of the life of Londonderry and its hinterland through all of those 400 years, and anyone interested in the Plantation, the Siege or the Troubles will gain insight into those great events by the light shone upon them by the recollections of those who lived through them.

This book is built from components housed in the school archive and can only represent a small fraction of everything contained in that archive. We are fortunate as a school to have retained such a wealth of material accumulated over 400 years. Even more fortunate is having people who care so passionately about the school that they are willing to maintain the archive and mine it for its wealth of detail. Amongst other things, I hope it will stimulate a response from others to deepen and enrich our understanding of the past of Foyle College.

Jack Magill (Headmaster 1994–2012)

Aristotle wrote: 'The whole is greater than the sum of the parts' and it is especially true when schools are moulded by people and events in the past and in the present. A school is a living entity, which grows and develops to meet the demands placed upon it by society. The staff, the pupils and their parents all contribute to that growth.

The 400-year story of Foyle is here recorded as we look forward to celebrating the school's quatercentenary in 2017. I hope that it will be of wide interest as the school has played a fundamental role in the life of the city and its surrounding area throughout its history. Anyone with an interest in our history can gain additional insight into those events through the light shone upon them by the recollections of those who lived through them as part of Foyle.

It is a delight, for example, to have the first register from 1814 containing the name and signature of George Fletcher Moore, the pupil who proposed the name Foyle College. I hope you enjoy reading *A View the Foyle Commanding*.

Patrick Allen (Appointed Headmaster, September 2012)

OPPOSITE: *Aerial view of the Foyle and Derry City, looking north-east.*

EDITOR'S INTRODUCTION

The task of writing the history of a school nearly 400 years old was daunting in prospect and exacting in fulfilment. A glance at the table of contents will show that the project required a working definition of what the school should be and reveals how Foyle has lived up to this ideal. Many aspects of school life are covered: a narrative history of Foyle showing how the school's story intersected with the history of Derry/Londonderry through the troubled centuries; some account of the 43 men and women whose tolerance shaped and moulded the schools under their titular care; the sometimes fraught relationship with the Irish Society; the beneficial relationship we had with the diocese of Derry (later Derry and Raphoe); girls' education in the city, especially the leadership provided by such pioneers as Frances Holmes, Jane Kerr and the Misses McKillip, who were determined that the standards of education should be the same as that of the boys; and an account of its sometime rival, the Londonderry Academical Institution.

Here the names of three men should be mentioned: Will Ferguson (1894–1972), Alan Roberts (1924–2012) and Robert Montgomery. During their lives, Ferguson as vice-principal at Foyle and Roberts as librarian in Magee collected and kept safe every item of historical interest about Foyle and the city and published many articles in the magazines. Dr Montgomery organised and catalogued that mass of material, thus creating an exemplary and enviable archive which made the writing of the history of the school, to which he contributed much material, much less onerous. William Lynn, as well as being an exemplary project manager, has contributed a number of colourful items that he has dubbed 'vignettes', describing such elements of school life as the Lawrence Medal, the War Memorial Board, the House System and the Ceremonial Sword.

Within the composite school history are found connections with Trinity College, Dublin, with Magee in Derry and with more exotic places like Norway, Australia, the US, Singapore, Hong Kong, India and Pakistan. I use the word 'composite' deliberately, as many strands went to make up the totality of Foyle today. The amalgamation with Londonderry High School in 1976 was a challenging and perhaps uncomfortable necessity, and the former had at least three different skeins woven into *its* fabric. We include accounts of the various preparatory schools, the pains

and pleasures of boarding, the trauma of the wartime years and the evolving curriculum.

School life is not all about confinement in classrooms while reluctantly learning or failing to learn; what Old Girls and Old Boys remember with greatest pleasure are the extra bits, the literally extra-curricular activities that cast a golden glow over the 'happiest days'. The most obvious outlet for energy was, of course, in sport, and the schools had a glorious record in hockey, rugby, cricket, athletics, swimming and fencing. Scouts and guides had their place as well, and in a sense the logical extensions of such activities are the flourishing Army Cadet Force and the Duke of Edinburgh Awards. The long tradition of school trips and tours continues as does school drama, all being covered in a series of signed articles which, while contributing to the book also provide increased material for the school archive. Debating still flourishes, with a fascinating new forensic development in the Bar Mock and Junior Magistrates competitions. Nor can we forget the hours of voluntary service that are of the essence of staff life.

Ecclesiasticus commands: 'Let us now praise famous men' – and women! It is perfectly appropriate that the school, while not forgetting its many thousand alumni should take pride in the careers of those whose special talents have made them famous. The sections on 'Foyle Lives' and 'Reminiscences of School Life' are intended to help complete the picture. Our main text finishes with 'The Future of Foyle', written by Jack Magill, the retiring headmaster. It is a future for Foyle that will be sited in a campus that will bear the name of Mathias Springham, whose vision persuaded him to invest his own personal wealth in the Free School.

Thanks are due to the many contributors to this book, alive and dead, and we are most grateful to The Rt Revd Dr James Mehaffey, Retired Bishop of Derry and Raphoe, who contributed the foreword, Ken Thatcher who headed the team given the difficult tasks of publicity and marketing, and Christopher Fagg and Susan Pugsley of Third Millennium, our publisher, for their helpful advice.

Ne umquam cesseris!
Sean McMahon

Editorial note: All unascribed text in the narrative history and Foyle Lives is the joint work (and responsibility) of Robert Montgomery and Sean McMahon.

CHRONOLOGY

1570
Dublin parliament passes act (Act 12 Eliz.Ch1) for the establishment of 'a free school in every diocesse of Ireland … the schoolemaster shall be an Englishman of English birth of this realm.' No school built in Derry.

1608
As part of the Plantation of Ulster James I orders: 'There shall be one Free School, at least appointed in Every County for the education of Youth and learning and religion'. Royal schools are set to be established in the counties of Cavan, Armagh, Tyrone, Donegal and Fermanagh. Londonderry initially intended but then overlooked.

1610
Rebuilding of the city of Derry commences after destruction during Sir Cahir O'Doherty's rising.

1611
Building of Derry's walls commences.

1613
Charter of Londonderry issued by King James I (29 March), renaming the city and county.

1617
Matthias Springham (1561–1620), Master of the Guild of Merchant Taylors builds within the walls of the city the Free School (at his own expense). Alone of the established schools of the Ulster Plantation it has no royal charter and survives thereafter with no endowments. The Irish Society 'allows 20 Markes stipend yearly.'

1618
City walls completed.

1624
'A schoolmaster now resident there.'

1625
Death of James I; accession of Charles I (27 March).

1633
Completion of St Columb's cathedral – first cathedral built in these islands since the Reformation.

1634
John Wood, master of Free School. John Bramhall becomes Bishop of Derry.

1641
Ulster rebellion; Derry place of refuge for Protestant settlers.

1649
Execution of Charles I, 30 January. First siege of city.

1656
Cromwell issues new charter for the Irish Society.

1660
Restoration of Charles II.

1662
New charter from Charles II. By its terms the The Hon., the Irish Society relieved from any obligation of endowing the school with a grant of land.

1668
Major fire causes extensive damage in Derry. Free/Diocesan School unharmed.

1682
The Irish Society increases the grant by 20 marks to maintain the school master and usher.

1683
John Morris MA (TCD) master of school.

1685
Charles II dies, succeeded by his brother James II. Ellis Walker BA (TCD) master of school.

1688
Symbolic shutting of the Ferryquay Gate by the apprentice boys from London against the forces of James II. Ezekiel Hopkins, Bishop of Derry, leaves the city on the following day. Ellis Walker, master of Free School also leaves. Joshua Pilott, school usher, joins defence force inside the walls.

1689
Siege of Derry. School evacuated and adapted by Robert Gregory as a horse-powered mill to grind corn and alleviate the food shortages. School building badly damaged by Jacobite fire.

1690
Battle of Boyne at which Revd George Walker is killed and Free School pupil George Farquhar, future dramatist, is present.

1691
William King appointed Bishop of Derry; the bishop requires the return to the school of Ellis Walker as master.

1692
Queen Mary, joint sovereign with William III, grants £1,500 for the rebuilding of the city, virtually uninhabitable for three years after the siege – a portion of the money being used for rebuilding the school. Diocese provides £40 per year for the master; smallness of the grant obliges him to become also curate of 'Iniskehin and Burt'. King buys the extensive library collected by Hopkins.

1694
Ellis Walker returns briefly and Revd David Jenkins BA succeeds him as master in July.

1695
Bishop King increases the master's annual salary to £60, apparently out of his own pocket. Coote Ormsby (1695–9), made dean by royal appointment, refuses to recognise the bishop's authority and stops diocesan payments to the Free School.

1700s

1700

The Common Council of Londonderry (later the Corporation) recommends that John Frier be appointed as usher.

1701

The Irish Society approves Frier's appointment and notes on the occasion of Jenkins' retirement to become rector of Urney that during his seven years of service 11 boys from the school enter Trinity College, Dublin, as undergraduates.

1702

Revd Roger Blackhall MA appointed to succeed Jenkins. During his 32-year period as master the school is substantially rebuilt (1707–8) with a grant of £60 from the Corporation.

1702–83

The mastership a family preserve: Blackhall is succeeded by his son-in-law John Torrence MA DD (previously an usher) (1734–73), succeeded by his son Thomas (1773–80) and nephew Roger Blackhall (1780–3). A list of ushers in the school, the awarding of the post in the gift of the Irish Society, includes Henry Gonne (1721) and John Torrence (1729). Strong links maintained during this period with at least 150 alumni attending the university; eight become fellows and Francis Andrews becomes provost. During this period the total enrolment averages 40 and all appointments have to be approved by the Irish Society, the Bishop of Derry, the Corporation of Londonderry and/ or the parliament in Dublin.

1729

On his death Archbishop King bequeaths his library to the diocese of Derry. It is given into the care of the Free School and the master becomes the Diocesan Librarian at £40 a year. The school now becomes known as the Derry Diocesan Free School.

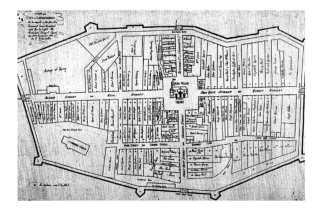

1783

Thomas Marshall, appointed to the mastership by the 'unanimous voice of the Earl Bishop of Derry, the Mayor and Corporation, the gentry of the city and county, and his fellow citizens.' The school had four boarders and 16 day scholars. School at a low ebb because of the prolonged (ultimately fatal) illness of Blackhall.

1790

On death of Marshall from a 'fever raging in the city' George Vaughan Sampson BA appointed as master. School numbers rise to 97, of whom 17 were boarders.

1794

When the Irish Society refuses to grant an increase of salary (£40 a year from the Society, £20 from the Corporation and £12 from the bishop) Sampson resigns to become Rector of Aghanloo. The late rector James Knox (1756–34) is appointed master.

1794–1834

Mastership of Knox: School seen to be in a poor state of repair. Intention is to cater for the growing city and find a new site outside the walls.

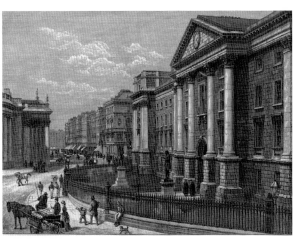

MATHIAS SPRINGHAM AR MIGER
AD HONOREM DEI ET BONARUM
LITERARUM PROPAGATIONEM
SCHOLAM HANC FUNDAVIT
ANNO SALUTIS 1617°

1800s

1803
William Knox (1762–1831), son of Viscount Northland, becomes Bishop of Derry.

1806
Bishop Knox offers a site on diocesan land on Strand Road, gives an initial £100 and institutes an annual endowment of £100. He also finds support from the Irish Society, the London livery Companies, the Grand Juries of the city and county and at least two private benefactors.

1808
First of two necessary acts of parliament before building could proceed, transferring patronage of the school from Lord Lieutenant to the Bishop of Derry. New school ('R. Elsam, Archt.') built in Lawrence Hill proves 'too dark' and is pulled down at a loss of £1,600 (with today's buying power: £128,000).

1809
Act to vest old school and allow Bishop Knox to lease the new site at a reasonable rent. Another building (architect John Bowden, who designed the courthouse) is begun.

1814
The school, now called Foyle on the proposal of George Fletcher Moore, one of the pupils, opens, though unfinished, on 19 August. School three storeys high, with north wing housing the Great Dining Room and private parlour for headmaster's family, and south wing with drawing room and Diocesan Library on ground floor.

1818
Knox now referred to as headmaster and has four members of staff, second master, two ushers and an English master. School numbers now 110, of whom 54 are boarders.

1823
Free Diocesan school building in Society Street pulled down.

1830
Knox, though 74, delays his retirement for lack of a pension; school no longer regarded as suitable for the sons of gentry.

1832
School closes for some months because of an outbreak of cholera; reopens 14 February 1833. On 10 August Knox reports to the Board of Education in Dublin that the school has 59 pupils: one boarder, 25 Free Scholars and 33 day scholars, with an age spread of nine to 18, and a modal age of 12 to 16.

1834
School declines as Knox ages; there are no boarders. Knox retires in August and is replaced by the Revd William Smyth, who remains as headmaster until 1841. Annual grants by Corporation and some Livery Companies withdrawn. Committee organised by Bishop Knox appeals to Sir Robert Peel, then Prime Minister. The Irish Society's increased grant allows school to continue.

1841
Revd John Hamilton Millar becomes headmaster in June; retires in December 1843: Drapers Company stops subscription; Cloth Workers (£25 a year) and Mercers (£50) continue support. 1847. School has 19 boarders, 62 day pupils and 20 Free scholars.

1846
April: The Irish Society increases grant to £220 a year plus a grant of £135 for school repairs.
1846–9: The Great Famine; Derry an important port of departure for massive emigration.

1848
Revd Robert Henderson BA MA becomes headmaster.

1851
Revd William Steele MA DD recommended as second master, or usher, on 29 December. A former pupil of Foyle, he becomes 13th headmaster of Portora on 23 June.

1853
Revd William Sweet Escott MA, fellow of New College, Oxford, Rector of Brompton Ralph in Somerset, exchanges offices with Steele and is headmaster until 1862. Influenced by Arnold of Rugby to run Foyle on public school lines, he begins to build a chapel that is consecrated on 30 April 1872. Adopts the name *Collegium Derriense* for the school.

1860
Strand House School for girls opened by Frances Holmes.

1862
Revd William Hunter Parrott becomes headmaster.

1865
Magee College opens.

1866
Revd William Percy Robinson MA DD becomes headmaster. Late master of Diocesan School, Sligo, he brings the boys of a number of significant Sligo families, including Pollexfens and Middletons.

1868
LAI is founded at 6 East Wall, a private house.

1869
Church Disestablishment Act passed. Prince Arthur (Victoria's third son) visits school on 28 April.

1870
Foundation stone of LAI laid in Haw Lane (later to be styled Academy Road) on 19 October. *The Birch*, first school magazine (first also in Ireland) runs from 16 November 1870 until 16 December 1871.

1872
Foyle College Monthly, first published 9 March, is still extant.

1874
Foyle College Act defines new constitution, with a board of governors comprising the Bishop and Dean of Derry, the Deputy Governor of the Hon., the Irish Society, the Moderator of the Presbyterian Church in Ireland and the Mayor of Derry. Revd Benjamin Moffett appointed headmaster. School maintains classical tradition with little regard for 'modern' subjects and dwindles until there are only eight boarders and about 40 dayboys. Lowest ebb in 1877, when Maurice Charles Hime MA LLD is appointed. Chapel is burned down with loss of communion plate.

1877
The Irish Society supports new headmaster with promises of new accommodation for headmaster, an infirmary and increase of grant for next eight years. Diocesan library transferred to diocesan offices in Artillery Street.

1878
January: Hime arrives with 30 Boarders, six horses and school magazine (later *Our School Times*) from Monaghan Diocesan School. Arrival delayed due to refurbishment of headmaster's house in Crawford Square, paid for by the Irish Society.

1878
The Intermediate Education Act.

1879
47 Boarders and 59 dayboys in Foyle. St Columb's College opens.
1882: Two boys bring bicycles into school; hope for a cycling club. Oliver Armstrong wins gold medal in Greek.

1895
The Irish Society suggests amalgamation of Foyle and Londonderry Academical Institution.

1896
Amalgamation Act (59 and 60 Vict. C. CXXXI) passed 20 July. Hime retires on a pension (first awarded); School magazine ceases to be published.

1897
JC Dick, formerly headmaster of LAI since 1878, appointed head of Foyle.

1899–90
Foyle wins Ulster Schools Cup.

1900s

2000s

1909
A link with Trinity College, Dublin allows students of Foyle, Victoria and St Lurach's to qualify for degrees, prizes and scholarships, through Magee. *Our School Times* again issued from April.

1911
Dick, a well-known classical scholar but a remote personality and a strict disciplinarian, retires and is succeeded by RF Dill, who comes from Dungannon Royal, bringing some pupils. Serves as headmaster for 17 years.

1912–15
Foyle in three Schools Cup finals, winning in 1915.

1914–18
World War I. 490 Old Boys serve and 72 are killed.

1921
School War Memorial unveiled.

1920–3
Northern Ireland and Irish Free State established.

1924
Intermediate examinations cease and new NI Ministry of Education establishes Junior and Senior Certificate examinations. School settles down to a pattern of teaching, with regular non-scholastic events such as swimming displays and galas in the school 'plunge', badminton and handball tournaments, Christmas entertainments, town and gown lectures, athletic sports, choirs and Feis appearances.

1928
Arthur Ernest Layng becomes headmaster.

1930
The Foyle Players formed, and a school orchestra; production of *Macbeth*.

1933
Ernest Perceval Southby becomes headmaster.

1935
WAC McConnell becomes headmaster and sets up an appeal fund, which nets sufficient income to buy playing fields at Springtown.

1939–45
Second World War witnesses the 'virtual disintegration of the school': LAI buildings, part of technical college, rooms in Miss Woodburn's house, Lawrence Hill requisitioned by services; boarding school closes.

1946
Post-war austerity and food rationing. School returns to Lawrence Hill and Academy Road.

1949
In March armorial bearings are granted to Foyle by the College of Arms; Lawrence Medal inaugurated.

1960
Vice-principal JS Connolly becomes headmaster; Board of Governors decides to build new school at Springtown.

1963
On 1 March the statue of John Laird Nair Lawrence, Lord Lawrence of the Punjab, Viceroy of India (1863–8) is unveiled at Lawrence Hill site.

1967
350th anniversary of founding.

1968
Duke and Duchess of Kent and Lord Erskine attend official opening of new school, 2 May. HRH unveils commemorative plaque.

1969
Civil Rights movement and beginnings of 'Troubles'.

1973
HW Gillespie appointed headmaster on retirement of JS Connolly in June.

1976
Foyle and Londonderry High School amalgamate to form Foyle and Londonderry College.

1994
WJ Magill appointed headmaster on retirement of HW Gillespie.

1996
Preparatory School moves from Dunseveric House to Springtown.

2003
Preparatory School closes.

2010
School takes ownership of Clooney army base on Limavady Road, which is renamed the Springham Campus.

2011
School reverts to former title of Foyle.

2012
Jack Magill retires and is replaced by Patrick Allen.

15

1

THE FREE SCHOOL

The history of any institution that has lasted for nearly four centuries is bound to be an account of success and disappointment, rise and fall, and involve many events and personalities. Unlike its sister colleges, the various royal schools in Raphoe, Enniskillen, Cavan, Armagh and Dungannon, it was denied the 'royal' because of the unusual nature of the plantation of County Coleraine that was renamed Londonderry because of the source of the investment – the Livery Companies of the city of London. The name of its chief borough, Derry, was

also given the honorific prefix. The earliest name of the city body given the task of planting the county was 'The Society of the Governor and Assistants, London, of the New Plantation of Ulster, within the Realm of Ulster', a rather cumbersome title that was changed to 'The Honourable, the Irish Society' on its restoration by Oliver Cromwell (1599–1658) in the year of his death.

This Irish Society, as from now on it will be referred to for convenience, took charge of the towns, customs and fisheries; implicit in this was

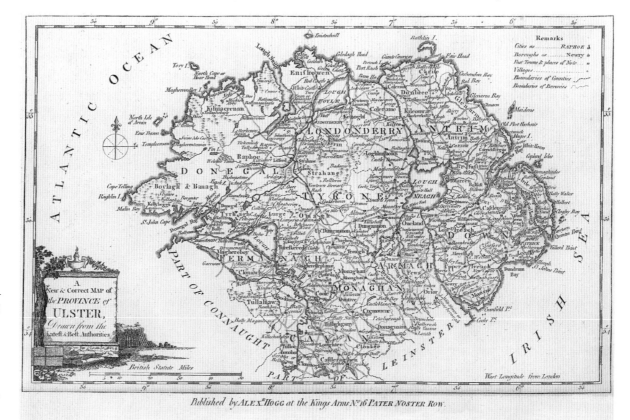

OPPOSITE: *King James VI and I of Scotland (from 1566) and England (1603–25).*

RIGHT: *The Province of Ulster, as it appeared in the late 18th century, from Henry Boswell's* Antiquities of England and Wales *(1786).*

17

the obligation first imposed on all the dioceses of Ireland by Elizabeth I in 1570 of establishing a 'free school'. The furnishing of the city with defensive walls was complete by 1618 but no royal school was formally established. A free school was begun in 1617 on the individual initiative of Mathias Springham Merchant Taylor of London. 'The City of London hath assigned a yearly stipend of twenty marks to be given to the schoole-master, but *our gracious King's grant is suppressed*,' as Bishop Downham noted on his visitation. The anomalous financial situation was to bedevil it for many years, and there would be constant argument and confusion between such interested parties as the city's corporation, the bishop of the diocese and the Irish Society about financial responsibility.

This uncertainty led to genuine hardship; one headmaster was forced to serve many years beyond his prime for lack of any superannuation scheme, and the same man's emolument for two consecutive years early in the 19th century was £0 and £5. This uncertainty about finance was mitigated somewhat by diocesan grants, both from the personal wealth of the incumbent bishop, and from occasional donations by individual members of the companies. In spite of this besetting poverty Springham's Free School and its successors provided an unbroken scholastic service through the troubled centuries except for the disruption after 1689, because of the Siege. The requisition of school premises by army and navy during World War II did not interrupt the school's scholastic provision and it survived (as did its future amalgamation partner, Londonderry High School) a number of changes of site.

The 'Flight of the Earls' in 1607, as the event has since become known, left a large portion of Gaelic Ulster leaderless, and the treason of which they were deemed to be guilty allowed their lands to be escheated to the Crown. 'The undutiful departure of the Earls of Tirone, Tirconnel and McGwyre', as they were referred to in contemporary documents, left the way open for plantation. James I had been tolerant of O'Neill's ambivalence, and with the best secret service in Europe was very well aware of the plotting of O'Donnell and Maguire, but like his predecessor he loathed war as dangerous, largely pointless and, most seriously, damnably expensive. The six counties that were to have plantations imposed upon them were those west of the Bann: Armagh, Cavan, Tyrone,

Hugh O'Neill, the Earl of Tyrone, c.1590.

Coleraine, Fermanagh and Donegal. Antrim and Down had already achieved the ideal of 'civility' by invitation and private plantation.

Ireland and especially the unregenerate Gaelic province of Ulster had to be tamed. Otherwise it could act as a backdoor to the forces of the Counter-Reformation and a return of popery. More importantly it was a colony that could be developed economically, much as Virginia was being exploited, with the same problem of aboriginal inhabitants but without their susceptibility to European diseases. And most pleasing of all to the frugal James was that it provided him with the opportunity to reward with grants of land the many to whom he felt indebted.

An important part of 'civility' was education, not to convert the wild Irish but to provide a necessary amenity for the intended permanent settlers. The schools to be established, one in each county, would secure not only the material welfare of the pupils but also their instruction in the Protestant religion. James's predecessor, Elizabeth I, had anticipated this necessity, and caused the Dublin parliament to pass in 1570 an act (Act 12 Eliz.Ch1) for the establishment of 'a free school in every diocese of Ireland ... the schoolemaster shall be an Englishman of English birth of this realm.' The legislation was largely ignored, particularly in Ulster, then still ruled by native chieftains.

In 1608 James found it necessary also to decree: 'There shall be one Free School at least appointed in Every County, for the education of Youth in learning and religion.' In this way Armagh, Cavan, Dungannon, Fermanagh and Donegal got their 'royal' schools. The case of County Derry – or more correctly County Coleraine – was different. Partly on the advice of Sir Thomas Phillips, who held lands around the mouth of the Bann, but largely because of an interest in the ruined city of Derry that he described as 'a Town of War and a Town of Merchandize', James I readily agreed to devolve the plantation of County Coleraine to the extremely reluctant city merchants of London. To whet their mercantile appetites he added all but that southwest corner of the barony of Loughinsholin, and agreed to the addition of the northeast liberties of Coleraine (3,000 acres), which was part of County Antrim, and the City and Liberties (4,000 acres) of Londonderry, which were in County Donegal – and named the county Londonderry.

Phillips' chief concern had been the reluctance of any 'undertakers' to face the endemic unruly nature of the territory – Ó Catháin country, mountainous, boggy and hostile, with lowland forests filled with

woodkerne – unattractive apart from the fertile basins of Foyle, Roe and Bann. As noted, the earliest name of the city body given the task of planting the county was 'The Society of the Governor and Assistants, London, of the New Plantation of Ulster, within the Realm of Ulster', changed to 'The Honourable, the Irish Society' on its restoration by Oliver Cromwell, and its members were drawn from the livery companies of the city of London. These groups, so-called from the distinct uniforms they wore on special occasions, had their origin in the old craft guilds that established conditions for membership, set professional standards and fixed wages, and now were essentially the controllers of the mercantile life of the city. There were 12 'great' companies who had a specific order of civic precedence, led by the Mercers (who were established in 1393) with the Clothworkers (1528) bringing up the rear. The positions of the Merchant Taylors (1326) and the Skinners (1327) as to which took sixth place in order and which seventh, caused such argument and violence that in 1484 Sir Robert Billesden, the then Lord Mayor of London, decreed that they should alternate positions in succeeding years. (This row is usually given as the origin of the expression 'at sixes and sevens'.) It was appropriate that the king should wish to involve the companies since they were essentially the magnates who controlled the finances not just of London but of much of the rest of Britain.

The companies were at first very dubious about the Ulster undertaking, but eventually 'great command o'erswayed the argument.' On 17 December 1613 a kind of lottery was held in the Guildhall in Gresham Street in the City, the headquarters of the livery companies. There the membership court, consisting of a governor, deputy governor and 24 assistants, supervised the parcelling out of land portions, each of an estimated 3,200 acres, in the new county of Londonderry. They were allocated as follows: Kilrea (21,600 acres) to the Mercers (originally dealers in textiles); Eglington [sic] (15,900) to the Grocers; Moneymore (38,800) to the Drapers; Ballykelly (24,100) to the Fishmongers; Newbuildings (11,005) to the Goldsmiths; Dungiven (49,000) to the Skinners; Macosquin (18,700) to the Merchant Taylors; Ballycastle (23,100) to the Haberdashers; Magherafelt (23,250) to the Salters; Agivey (19,450) to the Ironmongers; Bellaghy/Killowen/Articlave (32,600) to the Vintners; Castlerock (13,450) to the Clothworkers. (The Ballycastle assigned to the Haberdashers was

Oliver Cromwell, c.1650s.

part of the barony of Coleraine and not the town in northeast Antrim.)

That particular year the Merchant Taylors had precedence, and their 'assistant', [master] Mathias Springham (1561–1620), was to help found the Free School in Derry. The pace of the undertaking had been far too slow, and it was he who was sent to investigate. The three necessary improvements – walls, cathedral and school – were begun under his initiative, and the city remembers his name in Springham Street that leads from Lawrence Hill (another significant name) to Clarence Avenue, Springham Park at Springtown and in the name of the new campus at Clooney. The Merchant Taylors had been given 18,700 acres at Macosquin and Camus, effectively controlling the west bank of the Lower Bann, and it was at Springham's urging and that of Phillips that the piece from the east bank was added to the newly contrived County Londonderry to balance the piece taken from O'Doherty territory in the west, thus enabling the Irish Society through the Taylors guild to control the Foyle and the Bann.

Grants of land and therefore of income had already been made to Dungannon and Raphoe for the building of the 'royal' schools, and as Bishop Downham (1616–34) had already noted in his visitation book in 1622: 'both of these have fair proportions allotted to them for the maintenance of schooles; but the lands intended for the schools of Derry, has been swallowed up, I know not well by whom'. The venture had not been as successful as London had hoped and there were hints of sharp practice, but by the time of the bishop's comment there was as he noted 'a fair schoole-house built by Mathias Springham, Merchant-taylor of London, and the City of London hath assigned a yearly stipend of twenty marks to be given to the schoole-master, but *our gracious King's grant is suppressed*.'[his emphasis]

The history of the city for the rest of the 17th century was intermittently disturbed, though it was granted a sufficient time of peace for the building of the city walls (1611–18), the cathedral (1628–33) and the Free School, begun in 1617. Springham's personal initiative, though generous, meant that the school was not endowed, could not be called 'royal' and for 400 years found its position anomalous. It was the first of the new buildings to be completed, set in Free School Lane, where the significantly named Society Street now

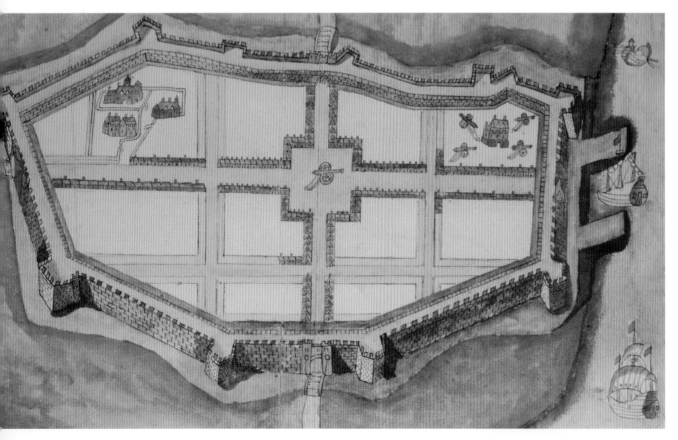

Early plan of Derry, 1620.

stands. The Society's annual grant for the school of 20 marks was characteristic of its persistent attitude to the school. (A mark was the monetary equivalent of eight ounces of gold and therefore a variable amount, but usually taken to be two-thirds of a pound sterling.) Its assumption of responsibility for the school was not only partial but changed over time and, being without statutory enforcement, was at the whim of the donor, whose generosity could stop at any time.

When Springham and his fellow guildsman Proby arrived to inspect the London companies investment they had a promise from the City of London that it would make ample provision for the maintenance of the school once it was built, setting aside 300 acres for that purpose. In fact the land was never granted, and Downham notes in his report that a petition from the 'Mayor, Commonalty and Citizens of the City of Londonderry' made in 1624 complained: 'which land hath bin and yet is by some undue means (as we conceive) detained, though the like guiftes unto other places are quietly enjoyed.' This plea fell on deaf ears and the position of the Free School and its later incarnations continued to cause fret and actual financial hardship.

The schoolhouse was 67ft in length, 25ft in breadth and of one and a half storeys in height and as such replicated the dimensions of the 'Free School of Fermanagh (1616–18).' The ground floor consisted of a schoolroom, a hall and parlour; the upper level had sleeping accommodation for the master, the usher and boarders. On a stone above the door was inscribed:

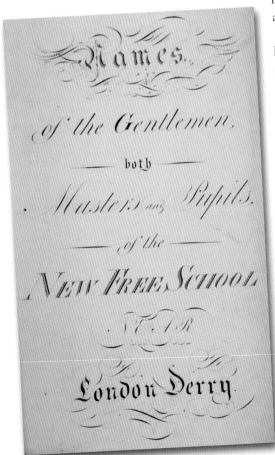

Mathias Springham A.R. ad honorem dei et bonarum literarum propogationem hanc scholam fundavit anno salutis mdcxvii ['Mathias Springham, Ar(miger) [Esquire] built this school to the honour of God and for the purpose of the furthering of classical studies, in the year of our salvation: 1617.']

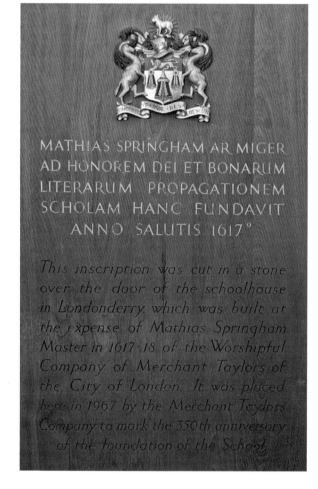

The curriculum was that of equivalent public schools in Britain, probably with a six-day week, with half-holidays on Wednesdays and Saturdays. They tended to work from dawn till dusk for practical reasons, making the schooldays in winter months somewhat shorter. The main subject was Latin and they probably used what remained a standard text for generations: William Lyly's *Short Introduction of Grammar*. Once assimilated by tedious rote learning so that Latin vocabulary was superior to English and the spelling of the dead language firmly assimilated (unlike English that took a century or more for standardisation), the possessor of the 'shining morning face creeping like snail unwillingly to school' went on to write prose, epistles, forensic speeches and finally Latin verse – and for relief entertainment acted in plays. It was simply a classical education that added to a deep knowledge of the doctrines of the Anglican faith and fitted, it was believed, a pupil for life. There was also some study of Greek and Hebrew appropriate in a diocesan school with a long series of ordained masters. For many,

LEFT: *The Ferryquay Gate, from an early 20th-century postcard view. One of the four original gateways to the city, it was famously barricaded against the king by the Apprentice Boys in September 1688.*

BELOW: *George Farquhar (dramatist, c.1690).*

however, the little bit of measuring and computation proved eventually more useful.

The Calendar of State Papers relating to Ireland gave this description: 'Near to the said church [the cathedral] is a Fair Free Schoole of lyme and stone, slated, with a base court of lyme and stone, about it, built at the charges of Mathias Springham of London Merchant deceased; and towards the maintenance of the scholemaister thereof the citty of London allows 20 Markes stipend yearly.' There is documentary evidence about one of these 'scholemaisters'; John Wood is named as master of the Derry Free Schoole in 1634 and he was replaced in 1641 by John Campion. In all there were 15 masters up to the time of the beginning of the great siege. The school continued with its double function of sacred and secular education through the troubled 17th century experienced by the city in the turmoil of the incredibly complicated politics of the time. A measure of this complexity was the relief of the first siege of the city in August 1649, when Owen Roe O'Neill, the northern commander of the anti-parliamentary forces, successfully attacked the royalists who were besieging its Presbyterian inhabitants during the 20-week attrition. The school could hardly have functioned during those summer months but there is nothing in the records to indicate whether the pupils were sent home during the fighting, as happened in 1689.

In 1638, following a report by the commissioners of Charles I, the Society was called to give an account of itself before the Star Chamber, and their mandate to manage the plantation (and the school) was withdrawn. The following year, when the sequestration of the Irish Society was in force, Bishop Bramhall

William III and Queen Mary, joint rulers from 1688 at the invitation of Parliament. Engraving, c.1692.

left the city in 1641 and did not return until 1648, but had to flee the city again in 1649 as a noted royalist when Cromwell offered a reward for his capture. He returned in 1660 at the Restoration and was succeeded by Bishop Mossom in 1661.

During the Protectorate the government showed a keen interest in schooling and providing salaries for teachers, both in Britain and Ireland. An 'Act for the Better Advancement of the Gospel and Learning in Ireland' was passed in March 1650 and the following year an Order of State was issued directing:

> *the commissioners for revenue for Ulster to appoint godly and able persons to preach the gospel or to be schoolmasters at five towns in the precinct of Ulster and to assign to these minister and schoolmasters such yearly stipends or salaries they in their judgement conceive their paines and parts in their respective employments to deserve, the same not exceeding £100 per annum for each minister and £40 for each schoolmaster.*

Londonderry was one of these five, and the likely consequence was the appointment of William Crofton as master in 1653. The birth of his daughter Anne on 6 February 1654 is recorded and his name on the Civil List for 1655 indicates that he was in receipt of a salary of £40. He was succeeded at Christmas 1656 by William Finch at a lower salary of £20, either due to his inferior qualifications or a diminishing in the status of the school.

That year Cromwell issued a new charter for the Irish Society, giving it the name by which it is still known, and Charles II, two years after his accession in 1660 virtually restored it to its former position and removed from it any obligation of endowing the school with a grant of land, Robert Mossom, bishop (1666–81), realising that the school was in need of repair, requested the Society in 1670 to increase the grant to the school. Then began tedious and lengthy negotiations between the Society and Londonderry Corporation. The school was one of the buildings that escaped harm during a major fire that did great damage to the city in 1668 and there was considerable relief when in 1682 the Society increased the grant by 20 marks to maintain the master and usher. The death of Charles II and the accession of his Catholic brother in 1685 did not at first cause any serious disturbance

(1634–61), the sequestrator, set aside money for necessary repairs, and it was on the basis of these funds that the school managed to carry on until the period of the Commonwealth, when the government made itself responsible for masters' salaries. Bramhall

to the city or the school, now with its new master Ellis Walker BA (TCD), but when the king chose struggle in Ireland to be the means of regaining the lost throne the city was soon engulfed in the longer, more destructive siege.

The first sign of trouble was the shutting in 1688 of the Ferryquay Gate by the apprentices against the king's men. Ezekiel Hopkins, Bishop of Derry, left the city the following day, unwilling to face the uncertainty of the diocese's future. Ellis Walker also left, while his usher Joshua Pilott joined the defence force inside the walls with the rank of captain. The city, now with a metropolitan prefix, played its famous part in the far-from-bloodless revolution and the end of the Stuart dynasty. Some of the Free School scholars played their parts in the siege of 1689 and at least one claimed to have fought on the Williamite side at the indecisive Battle of the Boyne. This was George Farquhar (?1677–1707), son of the curate of Liscooley, Castlefinn, who at 13 must have been one of the youngest soldiers at Oldtown. He was certainly the youngest and latest of the Restoration dramatists, dying of tuberculosis as *The Beaux' Stratagem*, his dark comedy, proved a success at Drury Lane.

During the siege the empty school was essentially in the front line. Its yard was used as the site of a mill to grind corn to feed the defenders, especially the soldiers. It was organised by Captain Robert Gregory, who in 1716 made a plea for recompense to he and his brother because 'they built a horse-mill and ground all graine for the souldiers free, maintaining men and horses to p'forme the work'. Gregory insisted that if the mill had not been built 'the whole garrison must have perished by want of bread'. It did not take much intelligence on the Jacobite side to realise that it was a prime target, and it was seriously damaged several times by artillery fire.

In 1692 James II's daughter, Queen Mary, fellow sovereign with her husband William III, granted £1,500 (£187,000 today) for the rebuilding of the city, virtually uninhabitable for three years after the siege. William King, who replaced Hopkins as bishop in 1691, required the return to the school of Ellis Walker as master and, having purchased the extensive library collected by Hopkins, arranged for the building of an extra apartment in the Free School to house it as the diocesan library. Walker assented to the decree when the bishop paid his travel expenses. He

found he could not live on the £40 a year provided by the diocese, and was obliged to act as curate, earning an extra stipend of £20 for the parishes of 'Iniskehin [Iskaheen] and Burt'. These livings are at least 12 miles apart by road and well fit the contemporary description of their location as *'in exterioribus partibus parochiae'*.

Walker's stay on return was brief, and by 1695 David Jenkins was master and glad to accept an increase in his annual salary to £60 that was paid, apparently, out of the bishop's own pocket. However, Coote Ormsby (1695–9), by royal appointment the resident dean in the city, refused to recognise the bishop's authority and stopped diocesan payments to the Free School until he retired in 1699. The following year the Common Council of Londonderry (CCLC – later the Corporation), the third party with joint responsibility for the school, recommended the appointment of John Frier as usher and in 1701, the Irish Society approved Frier's appointment and noted in its visitation report on the occasion of Jenkins's retirement to become rector of Urney that, during his seven years of service, 11 boys from the school entered Trinity as undergraduates.

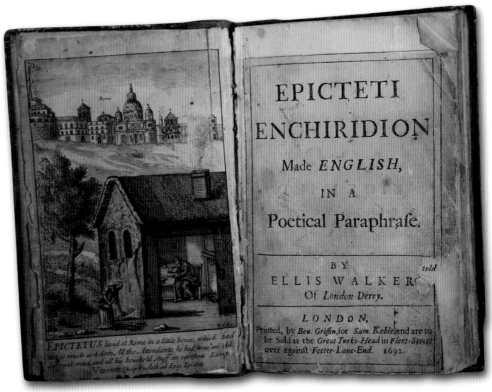

A book by Ellis Walker, 1692.

MATHIAS SPRINGHAM (1561–1627)

Mathias Springham, the founder of our school, was born in the city of London in 1561, the son of Richard who was a mercer, essentially a dealer in expensive fabrics. Mathias opted instead for the profession of merchant tailor and became a freeman of the Merchant Taylors' guild in 1588. By the time of the accession of James I in 1603 he already had trade dealings with Ireland. He was of sufficient stature in the guild to act as chief butler at a banquet given by the Merchant Taylors for the king in 1607 and from that date began to invest in such ventures as the Virginia Company. When at the king's behest some of the territory of Ulster became the concern of the city guilds, his company was assigned much of the county of Coleraine, the borough of Coleraine and the newly named London-derry.

Springham took very seriously his duties as commissioner to Ulster, like his master Sir Arthur Chichester, who declared he would rather 'labour with his hands in the plantation of Ulster than dance and play in that of Virginia'. By 1613 he was a senior member of the Irish Society and leader of the delegation that carried the new charter for Londonderry to the tiny settlement on the Foyle. They also brought a silver gilt communion cup with the inscription, *Ecclesia Dei in Civitate Derrensi Donum* ('For the church of God in the city of Derry', a gift from London). There he and his companion George Smithes had occasion to reprimand the local agents for inefficiency, sloth and even corruption, and insisted that work on the city's defences including the walls should begin at once. After all, James I [in his 1604 charter for 'the town or borough of Derrie'] had described it as 'a town of war and a town of merchandize' and these representatives of the city's masters in London required both aspects to be developed.

Education in the Irish colony had been a consideration since 1570 when the 12th statute of Elizabeth I had required that a free school should be established 'within every Diocese of this realm of Ireland'. This had been iterated in 1609 by the 'King's commissioners' who stated: 'There shall be one Free-School, at least, appointed in every county, for the education of the youth in learning and religion,' and four years later the Irish Society was similarly directed by the Privy Council. Springham and his associate Commissioner Peter Proby made specific reference to the matter in their report in 1616. They felt that both admonitions had been ignored and advocated the grant of land of 300 acres for a school that Springham would fund out of his own resources. However, as George Downham, Bishop of Derry (1617–34), reported in his Visitation Book of 1622:

As touching schooles it is well-known that his Majesty intended a convenient proportion of lands as well for Dungannon or Donegal, yet both these have fair proportions allotted to them for the maintenance of schooles; but the lands intended for the schools of Derry, have been swallowed up, I know not well by whom … Notwithstanding there is a fair schoole-house built at Londonderry by Mathias Springham, Merchant-taylor of London, and the City of London hath assigned a yearly stipend of 20 marks to be given to the schoole-master, but our gracious King's grant is suppressed.

It was as master of the Merchant Taylors' Company that he built the Free School, 'with a court of lime and stone'. The complicated story of why of the six planted counties of Armagh, Tyrone, Donegal, Monaghan, Cavan and Derry, it alone was not granted a royal school has been told elsewhere. Suffice to say that he deserves the plaque he had fixed above the entrance of his Free School:

Mathias Springham Ar(miger) ad Honorem Dei et Bonarum Literarium Propagationem hanc Scholam Fundavit.

Three years later 'being at this present sicke in bodye but of perfect minde and memorie' he made his will on 23 September 1627 and died almost immediately, being buried in the parish church of Richmond six days later. His memorial slab bears the inscription:

Matthias Springham Esquire
Who departed this life the
25th September anno 1627.
Here lieth interred under this stone
A man of charitie alone
Which while he lived did good to all.
He was an help to great and smale.
He left the world all full of sinn.
He lyved in Christ and dyed therein.
He hoped in God his soule to save
Among the saints which now they have.

He had little money left to leave to his family but clearly felt that it was his personal duty to make up the shortcomings, sloth and corruption of the commissioners who should have taken the corporate responsibility for the essential Free-Schoole that was an integral part of the project. One hopes he died unaware of the treachery of his colleagues. He is remembered in the naming of two streets in the city he helped to create, in the title of a house in his school's modern incarnation and in the name of the site of the new school.

How the Free School
Became the Diocesan Free School

The Act of 12 Elizabeth I c1 made provision for a free school to be built in every diocese in Ireland. Passed in 1570, the act was only sporadically observed and generally ignored. Initially the diocese of Derry was no different, but the act with later amendments would survive for three centuries, with its first effects observed in the city after 1656. On the recommendations of a commission under the Great Seal of Ireland, and an amendment passed on 27 March 1656, the bishops, deans and chapters within each respective county were required to support the free school and make up the revenue provided they did not exceed the allowance of £100 yearly.

In 1662 after the Restoration and on receiving its new charter the Irish Society had resumed the payment of 20 marks annually for the salary of the master. As this was less than was paid during the Commonwealth the payment was allocated to the usher (assistant teacher). Although the Society had been relieved of providing an endowment by Charles II it was still bound by its commitment of 1617 to provide for the free education of 14 poor scholars by paying the master 20 marks yearly.

The CCLC was now responsible for the cost of maintaining the school building, and the bishop and clergy of the diocese paid the salary of £40 to the master under the terms of the 1656 legislation. When in 1670 Robert Mossom, the Bishop of Derry, requested the Society to increase its payment to the school to £20, negotiations continued and an agreement was not reached until June 1682, with the Society then paying the increased amount in 1683. This was on the understanding that certain conditions had now been met,

and in the Foyle archives are statements indicating that the Society's position was that the school was now deemed diocesan under the terms of the 1570 and later acts. Hence it relieved the Society of the responsibility to provide additional support.

In 1695 the 7 William III c4 Act was passed. It confirmed the 1570 Act that 'a publick free Latin school shall be constantly maintained and kept within each diocese of this kingdom' and would further require that 'all other acts and statutes now in force in this realm shall from henceforth be strictly observed and put into execution'. In 1703 the Irish House of Lords set up a committee to prepare a bill relating to the free schools, and which when passed into law in 1704 would render the Act of Elizabeth more effectual.

In July 1707 the CCLC wrote to the Society asking it to contribute to the necessary repairs of the school. The Society replied mentioning the 1682 agreement and indicating that the school was now diocesan and not its responsibility. Clarification was sought by the CCLC from Charles Hickman, Bishop of Derry. In October of that year he wrote three letters, one to the CCLC indicating that he would pay for the repairs, another to the Society relieving it of any obligation to contribute and one to the Lord Lieutenant of Ireland stating that under the 1570 legislation, the Crown had the right to appoint the master. At the same time John Bolton, the Dean of Derry, agreed with William King (since 1703 Archbishop of Dublin) that a room could be built on to the school which would accommodate the library he had purchased from the executors of Bishop Hopkins. Archbishop King paid £100 towards the cost and arranged with Revd Chivers to have the library catalogued. By October 1708, the room was

OPPOSITE: *Charles II (r.1660–85).*

BELOW: *Queen Elizabeth I in a design for the obverse of the Great Seal of Ireland, c.1584.*

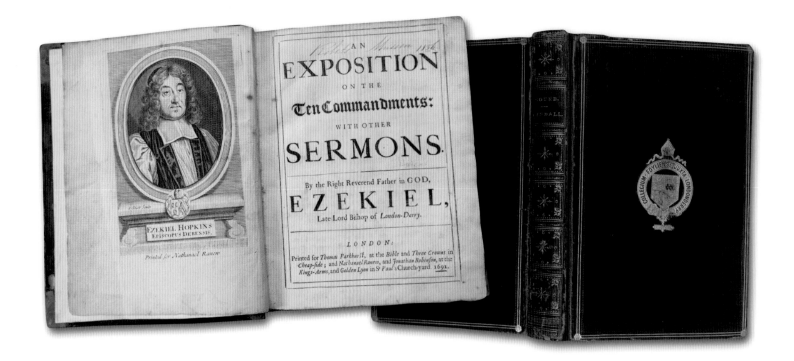

ready and Dean Bolton then transferred the books to their new abode. Revd Roger Blackhall MA, the headmaster, was made the diocesan librarian and paid £12 yearly by Bishop Hickman (and later bishops) to take care of the library.

In 1720 the Society exercised its right to appoint the usher and Henry Gonne was appointed. Following his death in 1726 Archbishop King left his library to William Nicholson, Bishop of Derry, and his successors 'for the perpetual use of the clergy and gentlemen of the diocese and as a public library'. The Derry diocesan library would remain with the school for the next 150 years and successive masters who were all ordained clergymen of the Church of Ireland during that time would retain the title of diocesan librarian. On 9 August 1734 Revd John Torrens was appointed as master and was the first Crown appointment under the 1570 Act. With the Crown exercising the right of appointment the Elizabeth legislation was firmly observed and the destiny of the school was with the bishop and diocese of Derry until the mid-Victorian period.

Later changes to the act were effected as follows. In 1755, the grand juries were empowered to levy sums on their respective counties to pay for repairs and building of diocesan schools. In 1782 a further act enabled the bishop to change the site of a diocesan school to a better one within the diocese. Under

that legislation Bishop Knox would later have the authority to move the school to Lawrence Hill. The legislation passed on 10 May 1788 (28 Geo. III c15) authorised the appointment of commissioners to enquire regularly about the state of the diocesan schools and publish reports. In the first report of 1791 the Derry Diocesan School was described as having 41 pupils, including four boarders and 31 day pupils, of whom six were free. The commissioners produced 14 reports during the next six years, with a final one in 1812. In the following year under another act: (46 Geo. III c107), the commissioners of education in Ireland were established and the Lord Lieutenant and Privy Council were empowered to fix the salaries of the masters. When the name of the school changed to Foyle College in August 1814, it was a change of name only, and the school retained its diocesan character. The 1827 report stated that Foyle had 32 boarders and 59 day boys, of whom 27 were free. The diocesan school system was to continue without much change, although many of the commissioners' reports were critical of its relative ineffectiveness.

The Irish Church Act of 26 July 1869 (32 and 33 Vict. c42) put an end to the diocesan school system. Foyle was no longer a diocesan school; major changes of governance then occurred and in May 1877 the diocesan library was moved to the diocesan offices close to the cathedral.

A book of sermons by the royalist Bishop Ezekiel Hopkins, whose library, left behind when he departed the city, became the core of the Derry Diocesan Library.

BISHOP EZEKIEL HOPKINS, ARCHBISHOP WILLIAM KING AND THE DERRY DIOCESAN LIBRARY

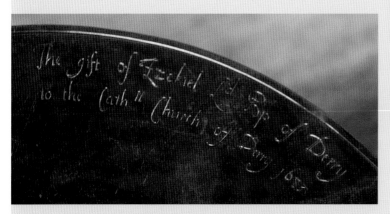

Ezekiel Hopkins, Bishop of Derry (1681–90), was a supporter of the monarch James II. After the closing of the gates of the city in December 1688 he quickly left Derry and went to Dublin. He died in London on 19 June 1690. On leaving Derry his library remained behind and these books were purchased from his executors by his successor William King, Bishop of Derry (1691–1703). On King's appointment as Archbishop of Dublin in 1703 the library stayed in Derry, but when in 1707 the repairs of the diocesan school were about to begin he negotiated with the Dean of Derry, John Bolton, in order (as we have seen) to have a room built which was capable of accommodating this library. He contributed £100 towards the cost and arranged for Revd Chivers of the Derry diocese to prepare the catalogue. In October 1708 the room was ready and Dean Bolton transferred the books there.

Negotiations continued between Archbishop King and his successor, Bishop Charles Hartman, Bishop of Derry (1703–14). with the result that the library was designated the Derry Diocesan Library and the headmaster became the diocesan librarian with a regular stipend. The agreement was to be binding on future bishops of Derry and Revd Roger Blackhall MA and his successors as master would receive £12 annually for this extra duty. Archbishop King intended to prepare a set of rules for the guidance of the librarian but apparently did not actually do so.

Substantial donations of books were given in the 18th and 19th centuries and the library stayed with the school until after the disestablishment of the Church of Ireland by the Irish Church Act of 1869. When the school moved to Lawrence Hill in August 1814 the library was then housed on the ground floor of the south wing – the rooms which would later be used by Messrs Gillanders and Mowbray in the 1950s and 1960s. In 1833 the Irish Church Temporalities Act resulted in the union of the dioceses of Derry and Raphoe. With the addition of the Raphoe diocesan library the library became the Derry and Raphoe diocesan library. It finally left the school on transfer to Synod Hall in the diocesan offices in May 1877.

Considered to be one of the most significant in Ireland, the collection is now currently housed in special accommodation within the library at the Magee campus of the University of Ulster. There are 5,600 books and pamphlets from 1460–1900 with approximately 700 from the 16th century, 1,900 from the 17th century and 1,400 from the 19th century. The oldest is a Latin breviary, printed in Venice in 1483. There is a first edition of Samuel Johnson's *A Dictionary of the English Language* (1755) and the work of early printers include Aldus Manutius of Venice and Anton Koberger of Nuremberg, both of whom were 15th-century masters.

ABOVE: *Silver donated to St Columb's by Bishop Hopkins, 1683 (see inscription, left).*

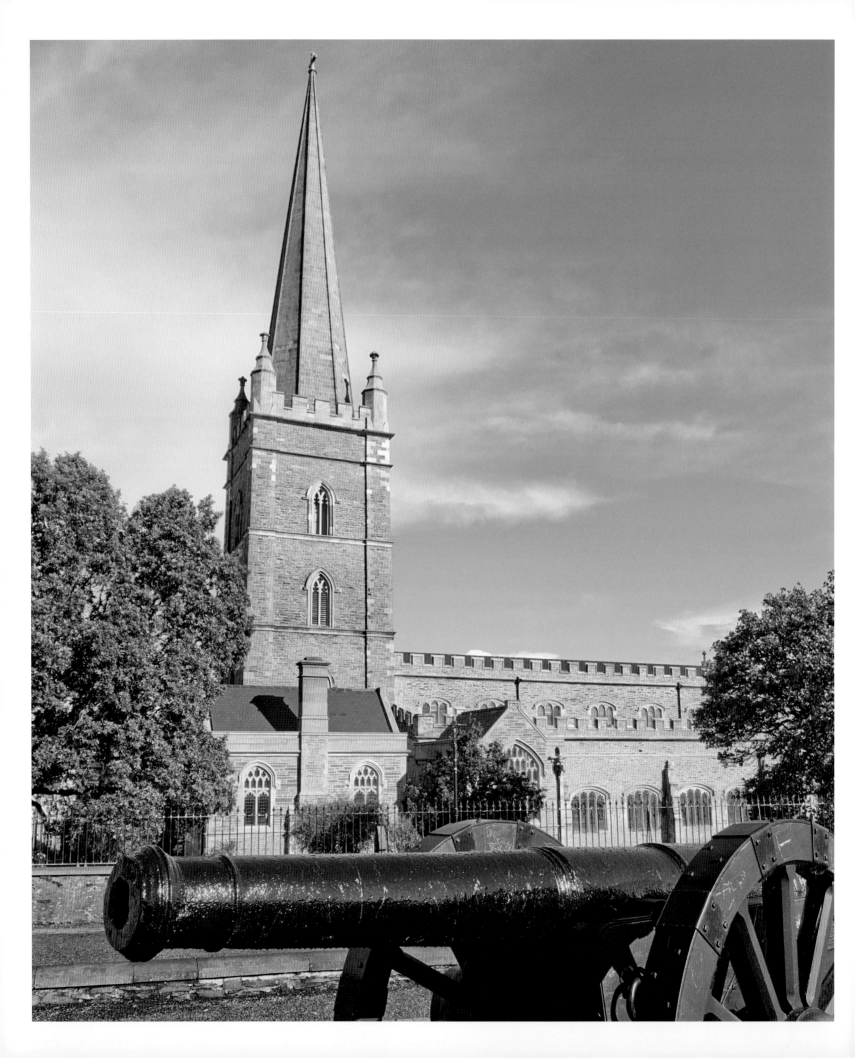

THE DIOCESAN FREE SCHOOL IN THE 18TH CENTURY

3

The 18th century was essentially a time of peace in Londonderry. The form 'Derry' was the common usage because of verbal convenience and the fact that the diocese retained the name. This usage would continue after the name of the school was changed to Foyle College, Derry, in 1814, although its working abbreviation was and still is Foyle. Apart from its busy port Derry was a quiet market town. Its population was essentially Protestant, with Presbyterians forming a strong and increasingly vocal minority. The Catholic population (mainly comprised of domestic servants) was so small and politically disempowered as to be insignificant, though it gradually increased as the years passed and the popery laws first fell into virtual disuse and were finally repealed. 'Derry Kay' became one of

the leading ports of emigration during the quiescent century, its clients mainly nonconformists, tired of the political and religious discrimination which they also suffered under the Penal Laws, and who left for America seeking greater tolerance and freedom. The school was entirely Anglican in its ethos (and staff), though of course the religious orientation of its pupils reflected that of the town. Its position in the life of the town was recognised in that the street in which it was set became known as Free School Lane. The thoroughfare was only later known as Society Street in deference to the ground landlords, the Irish Society, ostensibly one of the responsible parties in the running of the school.

This question of responsibility continued to vex, making what should have been a sound foundation

OPPOSITE: *St Columb's Cathedral.*

RIGHT: *View of Londonderry and the impact of the industrial age (c.1846).*

31

rather a metaphorical swamp. The full account of the gnarled and Byzantine complication of the school's funding is given in chapter 2. The school, still in the same foundation site, had been substantially rebuilt in 1710 and would remain there for more than a hundred years, unhappily insecure because of its

anomalous position, with all the trappings of a 'royal' school but without any royal emoluments. It was to mean in some cases real hardship for the teaching staff, in some cases necessitating a prolongation of service by some masters, through lack of money for a retirement pension.

In 1709 the CCLC had granted £60 (£6,370 with today's purchasing power) towards the re-building, and 20 years later Archbishop King in his will donated the diocesan library to the school. The new building had a specific ground-floor annex to house the volumes. For the next 80 years the mastership became almost a family preserve. Roger Blackhall who served from 1702 until 1734 was succeeded by his son-in-law the Revd John Torrens MA DD, who had previously been usher. When his term of office ended in 1773 he was replaced by his son Thomas, who stayed for seven years to be replaced by his cousin, Roger Blackhall, who was master until 1783.

During these years, though the average attendance was less than 40, over 150 went on to graduate from Trinity College, Dublin. Eight of these became fellows, and Francis Andrews rose to the exalted rank of provost of the university. During this period all appointments had to be approved by the Irish Society, the Bishop of Derry, the Corporation of Londonderry and/or the parliament in Dublin. It was after this that the school became known as the Derry Diocesan Free

ABOVE: *St Augustine's Church on the walls of Derry is adjacent to the site of the original Free School – now a car park.*

LEFT: *Revd Thomas Torrens, 1773–80.*

RIGHT: *Colonel George Vaughan entered Trinity College, Dublin, 1708.*

FAR RIGHT: *Francis Andrews was Provost of Trinity College, Dublin, 1758–74.*

School. By the time of Roger Blackhall's death in 1783 the school had again fallen into one of its recurring sloughs. Blackhall, like others, had been forced by economic necessity to stay longer than appropriate, professionally or personally. He had been incapacitated by a long and ultimately fatal illness and the school had suffered from his dysfunction.

The egregious Frederick Hervey had become bishop in 1768, and though he was very much an absentee, when he did come to Derry – or to his rural palace at Downhill – he was interested and genuinely concerned with diocesan matters. He approved the appointment of Blackhall's successor, Thomas Marshall, a native of the city, on 2 November 1783. Also formally assenting were the mayor and the corporation, the 'gentry of the city and county, and his fellow citizens'. This new broom had a salutary effect on the institution, soon increasing the number of boarders to its full complement and the number of dayboys to 80. Marshall fell victim to an outbreak of cholera that was raging in the city, dying on 10 September 1790. As WS Ferguson notes:

> *The master in charge in that period was the Revd Thomas Marshall BA, a former pupil who had entered Dublin University in 1775.*

He was then made a curate at St Columb's Cathedral before being appointed as the Master when the school was at a low ebb with only four boarders and 16 day pupils. The Revd Roger Blackhall, his predecessor had been ill but in Marshall's hands the numbers quickly picked up and when it had 17 boarders and 80 day-pupils it was probably one of the largest schools in the province. The 1788 government inquiry into the royal schools stated that Armagh had 66 pupils, Dungannon 15, Raphoe 20 and Enniskillen 24.

The boys found themselves in a happy community. Thomas Marshall proved to be a natural teacher who befriended his pupils and discipline was enforced with a light touch. As the school had only a small playground, the pupils were allowed to go into the town and the nearby countryside. If they had ventured down to the ship quay they would have seen the new wooden bridge across the Foyle being put in place by Cox and Thompson of Boston, New England. They could also have seen the Volunteers drilling. Special places were reserved for 'the gentlemen of the Free School' at the centenary commemoration of the Shutting of the Gates on 7 December 1788.

Thomas Marshall had friends with literary tastes whom he would invite to dine with the boys at the school. A visitor could have heard the star pupil, John Jebb (later Bishop of Limerick, Ardfert and Aghadoe) translate passages from Horace and Virgil. One visitor, Alexander Knox, developed a friendship with the young Jebb, which in 1834 would result in a publication, *Thirty Years of Correspondence between John Jebb and Alexander Knox*. The kindly and generous Thomas Marshall died young in 1790 and was buried a few yards from the school in St Augustine's graveyard. Bishop Jebb later recorded:

> … *my removal to Derry school, I cannot but consider providential. It has had a special influence on the whole colour of my life: on my studies, habits and pursuits: it has been the means of bringing me acquainted with persons whom I would not otherwise have known: of introducing me to those who have since been the chosen friends of my life: and my patrons and companions.*

His successor, George Vaughan Sampson, continued Marshall's good work for four years but, finding himself unable to live on the income that consisted of £40 a year from the diocese, plus £12 as diocesan librarian and £20 from the Irish Society for the usher, he petitioned for an increase, which they refused to grant.

He resigned in June 1794 to become rector of Aghanloo, near Limavady, to be replaced by James Knox, who had been the incumbent there. (It should be remembered that all headmasters of the Free School and Foyle were ordained clerics until the coming of Maurice Hime in 1877.) James Knox was to rule the school for 40 years until his retirement. In his time he would see the demolition of the old diocesan school, in a state of severe disrepair, the moving to the Strand Road site, a gift of the Hon. William Knox, who succeeded the Earl-Bishop in 1803, the further demolition of the replacement building because it was 'too dark' and the Lawrence Hill college that lasted until the opening of the new school in Springtown in 1967.

LEFT: *James Knox BA, Headmaster 1794–1834.*

BELOW: *Early plan of Lawrence Hill 1814.*

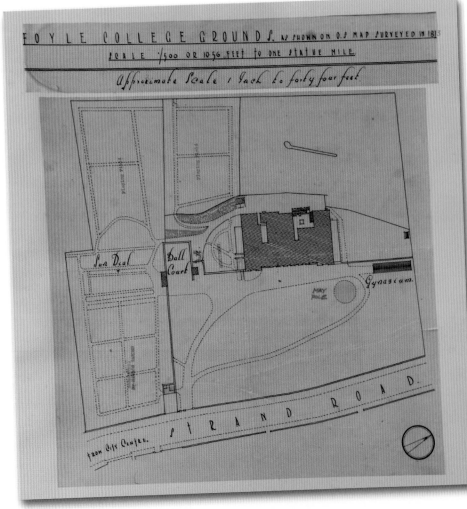

REVD GEORGE VAUGHAN SAMPSON BA MRIA HMGSL
Headmaster of the Derry Diocesan School (13 September 1790–1827 October 1794)

On graduating BA at TCD in 1782 at the age of 22 George Sampson was ordained in the Church of Ireland. He immediately went to France as assistant chaplain to the Duke of Dorset, the British ambassador at the French court. In 1789 he returned to Derry as a curate of Templemore parish, where he became a popular preacher. On the anniversary of the relief of Derry he took the centenary service in St Columb's Cathedral, which was attended by the bishops and clergy of the Roman Catholic and Church of Ireland dioceses. He later received public addresses of thanks from both bishops.

During his relatively brief period as headmaster he appointed masters to give a complete mercantile education, and his scientific interests included being a member of the Geological Society of London. He had been a classical scholar and was an excellent linguist who was fluent in French and Italian. In addition, he provided classes in music, dancing and fencing. In 1792, in order to encourage his pupils, the Londonderry Corporation funded the provision of six silver medals as awards. When in April 1794 it proved more expensive than estimated the corporation passed a resolution that 'in future not a penny more shall be given.' In 1794 there were 31 pupils of whom three qualified for TCD and in October he arranged to exchange livings with Revd James Knox, rector of Aghanloo.

In 1802 he published *The Statistical Survey of the County of Londonderry* and was made a member of the Royal Irish Academy. In 1807 he became the rector of Errigal parish, where he rebuilt the church and restored the glebe. He was the agent for the Fishmongers' company (1820–4) initiating many improvements in their estates before resigning in favour of his son Arthur. In 1813 he published a chart of the county of Londonderry including its fossil history and accompanied by a memoir. Revd George Vaughan Simpson died on 27 October 1827 in his 65th year.

View of Londonderry (c.1800).

THE NEW SCHOOL AND WILLIAM KNOX

William Knox, Bishop of Killaloe and Kilfenora, was rewarded for his support of the government when he voted for the Act of Union (1800) by being transferred to the bishopric of Derry, the richest in Ireland in 1803. There then followed a long conscientious episcopate in his new diocese characterised by his interest in educational provision and the support of many charitable causes. He offered a four-acre site on land on the Strand Road belonging to the see of Derry. His plans for the school were published in an article entitled 'The Diocesan School of Derry' in the *Londonderry Journal* of 25 March 1806. His plan needed to be approved by the Grand Jury at the spring assizes for two good reasons. One was that the site of the old school might be used for the new sessions (court) house and secondly under the Act 12 Geo. I c the grand jury had power to make a grant towards the building of the new school. A delay occurred when the owners of the old school site, the Irish Society, had to give their consent to build a sessions house. As the CCLC held that site without rent they agreed at their October council meeting to proceed with that request. When no reply was received, the grand jury at its spring assizes of 1807 approved the bishop's plan.

OPPOSITE: *College register, early 19th century.*

RIGHT: *Early engraving of Foyle College, 1814.*

37

THE LIVERY COMPANIES OF THE CITY OF LONDON AND THE SCHOOL

No records of livery companies' donations to the school prior to 1800 have yet surfaced. The main financial support provided by the London companies came after the appeal made in 1807 by Bishop William Knox, but after 1837 only a very few maintained an interest. With his definitive plans for the new school, Bishop Knox sent his request for funding to any company that had received land grants at the time of the plantation.

The Haberdashers, the Merchant Taylors and the Vintners did not respond to the bishop's appeal. The companies that did contribute (and the amounts) are given below:

Drapers: £600 between 1807 and 1815 and then £100 annually until 1837. From 1885 a Drapers' Company university scholarship of £40 per year for three years to each of two girls attending the Strand House School or the Londonderry Ladies' Collegiate School) and awarded on the results of the admission examination into the Royal University of Ireland. When Victoria College was founded one scholarship worth £115 over three years was given to the girl who each year obtained the best marks in an entrance examination of an Irish university. Grocers: £700 between 1807 and 1815 and then £100 annually until 1836. Between 1885 and 1909 an annual Grocers' Company scholarship of £25 at Magee

College was available by competition for one pupil attending girls' schools. Mercers: £840 between 1807 and 1815 and £105 annually until 1835. Then in 1840 a grant of £50 annually was provided to support two boarders at the school and at a reduced rate. That continued until 1871. Fishmongers: £600 between 1807 and 1815 and then £100 per year until 1816. Skinners: £600 between 1807 and 1815 and then £100 per year until 1829. Ironmongers: £420 between 1807 and 1815 and then £60 per year until 1823. Goldsmiths: £200 between 1807 and 1815. Salters: £200 between 1807 and 1815. Cooks: £60 between 1807 and 1815 and then £10 annually until 1820. Clothworkers: £25 in 1814 and from 1848 paid £25 annually for a boarder at the school. Brewers: £18 per annum between 1807 and 1815 and then £9 until 1830. Carpenters: £10 per annum between 1807 and 1815 and then £5 until 1835. Barbers: £5 per year between 1807 and 1835. Pewterers: £5 per year between 1807 and 1835.

All donations between 1807 and 1815 went into a building fund used to pay for the new school. Later payments were used to help finance it. When the Skinners' Company lost its legal case against the Irish Society in the Chancery Court London in 1835 there were considerable implications for the school. The remaining London companies withdrew their grants on the basis that the funding of the school was now a matter for the Society only. When an appeal went out for financial help in 1840 there was little or no response from the companies, with only the Mercers' Company and later the Clothworkers' Company making provision to support pupils from their local estates as boarders, and at reduced rates. And in more recent years the Merchant Taylors' Company has renewed its contact and has contributed generously to the school.

The CCLC voted £80 per annum at their meeting on 18 February 1807 in addition to the £20 they already paid each year. Knox next approached the Irish Society and presented his plan in person to their Committee of Accounts and Correspondence on 31 March. He indicated in a detailed statement that the present building was now in a ruinous state with a very small schoolyard and catered for 10 boarders and 40 day boys. Both numbers he hoped to increase with the offer of a second usher and with university scholarships awarded to 'exhibitioners' for four years at Dublin University. He stated his intention to donate £1,000 and the proceeds of the sale of the old school building. The court of the Society met on 7 April and approved a grant of £120 a year, together with a lease on the old school site to the CCLC for 21 years at a nominal rent so that the lease could be put up for auction. On 21 March 1807 he wrote to the clerks of the London livery companies describing this plan and suggesting a meeting with each court of the several companies. This was made possible by the fact that he spent only about four months of each year in Derry, the rest mostly in London.

Above: *Elevation and floor plan for the Gothic Lawrence Hill, 1812.*

Above right: *Foyle College, 1856.*

It is possible to follow the course of his negotiations with the Drapers Company and similar engagements with the other companies. He met the clerk of the company and followed that up with a letter on 15 May giving details of his scheme:

> *The greatest object which I have in view is to introduce such a system of education and such rewards for industry and talents as shall induce the landed proprietors as well as those engaged in commerce to educate their children at the school of Londonderry. The want of such an institution has forced the gentlemen of property to send their sons to English or distant schools and has prevented the rising and wealthy yeomanry such as the trading industry of the country must be considered from giving that education to their children as they ought to have.*

At their next court meeting on 16 July, the company approved an annual subscription of £100, and recommended that the school should be secured by an Act of Parliament. All donations received from the livery companies between January 1807 and January 1815 were allocated to the building fund, which was used to pay for the new school.

Bishop Knox now proceeded to obtain the legislative support required for the new school. The Duke of Wellington, the Chief Secretary for Ireland, secured the consent for the transfer of the patronage from the Lord Lieutenant, arguing that the proposed 'great school at Londonderry would act as a counterpoise to the democratical establishment proposed at Belfast' – a reference to the future Belfast Academical Institution which would open in February 1814. The bill became law on 8 April 1808. The Irish Society and the livery companies now sponsored the bill to allow the sale of the old school. This act 'to create a seminary amply sufficient for the purpose of extended education in all its necessary branches' was passed on 12 May 1809. Earlier, in November 1808, £500 was received from the Court of Common Council of London, and the bishop's letter of thanks on 6 December also expressed the hope that some of the gift could be used to provide exhibitions for boys to enter TCD.

Richard Elsam, a Dublin architect, was appointed and his plans for a two-storey Gothic building were published on 12 July 1808 in the *Gentleman and*

Charles Maginniss
Born 1813. Died 1896.
Entered T.C.D. from the Free Grammar
School, Londonderry, 1829.
Called to the Irish Bar. 1836.
Perpetual Curate Newtownsaville. 1844-72.
Rector of Dromore (Clogher diocese) 1872.

John Hamilton Magennis (Maginniss)
Born 1812.   Died 1837.
Entered T.C.D. From the Free Grammar
School of Londonderry in 1829.
Curate of Ballyboy, King's County.

LEFT: *The Maginnis brothers, Charles and John. Both entered Trinity College, Dublin, in 1829, although John, sadly, did not live long, dying in 1837.*

Builder's Companion. A lot of the preliminary work was undertaken and the building proceeded. But when it was reasonably advanced it became apparent that the rooms were too small and would be too dark. So it was decided to pull it down after £1,000 had been expended on the structure and another £600 was needed to remove it and reconstitute the site. So another architect, John Bowden of Dublin, was given the contract and it is thought work got under way later in 1809. Progress was slow, as work had to stop each year when the money ran out and could not restart until the next year's subscriptions were paid. In 1811 the Irish Society requested annual statements of accounts and details about the progress. Then the *Londonderry Journal* announced that the school was to be opened on 12 September 1813. This opening ceremony did not take place on that proposed date but was postponed until 29 August 1814.

An advertisement in the *Londonderry Journal* for Tuesday, 30 August 1814 printed a letter from James Knox, the master, written on 29 August: 'It is the Lord Bishop of Derry's desire that it should be publickly [sic] understood that a gentleman of high literary reputation and late candidate for Fellowship in our university, is expected immediately in Londonderry to take possession of his Apartments as Second Master of the new Free School which opened this day'. On 3 January 1815 the *Journal* carried another advertisement announcing that the 'New Grammar School' would open on Monday, 15 January and that the second master would be the Revd William Phelan, assisted by three other teachers. It did not use the name Foyle but it did refer to Knox as 'Head Master'. When the school was fully operational in 1815 it had 110 pupils, of whom 54 were boarders.

The financial statements up to January 1815 show the building cost £12,493-15s-1d with another £2,191-12s-1d of estimated expenses (interest on borrowed money, completion of the building and school furniture). With the sale of the old school for £1,400, another Grand Jury grant of £1,000 and donations from individuals, the result was that at the end of 1815 the accounts showed a small surplus. The diocesan school now had a magnificent Georgian building, which was to be its home for the next 150 years.

THE IRISH SOCIETY AND THE SCHOOL

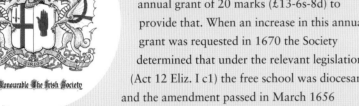

By its charter the Society was obliged to 'maintain a Free Grammar school in Derry', and from 1617 it provided for '14 poor scholars to be educated free of charge' at the school and made an annual grant of 20 marks (£13-6s-8d) to provide that. When an increase in this annual grant was requested in 1670 the Society determined that under the relevant legislation (Act 12 Eliz. I c1) the free school was diocesan and the amendment passed in March 1656 required the bishops, deans and chapters in each respective county financially to support their free schools. Negotiations continued for a decade until Ezekiel Hopkins, then bishop, accepted the responsibilities vested in him under the legislation.

With that agreement in place the Society increased its grant to £20 in 1683. Throughout the 17th century all bishops of Derry from Bishop Bramhall (appointed in 1634) on were involved in legal disputes with the Society over lands and fishing rights and those disputes were not settled until the following century. With their resolution, the diocese became relatively wealthy and remained so during the whole time that the school was diocesan.

The Society retained the right to appoint an usher from 1617 and we know that Robert Bonar was the usher in 1679. When further support was requested from the Society during the 18th century it was usually refused but it raised the grant to £30 in 1742 after insisting that the CCLC contribute a further £10. The grant was increased in 1808 to £110 and the local agent of the Society was appointed treasurer of the school. In 1826 £340 was given to cover the cost of repairs and the grant was raised to £140.

When the Skinners Company lost its case against the Society in the London Chancery court in 1835, almost all the London livery companies withdrew their financial support on the basis that it was now the Society's responsibility to provide for the school. So by 1846 it was providing £280 annually and that year it began to provide exhibitions of £30 per annum for each of five former pupils at Trinity College, Dublin. These scholarships would continue to be granted for over 100 years.

With the passing of the 1868 Irish Churches Act, the Society's role in its active management was incorporated in the 1874 Foyle College Act. The governor and deputy-governor of the Society were appointed to the board in recognition of the fact that it had now replaced the diocese as the sole financial supporter of the school. It continued to meet the costs of running the school but Foyle was not the only institution requiring its support. Both St Columb's College and (from 1869) the LAI sought and were given its help. The Society also contributed to the costs of building the gymnasium and swimming pool in 1888, and gave LAI annual grants of £210 from 1890.

In the early 1890s the Society found it was too costly to provide for both Foyle and LAI and so it used its financial clout to bring about their amalgamation in 1896. It continued its financial provision which, along with the school fees, would be the largest two sources of the school's income until 1948. In 1913 for example it provided £1,100 for the running costs and £180 for scholarships. The 1947 Education Act changed that, with the Government of Northern Ireland now responsible for the provision of education, and the Society gradually withdrew. It did continue to provide scholarships and give financial support for specific projects, but by the 1990s the scholarships were no longer provided.

Sketch of Irish Chamber, Guildhall Yard by Robert Randoll, 1913.

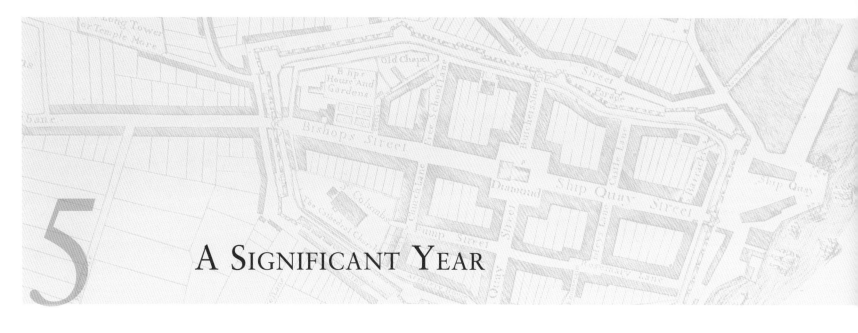

A SIGNIFICANT YEAR

WS Ferguson has described the academic year 1814–15 as one of the most significant in the school's history. It saw the problems of the move to Lawrence Hill surmounted and enabled the headmaster James Knox to place the following advertisement in the *Londonderry Journal* of 14 January 1815:

Free Grammar School Londonderry
Under the Superintendence of Revd James
Knox Headmaster and Revd William Phelan

second master and three assistants, the school will open on Monday 16 January.

Terms: To those not admitted as Free Scholars 7 guineas annually and 2 guineas entrance fee for tuition in Languages: Greek, Latin Composition in prose and verse. History and Geography – ancient and modern, with a complete commercial education by Mr Saunders who has here-to-fore been engaged in an eminent Commercial academy near London. Mr Saunders' course comprises English

OPPOSITE: *Foyle College, c.1880.*

RIGHT: *Assembly Hall, Lawrence Hill, c.1880.*

Foyle College, Lawrence Hill.

grammar, Arithmetic – vulgar and decimal, Algebra, Euclid's elements and bookkeeping according to the most approved modern systems. Use of the globe, Trigonometry, Mensuration and Navigation.

In addition to the above course, Logic, Ancient Geometry and Military Mathematics on the plan of Dr Hutton Woolwich by Revd Phelan. Terms 2 guineas annually.

Mr Saunders' English course separately: 4 guineas annually and 1 guinea entrance fee. Board and Lodging – 25 guineas with 6 guineas entrance fee.

French by Monsieur de Verney – 4 guineas annually and 1 guinea entrance fee. Dancing – Monsieur Perois.

The name the Free Grammar School was chosen in preference to the Derry Diocesan School as Knox knew that the income derived from the diocese was now much less than that provided from other sources. The staff comprised: Revd Knox, who had served 20 years as the Headmaster; Revd Phelan, who would become a Fellow of Trinity College, Dublin in 1817; William Smyth, who had been an usher since 1809; the second assistant William Stevenson, aged 17, who would enter TCD after the summer of 1815; and Henry Saunders, who had been appointed to lead the commercial and mercantile department. The salaries received by these men were considerably larger than had been envisioned by Bishop Knox in 1807. The second master received £150, free board and lodging, plus half a guinea from the entrance fee and two guineas from each pupil who

Foyle College.

Six Months	John Maginnis	L	s	d
	Board and Tuition	18	4	—
due Nov 1st	Pen, Ink, and Paper }	1	10	—
1st 1823	Fire in School, and Repairs }			
	French Master one Quarter Tuition & with Entrance Fee	2	5	6
	Weekly Allowance & Poor Box } Leather Cap	10	10	
	Books & Stationery —	14	10	
	Woollen Draper and Taylor			
	Shoemaker			
	Glazier, Lock Smith, &c.			
		23	5	2
	Entrance Fee reduced to one half	3	2	3
	£	26	16	5

Paid by order on Mr John Kelso March 1823

J. K. March 5th 1823

and dancing remained optional subjects but the fees that appeared on the school bills at that time indicate that French had acquired a new status.

Bishop Knox's proposal to provide exhibitions at TCD to pupils who distinguished themselves in the university entrance exams was first implemented in the autumn of 1814, when awards of £40 each were made to George Fletcher Moore and M Shaw who had gained the first and second places respectively.

It was George Fletcher Moore, one of the boarders, who first suggested that the school should be called Foyle College, Derry. It is said that it was while gazing at the river from a classroom window – there was nothing then to interrupt the view – he conceived the idea of calling it after the river that flowed so close by. He confided in some of his schoolmates and they approached the Revd Knox who accepted the idea. Moore afterwards became Advocate-General and Colonial Secretary for Western Australia. The name and the abbreviation Foyle persisted though in 1855 Revd William Sweet Escott MA, Fellow of New College, Oxford, the then headmaster, was anxious to run Foyle on public school lines. Strongly influenced by Arnold of Rugby he adopted the name *Collegium Derriense* for the school and initiated the building of a college chapel.

ABOVE: *Half-yearly bill for John Maginnis, 1823.*

RIGHT: *George Fletcher Moore was a boarder who first suggested the name Foyle College. In later life he became Advocate-General and Colonial Secretary for Western Australia.*

undertook the Logic course. The first assistant and the English assistant were paid £100 and free board and lodging while the second assistant received £50 plus free accommodation. The headmaster received £40 from the diocese, £20 from the Irish Society (which had been paid since 1663 to provide for the education of 14 poor scholars) and £100 for educating another 20 scholars without charge. He was also entitled to any profits from looking after the boarders and part of the fees from the day pupils.

The curriculum consisted of the three 'holy' languages, Greek, Hebrew and Latin. English and the more commercial subjects were to become increasingly emphasised because of their practical value. French

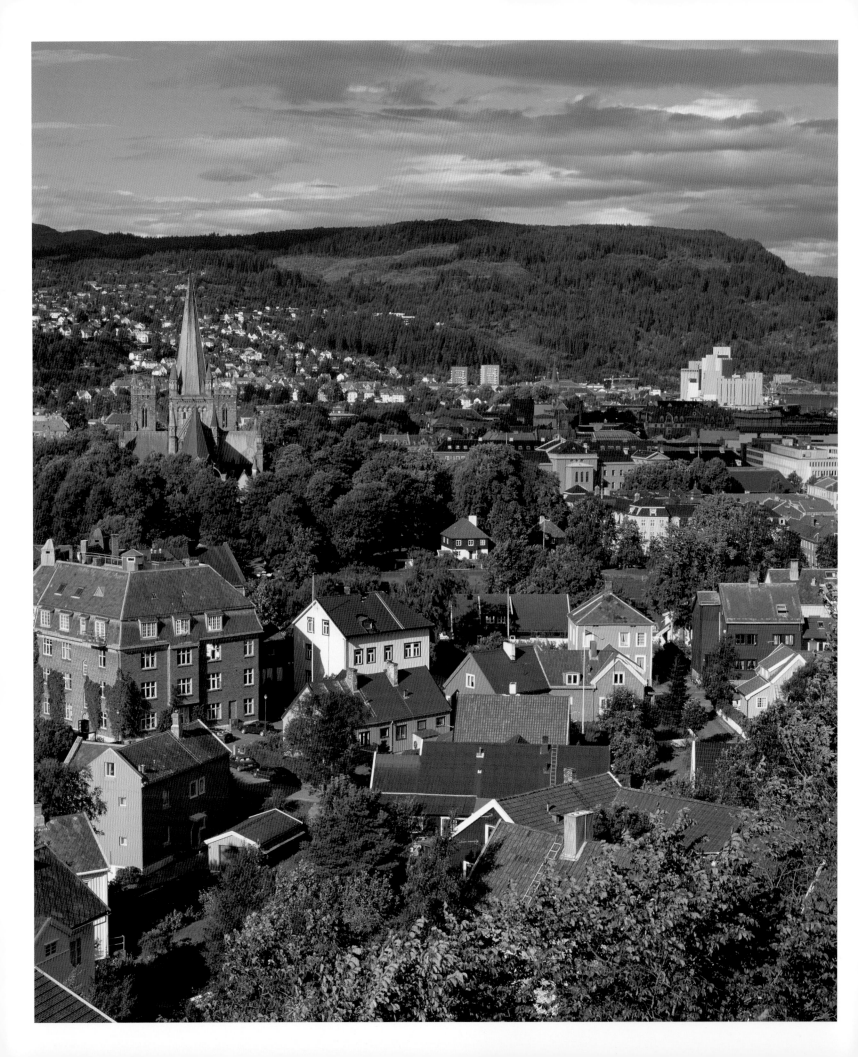

6 NORWEGIAN STUDENTS AT FOYLE

Nidaros or Trondhjem (today Trondheim) is an old town on the Norwegian coast. After a cathedral was built by the grave of St Olav in the 11th century, pilgrims gathered from all Scandinavia. This was a very important religious centre, as the Archbishop of Nidaros had a vast diocese including Norway, Iceland and Greenland, as well as the Faeroes, Shetland and Orkney Islands. Since the time of the Vikings this town has also been the main port and trading centre for the northern parts of the country. Many ships headed west for England and Ireland, while others went to Germany, the Netherlands, France or Spain. Besides necessities like grain and salt they brought all imaginable kinds of goods from all over the world – for those who could afford it. The main export articles were dried fish, copper and timber. Much of the timber was sent to Irish ports.

For centuries Norway was under Danish rule, and the officials all came from Copenhagen. In the period 1650–1800 for some reason many merchants from the little Danish town of Flensburg (now on the German side of the border) found their way to Trondhjem. They formed prosperous 'merchant houses' (companies) and literally took over all international trade.

In connection with the cathedral a Latin school was founded to provide a solid foundation for further studies of law or theology suitable for future officials at the University of Copenhagen. The merchants of Trondhjem, however, felt their sons had other needs: German, English and French, practical subjects like Bookkeeping, Economy and Trade, Geography and Navigation. For this reason, a new school was founded by some of the merchants in 1783: Trondhjem Borgerlige Realskole (*School of Modern Science*). After attending this school many merchant

sons went abroad for further studies, to practise languages and (to be hoped) form connections with other students from merchant families. At least a dozen attended Greenrow Academy, situated near Silloth in Cumberland in northwest England.

One of the major timber merchants was Hans Wingaard Finne (1758–1830). His oldest son attended Greenrow Academy but two younger brothers were sent to Foyle instead: Johan Thue Finne (1797–1865) in 1816 and Paul Nicolai Finne (1802–78) in 1818–20. The Finne brothers all returned to Trondhjem to work together with their father in their prosperous merchant company. Another Norwegian student at Foyle was Hans Peter Walther (1808–86), the son of a merchant in Kristiansund (a little town south west of Trondhjem). He later combined trade with working as a customs officer in the port of Kristiansund. There may also have been other Norwegian students in Derry in the time before 1814.

Another great timber merchant of the late 1700s was Johan Wideroe Thoning. Among his trading partners was John Allingham of Ballyshannon. It seems Allingham also wanted his eldest son Edward to study abroad, and in 1804 Thoning made arrangements for Edward and also for James Carson (the son of a Belfast merchant) to study at the Realskole in Trondhjem.

Otto Owesen was one of the young lads who came from Flensburg to Trondhjem to try his luck. Thoning appointed him as a trainee and Owesen worked his way up to partnership. Owesen spent much time in Ireland and in 1803 he married Jane, John Allingham's daughter (Edward's elder sister), in Ballyshannon. When a son was born in March 1804 he was given the name Johan Wideroe Thoning Owesen, as a token of esteem and gratitude to his father's partner. In August Owesen brought his family back to Trondhjem; a month later old Thoning passed away and he continued the business by himself. His brothers-in-law Edward and William (father of the poet) took turns at working with him as trainees

Sadly, in 1807 Jane, as well as their tiny daughter, died. Owesen had no family in Trondhjem and immersed himself in the business. He decided that young Thoning Owesen (as he was called for short) would be better off living with his grandparents in Ballyshannon. There he would also have young uncles and aunts for company. The youngest one, James, was actually the same age as himself. This was only meant to be for a period but, due to the Napoleonic wars, Thoning was never to see his father again before Otto died in 1812.

In March 1813 uncle Edward brought Thoning to Derry to begin his schooldays, and in May Edward reports in a letter to Trondhjem: 'He has commenced his Latin and Greek studies and has already received uncommon favours from his Masters, for goodness of disposition and application'. Thoning signed the register of Foyle in 1814 and remained until 1819. Apparently his young uncle James also went to the college at the same time.

It is likely that Thoning heard numerous stories about life in Trondhjem from his uncles, and probably read the amazing diary written by his Uncle William (parts of which are preserved in Trondheim's library). In 1820 Thoning was able to visit Trondhjem, and met at last his father's friends again, being welcomed like a long-lost son. Two years later Thoning returned to Norway – this time to stay.

When he came of age and inherited the money from his late father's merchant company he was able to buy the estate of Leren (Leira) in 1829. This is situated a few miles south of Trondheim and consisted of a manor surrounded by undulating farming land and many tenant farms, vast woodlands with more tenant farms, and a river full of salmon fed by a great waterfall, that also powered corn mills, sawmills and other industries. Thoning took part wholeheartedly in running the main farm and improving it in many ways, and is considered to have been the first to introduce fly-fishing in Norway. He led a simple and unassuming life, and was notably considerate and kind to his servants and tenants.

As Thoning neither married nor had children, he had to consider what should happen to the estate

after his death. There was a strong tradition of donations to charities in Trondhjem, culminating in the case of the rich Thomas Angell disinheriting his dissolute family in 1767 and leaving his estate to the poor people of the town. From this time they were well provided for. Life in the countryside was another matter.

Thoning's lengthy and very detailed will reveals a charitable heart and a practical mind. The family in Ireland was remembered, as well as his Norwegian friends and his servants. He also requested that a chapel should be built at Leira, with funds for maintenance. Three charitable institutions were to be founded for people living in the district around Trondhjem. These were an institution named 'The Love of Christ', a rescue home for pregnant unmarried girls where they could live for a couple of years, work and learn crafts that would enable them to earn a living, as well as be inspired to better themselves and lead a pure and Christian life, a school for poor, orphaned or deprived boys to be educated as above and a similar school for girls. Very detailed instructions were given, particularly about the rescue home.

The greatest part of his fortune, however, was to be used to establish an institution for blind people in the northern part of Norway, situated in Trondhjem. Here Thoning left the details to be decided by the Church Department. Thoning probably knew that a boarding school for blind people had been opened in Christiania (Oslo) in 1861. In 1881, the year of his death, the parliament passed a law that gave all blind children the right to education and decided that the national school for the blind should be situated in Trondhjem. I am sure that Thoning would have been very happy to see a school opened in Trondhjem five years later, although his donations were not released for use until 1900. This was the starting point for the building of the much larger Dalen blindeskole, which was opened in 1912. The street was named 'Thoning Owesens Gate'.

A considerable amount of money from Thoning's legacy was put aside as a special fund, where parts of the yielded interest would be used for equipment and other expenses. Blind and visually impaired people still benefit greatly from this fund today. For them and for the people worshipping in Leira Chapel, the memory of Thoning Owesen is still living, in gratitude.

Eva Hov

Eva Hov.

REVD JAMES KNOX BA
(Headmaster June 1794–June 1834)

James Knox was born in 1756 to a family with Scottish origins, whose ancestors on both sides moved to County Donegal at the time of the plantations in Ulster. His father, Revd George Knox DD, was the curate at Clonleigh and his mother was Catherine Nesbitt of Woodhill, Ardara. Following a classical school education at Drogheda Grammar School, he entered TCD aged 14 on 9 July 1770. On graduating with a BA he became an ordained clergyman and in 1781 he was appointed Rector of Aghanloo. In 1790 he married his cousin Mary Frances Nesbitt of Woodhill, and four years later, aged 38, he became headmaster of the Derry Diocesan School. The letter of approval from the CCLC stated 'from all we learn and believe this gentleman in morals, temper, inclinations, talents and requirements is eminently desirable to us'. And by accepting the appointment he suffered a drop in income. Both the Lord Lieutenant and the Earl Bishop approved the appointment.

On his taking up the post there followed a period of considerable stability for the school. In 1802 his predecessor described the school in the following terms: 'Over this institution my learned and amiable friend Revd James Knox presides with great diligence and zeal. The learned and modern languages with other branches of education necessary for the mercantile pursuits are taught in this seminary.'

With the move to Lawrence Hill the school drew its pupils from some of Ulster's oldest families and from the business classes in Derry. By 1818 there were 110 pupils, including 54 boarders, but before long the numbers began to diminish. In 1825 there were 96 pupils but by 1834 there were none, and 30 non-fee paying pupils had been taken on by Revd Knox in order to keep the school alive. After 1830 the income had dropped and there was little or no money to pay the headmaster, nor did he have any pension. Consequently it was difficult for him to retire. Some provision was then made by the Bishop of Derry, and the headmaster's son, Revd George Knox, was given the living of the parish of Tremone, County Tyrone. So, after 40 years as headmaster and at the age of 78, Revd Knox resigned in June 1834. With his wife, two unmarried daughters and two unmarried sisters, he moved to Carthage, Culdaff, where his wife's sister Marcia also lived.

During his time as headmaster we believe 40 of his pupils entered TCD. A number of his former pupils met shortly after his retirement and resolved that some expression of gratitude for his long service was necessary. Arrangements were made for that appreciation to take the form of a presentation of a solid silver tea service along with an accompanying address showing the highest esteem and warmest affection. The address was signed by over 140 of his pupils, former pupils and other prominent citizens mainly from the city, County Londonderry and County Donegal.

Revd Knox remained hale and active over many years, assisting at church services until December 1847. After a short illness he died on 14 January 1848, and was buried in Culdaff church graveyard, in the vault in which his wife would be interred the following year.

LEFT: *A page from Knox's register of 1814.*

THE LAWRENCE BROTHERS AND THE INDIAN COLONIAL ADMINISTRATION

Along with James Abbott (b. 1807) and Frederick Makeson (b. 1807), the Lawrences – George (b. 1804), Henry (b. 1806) and John (b. 1811), comprised the older generation of the Indian Administration. With their political acumen and skills they formed a group with James Abbott, Herbert Edwardes, Harry Lumsden, John Nicholson, Henry Coxe, William Hodson, Richard Pollock, Lewin Bowring and Henry Casie, whose abilities as colonial administrators were comparable to any elsewhere in the Empire. The next generation, who were about ten years younger, were trained by Henry and would later serve under John.

In addition the Lawrences married exceptional women who were prepared to support them through thick and thin, and willing to bear children in often inauspicious circumstances. Honoria, Henry's wife, was remarkable but all took their Christianity seriously. Their Alma Mater was described as 'a tough no-nonsense God-fearing institution that produced boys ideally suited to the East India Company's needs'. After military education at Addiscombe, George and Henry joined the Bengal Army as military cadets while John, after Haileybury, joined the East India Company as a writer and intending to be a civil servant. George came to India as a cavalry officer, to be followed two years later by Henry as a gunnery officer. John and Henry got on well but John and George found it difficult to work together.

In 1839 George joined the army of the Indus as a political assistant and soon became the military secretary to Sir William Macnaughten. In late December 1841, in a confrontation near Kabul with Akbar Khan, George was taken prisoner and his assistant killed. Retribution was swift, Kabul was surrounded by the army under General Pollock, and all British prisoners were released. On being taken to the relief camp outside Kabul, George was reunited with Henry.

Further conflicts with the Sikhs followed until they were defeated at the battle of Sobraon (February 1846), and the Punjab was then governed by the Regency of the Council of Sikhs, but with a British administrator in charge. Henry was appointed and promoted colonel. He made George his political assistant at Peshawar, and John, in the headquarters at Lahore, became the commissioner of the land between the Sutle and Beas rivers. To ensure fair tax assessments, George travelled throughout his area, negotiating with the tribal leaders, known as Khans. He learned about the injustices perpetrated by the Sikh leaders with their extortionate methods. By providing the Pashtuns of the Yusufzai (Sons of Joseph) with religious freedom and relief from their Sikh tax masters, he ensured their gratitude and cooperation.

Meanwhile, Lumsden, who had also gained the respect of the tribal elders and warriors, was given the task of raising a corps of loyal troops who would

GEORGE LAWRENCE. 1815-1819.
HENRY LAWRENCE. 1815-1819.
ROBERT MONTGOMERY. 1819-1824.
JOHN LAWRENCE. 1823-1825.
THIS TABLET
WAS PLACED HERE BY THE BOYS OF FOYLE COLLEGE
ONE HUNDRED YEARS
AFTER JOHN LAWRENCE LEFT THIS SCHOOL.

ABOVE: *John (left) and George (right) Lawrence.*

LEFT: *Memorial plaque marking the Lawrence brothers and Robert Montgomery.*

ABOVE: *Blue plaque commemorating Henry Lawrence on the original Foyle College building at Lawrence Hill.*

RIGHT: *Henry Lawrence.*

FAR RIGHT: *Illuminated manuscript from the Lawrence schools, India.*

BELOW: *The Lawrence medal and obverse.*

collect intelligence. Over his lifetime he built a mixed cavalry and infantry force with a mystique that made it the most famous unit in the Indian Army. George employed this force to protect the high Gundgurh country and to keep order on the Peshawar plain and the Burmer frontier. He knew from his 1830s experience of the Khyber pass that security could only be assured with the agreement of the local tribes. One of their rules of hospitality required them to provide a guard of troops, the *bedragga* ('bedraggled'), who guarded their territory to the tribal boundary and no further. That required patient negotiations but was the method used for the next century to protect the tribal areas.

In January 1848 Henry Lawrence returned to England on home leave, and Lord Dalhousie replaced Lord Hardinge as governor-general of the Punjab. A dispute over the control of the tax revenue then arose in Multan 200 miles south west of Lahore, and two envoys sent there were murdered on arrival. A serious delay in responding resulted in a worsening of the revolt. An attempt by George to move his family to Lahore failed, and with the fall of Peshawar they became prisoners of the Afghans in Khodat. This Afghan entry started the Second Sikh war (1848–9). Henry returned to India after receiving

his knighthood in April 1848. With the surrender of the Sikh army in March 1849, the Punjab with its four million subjects became part of British India. When Henry refused to comply with this new chain of command, Lord Dalhousie restricted his governing powers. He was made the agent in Rajputana, then the agent of the governor-general and died at the siege of Lucknow in 1857. Henry was buried in the grounds of the Residency in Lucknow.

George followed Henry as the agent of the governor-general until he resigned due to ill health in 1864. In 1866 he became a Knight Commander of the Star of India and retired from the army as an honorary lieutenant-general in 1867. He died five years after John in 1884.

John became the Chief Commissioner in the Punjab and at the end of 1863 he succeeded Lord Elgin as the Viceroy of India. He maintained a policy of non-interference in Afghanistan, and concentrated on extending the railway system, while improving irrigation and sanitation. In 1869 he left India and was made a Baron on his return to London, with a small estate on Salisbury Plain. He died on 29 June 1879 and was buried in Westminster Abbey.

WS Anderson

Browsing through the files held at Foyle I was struck by the long and close associations between Foyle and TCD. The first recorded entry into TCD was that of Thomas Hemsworth in 1682. We now have a complete list of the 297 students from Foyle who by the year 1834 had attended TCD. George Farquhar, one of the school's most famous alumni, entered as a sizar in 1684 under the patronage of the Bishop of Dromore. [For a fuller account of Farquhar's career see the Alumni section.]

Charles Hopkins, the son of Bishop Ezekiel Hopkins, entered one year after Farquhar. Henry Singleton, who entered in 1698, became Master of the Rolls. The list of famous alumni includes Thomas Skipton (1701), John Lecky (1723) and Basil Brooke (1724). Robert Boyd (1740) became a judge of the King's Court of Ireland and Recorder of Derry; William Richardson (1759) won fame as an important agriculturalist. Not all entrants from Foyle did well. John Graffan entered in 1708 but was expelled in 1710 for drunkenness and aiding and abetting Thomas Harvey in damaging the baton in the hand of the statue of William III at College Green. Later, Samuel Law Montgomery (1783) became Rector of Moville in 1812 and lived at Newpark. Alexander Curry (1814) also served as Recorder of Derry, along with three Babingtons, Richard (1781), Richard (1783) and GV (1815).

Francis Andrews entered Trinity in 1733 aged 15. [See profile that follows.] Another notable alumnus was George Hill (1780), who represented Derry in Grattan's parliament. He was present at the arrest of Wolfe Tone at Buncrana, and as they had been fellow students at Trinity there *must* have been a brief moment of recognition. Robert Torrens (1791) became a judge of the Court of Common Council of Ireland and Samuel Kyle (1788) became provost in 1820 and later Bishop of Cork. Percy French, one of our most famous entertainers, graduated from TCD in engineering in 1881.

When Maurice Hime came as headmaster of Foyle in January 1878 he brought with him one of our most distinguished scholars, John Bagnell Bury. [For a fuller account of Bury's career see the Alumni section.]

Sir John Herbert McCutcheon (b. 1885) entered TCD in 1903 and won the university welterweight boxing championship. Entering the Treasury he became Principal Assistant Secretary and in 1938 was appointed Deputy Master of the Mint. He organised the new coinage for Eire and in direct consultation with George VI designed the new George Medal.

Magee College was founded by Martha Magee in 1845 to prepare men for ministry in the Presbyterian Church. The present building dates from 1865. In 1880 it was incorporated into the Royal University of Ireland after a failure of a proposed connection with Queen's University Belfast (QUB) in 1867, and two years later Magee students could obtain their degrees. From 1909 Magee students were able to register as TCD undergraduates and were able to complete their third and fourth years there and have their degrees conferred there. This arrangement ended in 1972, when it became Magee University College, and it is

ABOVE: *Trinity College, Dublin.*

RIGHT: *Magee University College. Originally founded in 1845 on another site, it became part of the Royal University of Ireland in 1880, then in 1909 an annexe of Trinity College, Dublin, which Magee students went on to attend in their third and fourth years. It is now a campus of the University of Ulster.*

now a campus of the University of Ulster. The peak year for Foyle alumni at Magee was 1936, when there were 160 on the rolls. Nowadays only a small number go: one only in 2006 and 2008, none in 2007 and 2009. One of the causes is stringent entry requirement: students require more CAO points than the usual number of A-level results can generate, compared to those accruing from the greater numbers of subjects sat in the Leaving Certificate in the Republic of Ireland.

Dean Cecil Orr

FRANCIS ANDREWS (1718–74)

Francis Andrews was born in 1718 in Derry to a father of independent means. Having attended the Free School, he entered TCD in 1733 at the age of

14. He graduated in 1737 and read law at Middle Temple Bar, London, and was called to the Irish Bar in 1746, having become a Fellow of TCD in 1740. He was appointed Provost on 28 October 1758, the first layman in that post since 1626. He was the second of only three provosts during the 18th century, described by Sir John Pentland Mahaffy (1839–1919), a later provost, as 'a century of glittering magnificence'. He was unquestionably one of the most significant and influential of the TCD's provosts.

Andrews was Professor of Modern History (1762–9) and MP (in the Irish parliament) for Midleton, County Cork (1759–60), and Derry (1761–74). As a parliamentarian, he was an eloquent speaker, witty, frank, benevolent, good-humoured and cultured.

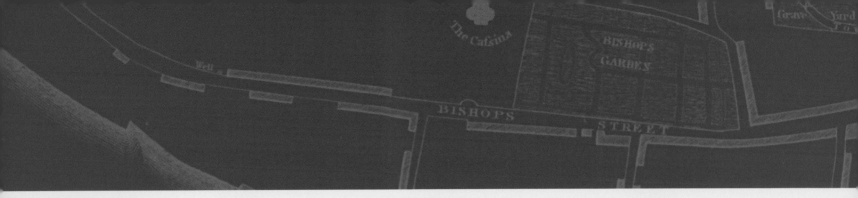

LEFT: *Provost's House, Trinity College, Dublin.*

BELOW: *Great West Front, Trinity College, Dublin.*

He made influential friends amongst the British and Irish aristocracy and persuaded Parliament to grant substantial funds for the rebuilding of the Provost's House and the remodelling of the Great West Front, which dominates the entrance to TCD to this day. He designed the larger Provost's House on a grand scale in which he could entertain on an equally lavish style. The exterior with its granite Doric pillars and Venetian-style windows was described as 'a monument to good taste' and the main reception room as 'the most elaborately and richly decorated room in Dublin'. Despite his provincial accent and manner, he held his own in high society at home and abroad. Described as a sensible and capable administrator, he instituted a system of public entrance examinations and cultivated music in the college, with a regular choir instituted in the college chapel. He was popular with his wide circle and managed to avoid the conflicts experienced by his predecessor, Richard Baldwin, and successor, John Hely-Hutchinson.

In his later years, following a period of illness, he travelled to Italy to convalesce. In Rome he commissioned a portrait by the artist Anton von Maroni, which hangs in the Provost's House. He died at Shrewsbury on the journey back from Italy on 12 June 1774 at the age of 56. He bequeathed a substantial sum of money to the college to build an astronomical observatory which was duly constructed at Dunsink, near Dublin, and the funding for a professorship of astronomy, first established in 1783 and suspended only in 1921.

SAMUEL KYLE (1772–1848)
Samuel Kyle was born in 1772 and attended the Free School until 1788, when he entered TCD, becoming a Fellow in 1798 and provost in 1820. He was one of the four provosts who served during the years 1799–1833, representing 34 years of relative obscurity – 'a twilight between the glittering magnificence of the 18th century and the solid splendour of the 19th century'. All four resisted the movement for Catholic emancipation and all resigned their posts for bishoprics in various parts of Ireland. Mahaffy describes the history of the period as 'the least creditable in all three centuries – the general atmosphere of the college was unwholesome, stagnant and disgraceful and its rulers criminally supine'.

Kyle resigned his post on 19 March 1831 when he was appointed Bishop of Cork, Cloyne and Ross. He died in 1848. He headed the college with competence but no special distinction during his 11 years.

SIR ANDREW SEARLE HART
After attending Foyle, he studied at Trinity, becoming a Fellow in 1835. He was bursar 1858–66, senior lecturer from 1866–87, registrar from 1873–6 and vice-provost from 1876–90. He was knighted in 1886 and died in 1890.

William Lynn

RIGHT: *Samuel Kyle (left) and Andrew Searle Hart (right), respectively from the Free School and its next incarnation as Foyle College, represented an involvement with Trinity College, Dublin, over a period spanning more than 70 years.*

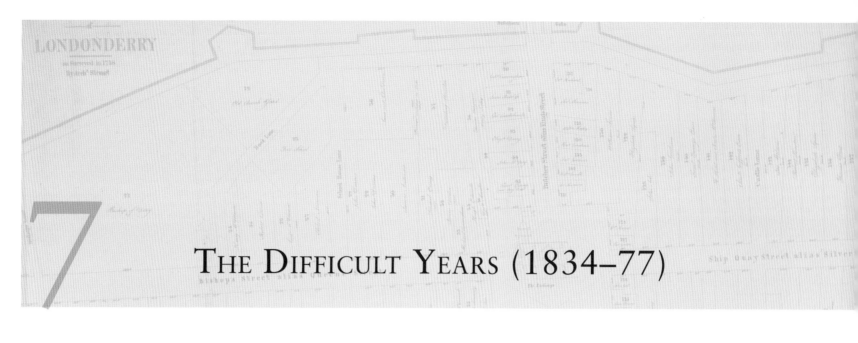

7 THE DIFFICULT YEARS (1834–77)

By 1830 the school's reputation had diminished. Knox was 74 years old and less able to run the school as formerly. Failing in health and increasingly incompetent he struggled on for four more years, finally resigning in 1834. The 'Report of the Londonderry Free School' issued in May 1835 spoke of him in the highest terms as 'a clergyman of the most exemplary character, and universally respected, and in every way qualified for the position'. It also suggested tactfully that 'forty years of work will wear out the strongest constitution'. His portrait by William Foy of Derry used to hang in Culdaff house until it was destroyed in the Irish War of Independence.

Knox's last years in office were relatively quiet, apart from the anxiety he must have had over money. Late in 1832 he was forced to close the school because of an outbreak of cholera, spread by the poor sanitation arrangements. It was able to open again on 14 February 1833 and Knox could advise the Board of Education in Dublin that the total enrolment was 59, consisting of 25 Free Scholars (the school maintaining its original role), 33 day pupils and one boarder. The age range was from nine to 18, with a modal grouping of 12 to 16. Knox's ambition of attracting pupils, especially boarders, from the grander families of the area had not been realised.

When he retired in August there were no boarders and the seven-year service of his successor, Revd William Smyth, was essentially an exercise in survival. Annual grants by the Corporation and some livery companies were withdrawn and a committee organised by Bishop Knox appealed to Sir Robert Peel, the Prime Minister, for necessary assistance. Probably because of Peel's intervention the Irish Society increased its grant sufficiently to allow the

OPPOSITE: *Revd John Hamilton Miller, Headmaster 1841–7.*

BELOW: *Derry Quay, 1846, by JN Gosset.*

the Revd William Sweet Escott MA, Fellow of New College, Oxford.

Escott was appointed in the spring of 1854 and became a vigorous new broom. Strongly influenced by the charismatic Thomas Arnold (1795–1842), who had made Rugby school, once the characteristic hellish English public school, an exemplar for the educational reforms that were long overdue, he decided to apply them to Foyle, though it had little if any of the violence and bullying that had been the hallmark of the older English model. During his nine years of office he tried to force it into the desired shape, giving it the title *Collegium Derriense* in 1855 and beginning the construction of a school chapel dedicated to St Patrick that was finally consecrated on 30 April 1872. It was deconsecrated five years later, when Maurice Hime became headmaster.

The school that Escott wished to make of Foyle was essentially inappropriate for the burgeoning city that had at least as many Presbyterians as Anglicans. There was need of a scholastic reform as well as a moral one if its young men were to fit themselves for the economic future of their city. This movement contributed to the setting up of the rival Londonderry Academical Institution. Escott retired in 1862 to be replaced by William Hunter Parret.

school to continue. Revd John Hamilton Millar took over in June 1841 and two years later the Drapers company ceased to contribute to the school.

Millar's tenure was marked by the visitation of the Great Famine, the most cataclysmic event in modern Irish history. The scholars were more or less protected from the awareness of the pestilence but it must have been clear even to them that Derry Quay had become the main port of huge salutary emigration. Even in the blackest year, 1847, Millar could show an improvement in enrolment with 19 boarders, 20 Free Scholars and 62 day-pupils.

An increased grant from the Irish Society of £220 a year in 1846 with a special payment of £135 for repairs had clearly enhanced the school's reputation and Millar was able to hand over to Robert Henderson, his successor, in 1848 a more vibrant institution than he had been given. On 29 December 1851 he welcomed to the staff as usher an old boy of Foyle, the Revd William Steele, who on 23 June 1857 was appointed the 13th headmaster of Portora and continued in the post for 34 years. In the summer of 1853 Henderson decided that the struggle of maintaining the school had become too wearing and in October he announced that he would retire to Brompton Ralph in Somerset, exchanging livings with

ABOVE LEFT: *Revd William Sweet Escott, Headmaster 1854–62.*

LEFT: *Revd W Percy Robinson, Headmaster 1866–74.*

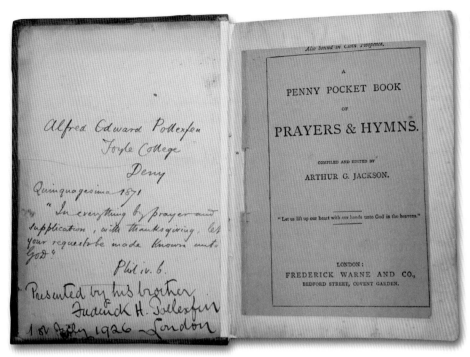

Society, the Presbyterian moderator and the mayor of Derry.

The school continued to grow; Robinson's account books for the years 1867–72 indicated that of 107 pupils, two were expelled, two were withdrawn, one was 'very nearly expelled', five were allowed to stay after a 'smoking affair' and one was allowed to stay despite being 'suspected of dishonesty'. *The Birch*, the first Irish school magazine, appeared on 16 November 1870 and lasted until 16 December 1871. One of the founders was Percy French, who spent some time at Foyle to improve his mathematics so that he could do engineering at TCD before becoming in his own words, 'an inspector of drains'. The following spring came the first number of *The Foyle College Monthly*, published on 9 March 1872 and lasting until the end of 1873.

When Robinson retired in 1874 Benjamin Moffat became the first headmaster of a school defined by its own act of parliament. The classical tradition continued with little regard for 'modern' subjects and dwindled until there were only eight boarders and about 40 dayboys.

When William Percy Robinson, Parret's successor, became headmaster in 1866 he determined to continue the school's strong diocesan links and maintained the devotional element that Escott had initiated. Robinson had been head of Sligo Grammar and brought with him a number of children of that town's leading families, notably Middletons and Pollexfens. Competence in Latin and to a lesser extent Greek was essential for entrance into Trinity College in Dublin. Already there was evidence of change. Five years before the foundation of Magee, a distinctly independent institution, the opening of Strand House School for girls by Frances Holmes signalled the beginnings of a movement that would have unprecedented and remarkable effects.

In the second year of Robinson's headship Foyle was faced for the first time in its history with a serious rival in the LAI, and as a result Foyle modified its curriculum. The Irish Church Disestablishment Act of 1869 weakened the school's diocesan support, since most of the Church's income was now transferred to the Treasury to supply the finance for the 'rewards' system that was part of the Intermediate Education (Ireland) Act of 1878. It was not until the Foyle College Act was passed in 1874 that the new constitution of the school was defined. Its new governing body was to comprise the Bishop and Dean of Derry, the deputy governor of the Irish

8 THE LONDONDERRY ACADEMICAL INSTITUTION (1868–96)

OPPOSITE: *Londonderry Academical Institution, c.1890.*

RIGHT: *Robert McCrea Chambers MA, 1868–75.*

BELOW: *LAI medal.*

After 1814 Foyle continued as a diocesan school in the Anglican tradition, the Bishop of Derry being the Patron of the school and its management firmly under the control of the Diocese of Derry. Meantime the city was developing and by the mid-19th century Derry was an active port, with railway links to other parts of Ireland and a ship-building industry, while the shirt factories, for which it was later to be famous, were already in production. This growing trade was in the hands of a progressive group of citizens who were not impressed with the classical education that the school offered.

When pressed for a commercial and mathematical course to be made available, Foyle's headmaster, the Revd William Percy Robinson MA DD, was not initially willing to accede to those demands. It was decided by the Nonconformist merchants and businessmen that a new school was needed, and on 8 January 1868 a public meeting was held in the Corporation Hall. The Revd JT McGaw, professor of logic, belles-lettres and rhetoric at Magee, convened this meeting, and Revd William McClure, the minister of First Derry Presbyterian Church presided. The following resolutions were carried: that there was a need for an additional intermediate school in the city; that it should be established immediately; that it would be called the LAI and that it would provide a sound, classical, mathematical and commercial education, and also provide careful, moral and religious training along non-sectarian lines.

LAI began on 14 February 1868 at 6 East Wall with two divisions, each with its own head. Robert McCrea Chambers MA was in charge of the Classics and English department while David Galloway Kimmond MA looked after the commercial and mathematics department. Mr Kimmond took boarders into the makeshift accommodation and it was apparent that they needed to build more suitable premises. The register shows 21 pupils entered on the first day, and at the end of 1868, 67 had been enrolled. On 15 January 1869 the preparatory department opened and 'it was intended for little boys from six to ten years, and is conducted by Mr Allison, a Magee College student, from 10am until 1pm'. To ease the overcrowding, in the following April, 16 Queen Street was acquired to accommodate the boarders under Mr Kimmond.

Londonderry Academical Institution staff and pupils, 1871.

Initially the Irish Society itself was not supportive but the school governors indicated that rivalry was healthy and that the Society should either grant a site for the new school or contribute to the building fund and provide an annual endowment. Soon afterwards, however, the Irish Society was won over. The government of the school was modelled on the Royal Belfast Academical Institution (RBAI), with the departments relatively independent of each other. The board of management consisted of those who had subscribed £50 or more to the funds. Hence there were 13 elected managers and 14 ex officio governors. The board also had authorisation to appoint the masters and determine their duties, to decide the courses for study, and make the rules, bye-laws and regulations.

On 21 December 1869 a site for the new school of just over four acres was obtained in Haw Lane (later the Academy Road). In July 1870 the advertisements calling for tenders to build the new school in an Italianate style of architecture, based on the plans of Messrs Turner and Williamson, were placed in the local papers, and on 1 September of the same year, the LAI trustees accepted the tender of Matthew McClelland, with the cost estimated at £3,576-12s-6d. On 26 September, the foundation stone was laid by the governor of the Irish Society, Col Sir WA Ross, at a public ceremony attended by many prominent citizens. The Irish Society contributed £1,000 to the cost, and would continue its financial support during the whole lifetime of the Londonderry Academical Institution.

Over £3,000 was raised from individuals, with William Tillie JP and William F Bigger heading the list of donors, each giving £350.

The new building was first occupied on 22 August 1871 and shortly afterwards Mr Kimmond took an appointment as head of the Mathematical and Science Department at Dollar Academy. Mr Chambers became the resident master in the new building, with responsibility also for the boarders. George Gordon MA came to replace Mr Kimmond but stayed for only two years before going to Cape Colony. His place was taken by John Young BA, who remained at the head of the commercial and mathematical department for the next 17 years.

The LAI always had a lack of money. When McClelland and Co furnished their final account of £3,846-19s-1d on 2 March 1872, the trustees found themselves with a debt of £1,000. On 14 March a 'Ladies' Committee', with Mrs Tillie and Mrs Osborne joint treasurers and Mrs Bigger and Mrs Joyce joint secretaries, was formed. They

then announced that a bazaar would be held in order to raise the funds. This was held on 11 and 12 December in the Corporation Hall, and at Christmas the Ladies Committee handed over £876 to the trustees. So with other donations the debt was wiped out and the trustees were able to consider further plans for the school.

In the early 1870s games were infrequent and there were few matches with other clubs or schools. But the real prowess on the sporting fields would have to await the appointment of Mr JC Dick in the autumn of 1879, which not only transformed the outlook of the boys but made the LAI a formidable force on the rugby and cricket fields of our province.

Meanwhile the preparatory department at the LAI had only eight pupils on its rolls in March 1873 and was not viable. In July it was decided that it should have a female teacher and so, on the recommendation of Mr Bole, the Inspector of National Schools, Miss Jane McKillip was appointed on 5 August 1873. She was paid £40 per annum and the hours were

LAI c.1880.

10am–2pm on weekdays and 10am–12 noon on Saturdays. By October only 13 boys had enrolled, and in January 1874 the board gave Miss McKillip permission to enrol girls on similar terms as the boys. The teaching staff was not consulted and when Mr Chambers objected in writing, he was overruled. On 18 October 1875 the board accepted his resignation. The numbers of pupils continued to rise and in the quarter ending 17 June 1875 the total had reached 100, with 15 boarders.

On 2 December Edward James Chinnock BA LLB replaced Mr Chambers as headmaster of the Classics and English department. Since Mr Chinnock did not enjoy the full support of the board he resigned in September 1878 in order to become the Rector of Dumfries Academy. John Clarke Dick MA came in his

place and he, along with Mr Young, would for more than a decade provide the leadership and excellence of education that would bring success for the pupils in the examinations of the Intermediate Education Board for Ireland, and also on the sports fields. By February 1883, the school had 157 pupils, including 31 boarders.

Games, particularly rugby, now became central to the life of the school, as may be gathered from the separate article on school rugby. Mr Dick supported cricket and the school has photographs of the 1st XIs in the 1880s and 1890s in which he appears. In November 1886 he asked the board to provide a gymnasium and swimming pool. After the tender from Colhoun Bros of £825 to build the gymnasium was accepted, the new facility was ready for use at the end of 1888. The board then resorted to its tried and tested method of raising funds. The Ladies' Committee got organised and held 'A Grand Fancy Fair' in aid of both the gymnasium and swimming pool, and which was held in Magee College on 9–11 April 1889. Thus £1,960 was raised and on 8 July the board authorised the Colhoun Bros to proceed with building the swimming pool at a cost of £1,223-15s-4d. It had been agreed that these new facilities would be available for the use of the public and in particular for the girls' schools of the city.

On 19 April 1890 Mr Young resigned and was given a glowing testimonial for his long service from a grateful board. Mr Dick became the sole headmaster from July 1890. Pupil numbers in the preparatory department had dropped to eight, and in February 1892 it was closed when the remaining pupils were transferred to Gwyn's Institute. In February 1893 Mr Dick gave up the responsibility for the boarding department, and in April Mr Alex Larmour MA was appointed to teach mathematics.

With the advent of Intermediate Education legislation the Irish Society was increasingly called upon to fund both the LAI and Foyle. After 1891 it also provided scholarships for the successful pupils to attend Irish universities. From November 1894, the Irish Society strongly advocated the amalgamation of Foyle and the Londonderry Academical Institution, and managed to persuade both parties that it was in their best interests to do so. After much debate, the draft of the bill, the Foyle College Act, was passed and became law on 20 July 1896. To facilitate the union, the headmaster of Foyle, Dr Maurice C Hime, retired.

The school continued as Foyle, and the LAI building was used for the boarding school and its sporting facilities, including the (usually unheated) swimming pool which was still in use in the 1950s.

A measure of the success of a school is usually reflected in the careers of its pupils. The LAI sent forth moderators of the Presbyterian Church in Ireland, two Moderators of the Presbyterian Church of South Africa, university professors and headmasters, surgeons with international reputations, physicians and military men. Special reference should be made to Matthew Robinson (1872–1929), the engineer who had the foresight to supply Derry with water from the Banagher dam. [See Box 11] Following the amalgamation, JC Dick was appointed headmaster, going on to integrate the traditions of both foundations and provide distinguished leadership until his retirement in 1911. The register of the LAI is in the school archive and we estimate that 1,150 boys attended the school during its short life of 28 years.

ABOVE: *Rugby at LAI c.1890; the sport was revolutionised by the arrival in 1878 of John Clark Dick, headmaster from 1890 (and subsequently headmaster of Foyle).*

RIGHT: *John Young, LAI 1878–90.*

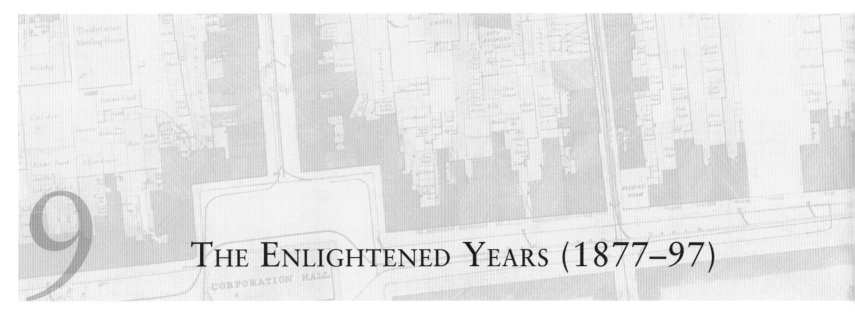

9 THE ENLIGHTENED YEARS (1877–97)

Foyle was at a low ebb when Maurice Charles Hime MA LLD, its first non-clerical headmaster, was sought out for the appointment from Monaghan Diocesan School in January 1877. He negotiated with the Irish Society and obtained special terms before accepting the post. As Foyle had only four boarders they were transferred to Monaghan and in January 1878 they returned to Foyle along with 40 other boarders from the Monaghan school, whose parents agreed to move their sons to Foyle. Dr Hime brought his young wife, his family of two boys and two girls, along with his widowed mother. The Monaghan school magazine *Our School Times* came as well, and was published under the Foyle banner from May 1878. One month later, at his instruction the Monaghan Diocesan library was also transferred.

The most significant educational change in the early years of Hime's headship was the Intermediate Education Act of 1878 that gave a great impetus to women's education and also to Catholic secondary education. This proved beneficial to St Columb's College, which opened on 3 November 1879. Strictly a junior diocesan seminary, its primary purpose was the provision of a secondary education for the future priests of the diocese. Now at last it had a site and buildings commensurate with its purpose, which was maintained for many years, while supplying much-needed education for a growing Catholic middle class. Foyle had been the only secondary school for boys in the city and its pupils included some future diocesan priests, who praised the non-sectarian nature of the school. Both schools took advantage of the act and made their mark in the yearly examinations.

School concerts were held to raise funds for various charities, including the Buncrana Relief Fund (where Hime had his holiday home) and for the Masonic schools. The now famous Percy French volunteered to entertain at some of these, and they were usually held in a public venue. School reports including exam results were produced every six months and, if results in the Intermediate exam were up to par, a one-day's holiday was declared to such venues as Buncrana, Moville, Castlerock or Portrush. So formidable a record of success in the public exams was achieved that from 1891 until the Northern Ireland state system came in, Foyle had the best results of all the Protestant schools in Ireland.

By 1894 there were in practice two Protestant boys schools in Derry, both financed by the Irish Society, who now pressed for amalgamation. After much debate, another Foyle College Act was passed on 20 July 1896 and Hime retired on a pension, the first

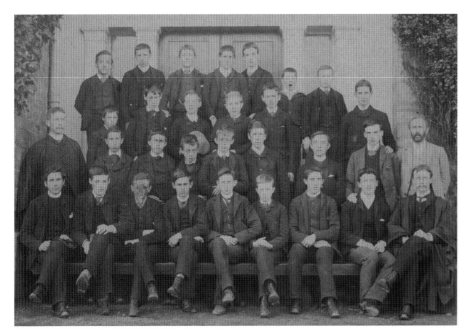

Foyle College, 1895, prior to the merger with LAI.

such granted by the Irish Society. He continued to play a vigorous part in all aspects of Derry life, political, social and charitable.

As we have seen, JC Dick – who had given the LAI its distinctive culture – appropriately became the headmaster of the 'new' Foyle in 1897, and as an indication of future success it won the Ulster Schools Cup in the school year 1899–1900. He retired in 1911, and was granted a pension by the governors of the school. His successor, Robert Foster Dill, would see the school through the trauma of World War I, in which 490 Old Boys served, with 72 of them making the supreme sacrifice. The post-war violence that accompanied the partition of Ireland and the establishment of the Northern Ireland state did not impinge much on the school, since the minuscule civil

war was at its most violent during the summer of 1920, while the school was on vacation.

In 1924 the newly established Ministry of Education of Northern Ireland introduced the Junior and Senior Certificate Examinations and soon the school, like the city as a whole, accepted the new situation. The sterner disciplines of earlier centuries relaxed somewhat and a wholesome balance of formal education and extra-curricular activities prevailed.

Arthur Edward Layng replaced Dill in 1928, to be followed in 1933 by Ernest Percival Southby. The latter resigned two years later and was succeeded by William Alexander Cuthbert McConnell, the headmaster during the Second World War, when the school suffered virtual disintegration, with most school buildings being requisitioned by the War Office. (See separate account.)

RIGHT: *Arthur Edward Layng, headmaster 1928–33.*

FAR RIGHT: *Ernest Perceval Southby, headmaster 1933–5.*

MATTHEW ROBINSON AND DERRY'S WATER SUPPLY

Matthew Alexander Robinson was born in Ballykelly on 26 March 1872, the son of the Revd WC Robinson, a Presbyterian minister. He was educated locally and at Limavady Intermediate School before attending LAI and later QUB. He qualified as an architect and civil engineer, beginning practice in Derry in 1898. At the age of 36 he designed the new Guildhall after the older building had been destroyed by fire in 1908 and became city surveyor the following year.

His great claim to fame was his contribution to the city's water supply, having been made only too aware of the inadequacies of its existing system. When the fire service attempted to deal with the Guildhall conflagration they found that there was not enough water for their appliances. A series of dry summers had had a dire effect on reservoir supplies and in 1911 there was an official 'water famine' declared. Robinson realised that dramatic action was required and began searching for possible sites for a dam, travelling around County Derry in his Model T Ford.

In 1915 he found the ideal site in Banagher Glen near Dungiven: a valley with a deep burn and of sufficient height to allow a gravity flow into Derry. It was also virtually unpopulated. Now came the problem of cost, which would include the construction of an access road before work on the dam could commence. He estimated that the cost would be £400,000 (more than £15m today) and began a three-year campaign with the Londonderry Corporation and the Westminster government. It required an act of parliament in 1918 before work could begin.

By 1925 construction was begun of the 19-mile aqueduct trench to Corrody Hill, overlooking the city, a project that required the bridging of 12 rivers and two railroads. The scheme took ten years to complete, but from the time of its inauguration in 1935 to 1985 no major work was necessary. Derry never again ran short of water; the dam's capacity is 500m gallons and because the average rainfall is 57in and the catchment area 1,500 acres it delivers 3m gallons of water daily.

Robinson did not live to see the success of his crusade. A workaholic, while engaged on the Banagher project he was also working on designing the new Craigavon Bridge. He died suddenly of heart failure at his home in Crawford Square on Saturday, 16 February 1929. He was not quite 57 years of age.

MAURICE CHARLES HIME MA LLD
Headmaster (1877–96)

lighter material includes *A Plea for Cheerfulness* (1924), a book of light verse illustrated by his own caricatures, and *Wild Oats,* subtitled 'A Sermon in Rhyme'. He did not forget, however, the high moral purpose of his avocation; two volumes 'addressed to young men' were called *Morality* (1884) and *Home Education* – 'Irish Schools for Irish Boys' (1887).

By the time of the amalgamation Dr Hime had taught 564 pupils and the school had an average annual enrolment of 94. After 19 years in the post and aged 56, he was awarded a pension of £220 per annum by the Irish Society. He moved to the Waterside and was made a JP for both the city and county of Londonderry and was later elected to the Corporation. He was the High Sheriff for the city in 1906, a member of the Synod of the Church of Ireland, active in Masonry and the treasurer of the Masonic Orphan schools of Derry and Donegal. Dr Maurice Hime died on 14 November 1924 and was buried in the City Cemetery.

Dr Hime was educated at Portora and entered TCD to study Classics in 1858. He was the top student in his year and obtained a first class honours BA. He became headmaster of Monaghan Diocesan school in 1868 and in 1869 became an MA (TCD). In January 1877 he became the first layman to be appointed as headmaster of Foyle.

He ran the school with a non-sectarian but Protestant ethos as stipulated under the 1874 Foyle College Act. Prayers were held three times daily. Dr Hime disapproved of corporal punishment, believing that moral persuasion was a more effective means of discipline. TCD awarded him the LLB and LLD degrees, but when called to the Irish bar in 1884 he did not practice. School concerts raised funds for various charities including the Masonic schools and the Buncrana relief fund in 1880.

Hime was also a belletrist of note, with books of verse and occasional essays in contrast to school textbooks such as *Introduction to Latin* (1878), *Introduction to Latin Prose Composition* (1893), *An Introduction to the Greek Language* (1891). The

SCALE OF MARKS.

	Out of Maximum of 20.	Out of Maximum of 10.
Best	20	10
Very Good ...	18	9
Good ... ... {	16	8
	14	7
Middling	10	5
Scarcely Middling	8	4
Bad ... ... {	6	3
	4	2
Very Bad	2	1
Worst	0	0

N.B.—This Judgment Book is made up each week by the Master who signs it, and is sent home with the Day-boys each Saturday to be inspected, and *Signed* by their Parents or Guardians. It is to be returned, without fail, on the following Monday morning, otherwise it cannot be made up for the ensuing week.

(Signed)

M. C. HIME, M.A., LL.D.,
HEAD-MASTER.

LEFT: *Dr Hime's scale of marks: 'Scarcely Middling' has a benevolent rather than severe ring to it.*

JOHN CLARKE DICK MA
Headmaster, Classics Department, LAI (1878–96); Headmaster, Foyle (1896–1910)

John Clarke Dick (JC) graduated with a first class degree in 1872 from Queen's College, Belfast, and obtained an MA with gold medal in 1877. Prior to his appointment at the LAI he had been an assistant master at RBAI. He arrived in Derry with a formidable reputation as a sportsman, for he was an all-round cricketer, had played for the North of Ireland 1st XI team and had reached championship level as a high jumper. He was also an expert angler and a good shot. At the LAI all the masters coached rugby but JC was the first to organise competitive sport. By 1890 the school had both a gymnasium and a swimming pool, the only grammar school in Ireland to possess that latter facility.

As headmaster, following the amalgamation, he employed his skills with great efficiency to integrate both traditions. His standards were high and his business-like outlook brought results, as the boys responded by working hard. When his pupils won scholastic awards he was almost dismissive: 'Of course Foyle is used to winning distinctions of that kind'. On 8 November 1910, after two bouts of influenza and pneumonia, he notified the board of governors of his intention to retire due to ill-health. After 13 years as headmaster and 32 years of teaching at the LAI and

Foyle a grateful board awarded him a pension of £200 a year for life and he retired to Parkstone, Dorset, where he died on 4 March 1922. When the post was advertised in December 1910 there were 94 applicants who wished to succeed him.

BELOW: *Foyle College Group, 1904.*

BELOW RIGHT: *Exam book, 1908.*

ROBERT FOSTER DILL MA
Headmaster, Foyle (1911–28)

Robert Foster Dill was born in 1859, the son of Professor Samuel Marcus Dill DD, who held the chair of theology at Magee College. The family lived at Braehead House and Robert entered Foyle on 17 January 1871. He stayed until 1877 when he moved to Belfast, lived with his mother at Knock, and attended RBAI prior to entering QUB later that year. He obtained a BA in 1879 before he proceeded to Lincoln College, Oxford, and was awarded a MA by Oxford University in 1882. Thus he followed in the steps of his older brother, the eminent classical scholar Sir Samuel Dill, who was later professor of Classics at QUB.

On returning to Belfast he taught at Methodist College (Methody) and was thereafter appointed headmaster of Monaghan Diocesan School. In 1891 he became headmaster of Dungannon Royal School, finally coming to Foyle at Easter 1911. He is remembered as a strict, exacting but popular headmaster, who maintained a high level of culture and learning in the school. He was also genial and kindly and enjoyed the confidence of the staff and pupils.

His time at the school included the immediate aftermath of the First World War, and the turmoil associated with the setting up of Northern Ireland in early 1920s. His leadership was recognised when he became a member of the Departmental Committee on Educational Services in Northern Ireland, the body which would produce the NI Education Act.

On retiring he moved to River Bank, Hereford and he often attended Old Boys reunions, when he would contribute as an informative and witty speaker. His unfailing interest in the school and his former pupils was recognised when he was elected president of the Foyle College Old Boys' Association (FCOBA) in 1945–6. Robert Foster Dill died on 12 February 1947 in his 88th year.

BELOW: *Foyle College Group, 1928.*

WILLIAM ALEXANDER CUTHBERT MCCONNELL MA
Headmaster, Foyle (1935–60)

WAC ('Archie') McConnell became headmaster in January 1935 at the age of 39. He was born and brought up in Scotland where he attended Glasgow Academy. Graduating with an Hons MA in Classics in 1915 from Glasgow University, he was commissioned from the Glasgow University OTC into the 5th Battalion Scottish Rifles, serving with them from December 1915 until July 1919 except for a period in France in 1917 with the King's Royal Rifle Corps. Until October 1921 he worked for the Ministry of Labour and took charge of the Scottish Education Department's scheme to provide university grants for returned soldiers. He then joined the department of Classics at Hutcheson's Grammar School, and from 1922 was also the games master – by 1935 he had set up seven school rugby XVs and three cricket XIs there.

He maintained the classical tradition of Latin and Greek studies at Foyle, but by the 1950s scientific subjects were increasingly accommodated. In 1939 a regulation school uniform was adopted: the previous colours of black, red and yellow were changed and the school organised along grammar school lines. A prefects' council came into being and a house system with an elaborate arrangement of colours and half-colour awards introduced. He set up an appeal fund which enabled the school to acquire the playing fields at Springtown in 1938. He also initiated the annual general knowledge quiz taken by all the pupils at the end of the autumn term.

The Second World War brought considerable disruption to the life of the school. Mrs McConnell took complete charge of the domestic side of the boarding school, managing skilfully despite rationing and associated difficulties. The school's record in work and games was preserved, and the boys were still able to sit their certificate examinations. After the return to Lawrence Hill in 1945 the school slowly returned to normal, and Mr McConnell's enthusiasm for rugby would shortly be reinforced by the achievements of the 1946–7 XV captained by Noel Henderson. From 1953, Mr McConnell was President of the City of Derry Rugby Football Club (CDRFC).

Music and drama were pursuits of major activities between 1950 and 1958, when the school produced eight Gilbert and Sullivan operettas. He was equally supportive of the school orchestra and the Easter end-of-term concerts. Thanks to Mr McConnell's meticulous efforts in continuing the school register, the archives hold an excellent record of its pupils from 1896 until 1960. He is remembered for his gentlemanly character, his broad culture and his devotion to the school. On his retirement in 1960, Mr and Mrs McConnell went to live at Marino, County Down, and he died at his home on Saturday, 6 October 1962.

BELOW: *Portrait of WAC McConnell towards the end of his period as headmaster.*

10 THE WAR YEARS

Our *School Times*, printed during the two world wars, provides a valuable and poignant insight into how events impinged upon the everyday life of the school. The editorial of June 1915 stated that even within the walls of the school the shock of war was felt as we grieved for brave young lives suddenly cut short. The names of the first five Old Boys were listed with the details of their regiments, date of death and a short obituary. Such announcements over the next four years would become grimly familiar:

Pro Patria:
Valentine Gilliland, captain, 3rd Royal Irish Rifles. Killed in action on 8 May 1915. Captain Gilliland is, we believe, the first Old Foyle Boy known to have been killed in action.

Of hundreds of Old Boys who fought in the conflict 72 are known to have made the supreme sacrifice, and as the war progressed some staff members joined their ranks. Pupils were torn between terminating their studies at the earliest opportunity or remaining in school. A boy leaving school to join a regiment was often aware that he could never hope to take up where he left off. The headmaster cautioned the boys to follow the safest and wisest course, which was to wait. During the conflict the school did its utmost to nurture a sense of normal activity, including the marking of the tercentenary of the foundation of the Free School.

Those serving submitted interesting accounts of trips and other events, including detailed eyewitness accounts from places as diverse as Archangel, Neuve Chapelle, Rouen, Flanders, the Dardanelles, Egypt, Greece, Mesopotamia and the Cameroons. Accounts of Zeppelin raids on London, the opening stages of the Battle of the Somme and even an account of the Sinn Fein rising in 1916 are all recorded. Professor Woodburn wrote: 'Foyle now for three centuries has looked out on the noble river that flows by the walls of Derry, and during these three hundred years has shared in all the changing fortunes of the city'.

No detailed record has been kept of Old Girls who served their country during the Great War but it is evident from accounts by Miss Margaret MacKillip, headmistress of Victoria High School, that many were involved, chiefly in Queen Alexandra's Nursing Corps and in other branches of war service such as transport. The girls in Victoria College raised funds for the war effort, and a detailed account of their range of activities and where the donations were directed may be read in a letter from Miss MacKillip (see illustration).

OPPOSITE: *World War I Roll of Honour at Springtown (see p78).*

RIGHT: *Wartime letter form Miss Mackillip to the Girls of Victoria High School.*

The publication of a Roll of Honour, comprising lists of those killed, wounded or missing, those decorated by the king and those mentioned in dispatches, became the norm. The sacrifice demanded of so many is perhaps best illustrated by the four Williams brothers, all keen sportsmen and rugby players. JA (a member of the 1915 Cup team), EJ (captain of the 1909 cricket XI) and CB Williams (all commissioned in the Royal Irish Rifles) were killed in action. The only survivor was Captain HP Williams MC. Sir Douglas Haig could claim in April 1917 that 'In every country in which are British soldiers, Old Foyle Boys are to be found fighting and dying for their motherland'. The headmaster initiated the Roll of Honour that would lead to the unveiling of the war memorial in 1920 in the assembly hall. By November 1917, the school magazine had published a list of 51 names under the title *Morts Au Champ d'Honneur* of those who had been killed.

By December 1918, the editor was able to say that:

The present volume of Our School Times *is one of joy, since our country and her allies have gained victory in the greatest war that the world has ever known. The sacrifices of the past four years have seen the downfall of Germany and all those principles for which she stood. Foyle has played a gallant part in that great struggle, the Alma Mater who in the past has given the British Army some of its greatest soldiers, has proved in the last four years that the same indomitable spirit which inspired her sons of yore inspires them still.*

Later a further 12 names were added to the list of those killed in action, and their names and regiments were listed on our war memorial at Springtown. On the anniversary of the armistice in November 1919 the boys were drawn up in lines in front of the Lawrence Hill school and the headmaster read the names of the fallen, followed by two minutes of remembrance observed in silence, a tradition honoured to this day.

In addition to our original source of information, the school magazines, there are many accounts of lived experiences during the period 1939–45. The tenor of the magazines for this period differs from those published during World War I. Each editorial begins with a detailed update on the progress of the war and it lists those killed in action, wounded, decorated and

Dedication of World War II Memorial, 1946 (see p78).

mentioned in dispatches. The editorial of December 1939 laments:

The world has not had twenty-one years in which to be healed of the distresses caused by the last war. Once more the same nation, animated by the same spirit, has appealed to war in the hope of obtaining her ambitions. Though we in Derry live in a remote corner of the British Isles, we share to the full the hopes and anxieties of our fellow citizens in Great Britain. Many Old Boys are serving in the forces or are rendering national service of some kind. Evidence of the effect that the war has had upon the school itself is abundant. Three members of staff, Mr GC Gillanders, Mr NL Sampson and Mr J Kershaw have been called up for service and left us.

The school constructed three large air-raid shelters at Academy Road and blackouts were put in place in all school buildings. Evening meetings and many sporting fixtures were cancelled. Pupils practised air-raid drills using the newly constructed shelters at Foyle; at Londonderry High School, the cellars of Duncreggan served a similar purpose. In World War II it was impossible for the schools to function with the same degree of normality as obtained in World War I.

With the collapse of France in late 1940, many pupils joined the newly organised Local Defence

Volunteers (LDV), forerunner of the Home Guard; others in various civil defence forces prepared to meet the increased danger of invasion and air attack. Many spent their summer holidays working on farms to help the nation's food supply. Form I pupils put together parcels of clothes for evacuees living in hostels in England. The first air raid alarms sounded across the city in late 1940 – Derry, with its naval port and shipyard and as a staging point for Atlantic convoys, was considered a strategic target. The bombs which fell on Messines Park in April 1941 had profound consequences for the schools, especially for the boarders. The Army occupied Academy Road, the Navy Lawrence Hill and the RAF Londonderry High School: 45 Londonderry High School boarders spent the war isolated from the rest of the school at Greenfield, Strabane.

The experiences of girls and boys who were boarders during these years give a real flavour of life in wartime:

In the autumn of 1940 I left my home in Dublin as my parents feared that Germany would invade Britain via southern Ireland. So I was sent as a refugee to board at Londonderry High School where my aunt, Miss Park (Puce), was maths mistress and I would be with family.

When we were moved to Greenfield we experienced the novelty of sleeping in bunk beds. Teaching staff travelled daily from Derry and we had lessons 'at home'. It was all very pleasant and I have many happy memories of all my friends there and the fun we had. Once some of us were caught talking to boys at the school gate – imagine,

boys! Our parents were written to and we were severely punished; nine months later I was at TCD and surrounded by boys!

Joan Matthews (née Moon)

It was in 1941 when the boarders were evacuated to Greenfield and the daygirls continued with lessons at Duncreggan. With the introduction of clothing coupons our uniform had to be modified; instead of the velour and panama hats (seven coupons out of our annual allocation of 20!), we wore royal blue berets with the school crest on them, and in summer cotton dresses were allowed. For that reason Miss McIlroy insisted that we wore the uniform five out of seven days a week. I remember we had regular 'bug-raids', when the district nurse checked each girl's head for lice in private! But this practice was dropped when war began.

Margot Robertson (née Knox)

In September 1942 I was delivered with my older brother Harry, together with a large wooden box containing our full clothing requirements, as boarders to Upper Foyle in Academy Road. The boarding school was small – five tiny dorms on the top floor for all 16 of us. Not many could be accommodated because the Navy had taken over Lower Foyle, using only the ground floor as a naval canteen as marked on the sketch map handed to all naval personnel. The rest of the building, including the science labs on the first floor, remained available for teaching purposes. The dayboys also attended Upper Foyle, although there were just under 200 pupils at the school.

Everything was rationed – all foodstuffs, clothing, footwear, even sweets. Buying and selling sweet coupons was the first thing that set me on a business career. We got to know the teaching staff very well, since they took it in turns to supervise us in the evenings. The staffroom was on the top floor and I remember that this room was filled with dense cigarette smoke. When my father had a stroke during Easter 1945 my mother requested my immediate return to help on

Greenfield, Strabane, was home to 45 boarders during World War II.

the farm. I returned briefly to take my Junior Certificate examinations and managed to achieve the requisite nine passes.

Looking back on my three years at Foyle, while academically I gained a Junior Certificate, I consider that my sojourn as a boarder was of much more benefit to me in life. We boarders were like a large family. Five of us from the Donemana district, two from Claudy, several from Donegal, one from Belfast (away from the Blitz), one from Kenya and one from Czechoslovakia – a refugee who was adopted by a local doctor.

Alfie Danton

When World War II started, I was living with my family in the Cregagh area of Belfast. An evacuation scheme for primary school children came into operation in June 1940 and I was relocated to a family near Newbuildings and was to go to school at Foyle. I entered Foyle in September 1940. We used rooms at the back of the Technical College and I became a boarder in September 1941.

The kitchen in Academy Road had a large steel table which was designed as an air raid shelter, under which we sat during air raids. During the year we decided to raise money for the 'Spitfire Fund' and so we produced a variety concert. We wrote a short play and filled our programme with poems and songs performed, under duress, by my friends and other boarders. We also made scenery and spotlights.

THE WAR MEMORIAL BOARDS

Two oak memorial boards located in the assembly hall at Springtown bear testimony to the supreme sacrifice by former boys of the school during the two world wars. The World War I board was erected in 1919 and is constructed from reclaimed oak from battle ships decommissioned at that time. It contains the names of 72 former pupils, their ranks and regiments who gave their lives during World War I. World War II board, constructed from a lighter oak and unveiled in 1946, bears the names of 39 former pupils who gave their lives during that conflict.

A moving tribute is paid each Armistice Day in the form of a remembrance service to mark the sacrifice of the fallen, during which the assembled pupils and staff sing 'Abide with Me' followed by the sounding of the 'Last Post', which signals a two-minute silence and 'Reveille', and culminates with the placing of a wreath on each board. The wreath is placed on the World War I board by a representative of the Old Boys' Association and that on the World War II board by the current head boy and head girl. The ceremony ends with the singing of the national anthem.

William Lynn

With several of my friends I joined the Londonderry Sea Cadets. Most of the cadets were not from the college so this was an exceptionally good experience for us 'Foyle Boys'. We all did well and I earned my Leading Seaman's 'Hooks' before retiring in 1945. That year, the war came to an end and German U-boats surrendered at Lisahally. The headmaster allowed me to take his bicycle to Culmore Point to see the U-boats come up the river and I felt that here was proof that the war was really over.

Fred R Wright

Throughout the war years the changing fortunes of the Allies were chronicled in the editorials of the school magazines. Although losses were not on the scale of World War I, the magazines listed former pupils killed in action. The names of 39 alumni are recorded on the war memorial board in the assembly hall at Springtown. In March 1943 the editor commented that:

Attempts to predict an early conclusion to the war are singularly out of fashion at this present time. Even Hitler, that super-

THE TWO SWORDS

THE LAWRENCE SWORD

This sword is presented annually at the prize distribution to pupils deemed to have given outstanding service to the school during their final years. Its full title is the General Sir George Lawrence Sword. It was a gift of Mr Reginald Simmons, who was a member of the Board of Governors when the existence of the sword and a photograph of Sir George Lawrence were discovered in 1975 by Mrs Jane Jacobs, who had inherited the items and was aware of their significance. The items were purchased by Mr Simmons, who donated them to the school. The sword was first awarded at the annual prize distribution in 1976, the first occasion following the amalgamation of Foyle College with Londonderry High School, and has been awarded each year since then. Although it is generally awarded to a senior boy, it has on a number of occasions been awarded to a senior girl.

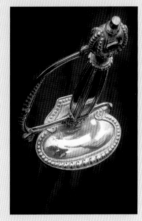

JAPANESE CEREMONIAL SWORD

The ceremonial Japanese sword was forged by Morikage about 1,200 years ago. It was owned and inherited by the ancestors of Captain Kubo of the Imperial Japanese Army, commander of the prisoner-of-war camp headquarters in Java. It was surrendered at the close of hostilities in August 1945 and was presented to Foyle by Wing Commander WC Pitts OBE, a former pupil of the school.

William Lynn

optimistic timetable specialist, has refrained from forecast. However the fall of Tripoli, after a brilliant advance by the Eighth Army, whose ranks include many an old Foyle boy, has engendered hopes. By June 1943 the tide in North Africa had turned with spectacular successes in Tunisia and Libya.

The careers of the three members of staff on active service were followed with interest. All had served in the Middle East since the beginning of the war. Lieutenant G Gillanders had returned to England to undergo special training; Captain J Kershaw and Major N Sampson were still abroad, and the latter was congratulated on being promoted to commander of the Hong Kong and Singapore Regiment.

The March 1944 editorial noted that, 'the British war effort has intensified with frequent air raids on Germany. Naturally, but unhappily, this has involved the loss of many airmen and old Foyle boys are among those who have suffered', and that:

By September 1944 troops were beginning to return to the city. Derry was in a state of expectancy. Crowds gathered at the railway station to welcome the troops. Among them were many old Foyle boys and two members of staff – Major Sampson and Captain Kershaw.

Pupils at both Foyle and Londonderry High School bore witness to the euphoria of the VE day celebrations. Searchlights blazed, horns blew, bells rang and bonfires were lit. The first surrendering U-boats sailed into Lisahally followed by many more in the following days. Many boys had trained through the Air Training Corps, the Army Cadet Corps and the Sea Cadet Corps, although in practice they were not needed. Others, both boys and girls, had contributed to the war effort and were justified to feel that they had played their small part in the victory.

In August 1945 the war in Japan ended and many of the prisoners released were old Foyle boys. This was a great cause for rejoicing, and the editor noted the fact that the world was now at peace. Much credit was due to the teaching staff, who maintained as normal a school life as possible during those difficult years.

William Lynn

11

GIRLS' EDUCATION IN THE CITY

OPPOSITE: *Aerial view of Duncreggan House, 1930.*

BELOW: *Prospectus for the newly named Strand House School, 1860.*

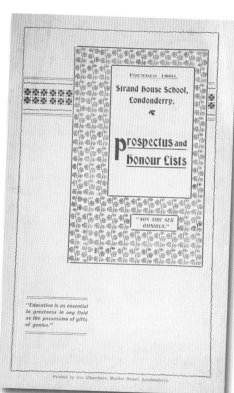

Until the middle of the 19th century female education was informal and local. In 1814 the Revd George Vaughan Sampson notes that: 'for the tuition of young ladies there are within the city two boarding schools'. He also describes a school for poor girls, superintended by Mrs Knox, wife of the Bishop of Derry, and another girls' school run by Miss Hennis. The Sisters of Mercy order, invited to Derry by Bishop Edward Maginn (1802–49) in 1848 to help deal with the influx of population because of the Great Famine, started the first convent school in the province in Pump Street, now part of the Playhouse complex. The sisters provided a day school in Pump Street until their Thornhill premises on the Culmore Road were opened in 1932.

With the demand for secondary education for girls, several individual independent institutions were established from 1860 onwards. Miss Frances Holmes established in 1860 a school for girls in Hawkin Street close to the wooden bridge across the Foyle. It moved to a larger house on Strand Road and thereafter was known as Strand House School, the name suggested by the pupils. It kept that name even after it moved again in 1865 to an elegant Victorian mansion beside the Great James Street Presbyterian Church. In 1877 the second strand, the Londonderry Ladies Collegiate College, was opened at 11 Queen Street by the Misses MacKillip.

In Ellis's *Irish Education Directory and Scholastic Guide* (1886), five

Londonderry schools are listed: 'Clarendon-street School, with headmistress Miss Jenkins; Convent of Mercy School, run by Miss Casey; Ladies' Academy, Miss ME O'Flanagan; Ladies' Collegiate School, Misses Mackillip [sic] and Strand-house Coll. School'. The Model School is asterisked as accepting both male and female. Ellis indicates that by the late 19th century girls' education, especially at secondary level, was regarded with appropriate gravitas in Derry. As the city grew in prosperity the merchant class began to appreciate the benefits and aesthetic value of educated daughters.

The education of Catholic girls was provided by such orders as the Ursulines, Loreto Sisters, Presentation Sisters and the Sisters of Mercy. The success of the National School system had an upwardly knock-on effect. A similar properly organised scheme for the secondary education of women was inevitable, and the glittering prize of university entrance became a worthy objective.

Three main skeins went to fashion the silken fabric that became Londonderry High School in 1922. These were the Strand House School, the Londonderry Ladies' Collegiate School (founded 1877) and St Lurach's (1900). By 1873 a preparatory department for boys under 12 at LAI was run by Margaret MacKillip who founded the 'Collegiate' four years later with her sisters. A sketch by the well-known local antiquary Mabel Colhoun with the title 'Foyle Bridges and Education for Girls' names the first address of the Collegiate as 11 Queen Street. Helen M Williams (née Buchanan), one of the its first pupils, describes the 'bright September morning' when she and her sister Emily (one aged 10, the other 11½) walked into the 'gloomy house opposite Hogg's factory, little thinking they were founding the famous Londonderry

81

ABOVE: *The MacKillip medal.*

LEFT: *Miss Margaret MacKillip, head of Victoria High School 1920–7.*

Sara taught mathematics and 'made of a dull subject a most interesting and absorbing study'.

Helen Williams records that Mary was studying for her BA and later taught in the school and 'Carrie, a young girl like ourselves' who eventually took charge of the kindergarten. She adds: 'Behind all this was dear Mrs MacKillip [sic] a mother to us all who kept up the tone of the school'. Clearly Jane was the mother of the school in every sense.

The passing of the Intermediate Education Act (1878) established a viable structure for secondary schooling. There was no longer a perception that secondary education was the exclusive right of males; women were eligible for the same rewards and the establishment of secondary schools for girls was made easier. Giving evidence at a commission meeting in 1899, Miss MacKillip described the act as revolutionary. She saw it as a rationalisation of education for women, and two years after the act became law her Collegiate School won 12 exhibitions and medals. By 1901 Victoria High School was the third-largest girls secondary establishment in Ireland.

The entry in the Londonderry Directory of 1884 indicates that English, Latin and Mathematics, Greek, Conversational French and German were taught in the Crawford Square school. There were no fewer than five pianoforte teachers – traditional female accomplishments were not neglected. The MacKillips also employed governesses, perhaps to deal with the younger pupils. One such was Alice Milligan (1866–1953), who after education at Methody and King's College, London, was appointed to the staff in 1887. Later famous as a nationalist editor and poet, she was a Gaelic League enthusiast who wrote the first playlet in modern Irish, Her two fellow governesses were Mlle Cazalong, who taught French and called Alice 'Meeligano' (Alice named her 'La Marsellaise'), and Marjorie Arthur, with whom Alice shared a room and christened her 'The Highland Lassie' because her mother was a MacDonald from Skye.

In Strand House School there were classes in English, mathematics, Classics, French and German. The total number of teachers, including the organists of both St Eugene's Cathedral and Christ Church, was 15, and its prospectus shows a remarkable similarity to that of Victoria High School. It offered 'an Education not inferior to any in the United Kingdom' and advises that 'the strictest attention is paid to the moral and religious training … while endeavouring to develop

High School in years to come'. In fact she became the first president of the Old Girls Association. The Londonderry Ladies' Collegiate School became Victoria High School in 1887, a royal title graciously granted as part of the queen's golden jubilee, and 12 years later it joined with Strand House, the composite school continuing to use the Victoria High School title.

Alan Roberts gives a summary of the various duties and responsibilities borne by the sisters and other members of the staff: Margaret: English (as eldest, referred to as 'Miss' MacKillip); Miss Sara: mathematics; Mrs Jane (the widowed mother): matron in charge of boarding; Caroline: kindergarten; Mary: Classics; Miss Violet Bolton, a niece, a graduate of Girton College, Cambridge, also taught Classics. Her mother, Ruby, the fifth Miss MacKillip, had married Mr Bolton. Margaret was the founder, responding to the call for 'higher education of women', and when pupil numbers increased the school moved to

> *larger quarters in Great James' Street, where it was carried on most successfully until the fine new buildings were completed at the top of Crawford Square … here Latin [and] Mathematics, unheard of subjects for girls, were taken up with energy.*

the intellectual, moral and physical capabilities, to teach habits of self-respect and ladylike deportment'. As well as the description of the school's curriculum by the headmistress, there is a sketch of 'the splendid new buildings in Asylum Road' from the *Derry Standard* of Friday, 30 October 1903. By comparison Clarendon Street school's brochure lists five teachers including the principal, Miss Jenkins. From the various extant prospectuses it is clear that some kind of amalgamation, of the sort actually that occurred in 1922, was regarded as inevitable.

The third skein of the final Londonderry High School fabric was St Lurach's, a large house at the top of Lawrence Hill. It was founded in 1900 by Jane Kerr from Maghera. Because her sister was the wife of Professor Woodburn of Magee, St Lurach's girls were allowed to use the tennis courts there. In 1917 on the death of Jane Kerr the headship St Lurach's was taken over by two sisters, the Misses Kyle. In 1921 the Northern Ireland state was established and soon Victoria High School and St Lurach's were amalgamated to form Londonderry High School with again, inevitably, a MacKillip – this time Sara – as headmistress. She was singled out for praise in inspection reports because of the 'perfect discipline' in her classes: 'Although Miss Sara MacKillip's

Above: *1877 prospectus and calendar for Victoria High School.*

Above left: *Victoria High School in the early 1900s and as it would have been in 1877.*

Far left: *St Lurach's, founded in 1900, was merged with Victoria High School to create Londonderry High School.*

Left: *St Lurach's uniform.*

LONDONDERRY HIGH SCHOOL
1928

back was turned to half the class the discipline was admirable'. The inspectors especially praised the teaching of mathematics as 'certainly above the average of that which prevails in most girls' schools'.

Claire Rush, in her essay 'The Cradle of Girls', gives some interesting details about the running of Victoria High School:

A majority of boarders were from Dublin and wealthy farming backgrounds in Killarney, Tralee and Galway'. In 1901 the school had seventy boarders and 110 day pupils, taught by thirteen female teachers and three male instructors. The school day lasted from 9am to 3pm with an hour for lunch, rather more leisured than today's time table.

One of the Misses MacKillip summed up the great advantage of the Intermediate Act as furnishing 'a most expensive education at a cost which brings it within the reach of many clever and ambitious girls who would otherwise be debarred from it'.

Pupils used their prize moneys to fund their own education and that of their sisters. The headmistress obtained university scholarships for her pupils from the 'London Cities Companies'. Claire Rush quotes a

'former pupil' of Margaret MacKillip: 'She was a pioneer and original thinker. Her mind absorbed all that was best in educational thought up to her time and contributed much that was new … We who had the privilege of Miss MacKillip's inspiration feel we owe a deep debt of gratitude to her memory. With us she cannot pass away'.

Alan Roberts' article 'Two Eminent Victorians' (*FPA Magazine*: February 1994) gives some word-of-mouth descriptions of the lighter side of Crawford Square life. The Ross sisters had come from Victoria College in Belfast when their father's job brought him to Derry. Evelyn was deprived of hockey, at which she excelled, because the playing-field was too far from her home and her mother would not allow her 'to remain after school to go with the boarders'. However she played golf at Lisfannon every Wednesday afternoon. Unable to play tennis at school she managed nevertheless to play near her home in Shantallow, and later excelled in both at TCD. Evelyn became a pioneer in contraception and Olive held the chair of French and German at Magee.

A Prospectus and Calendar of Victoria High School, Londonderry (1917) has as frontispiece a photograph of the school with groups of pupils and

ABOVE: *The prospectus of LHS still proudly looked back to its 1877 foundation as Strand House School.*

ABOVE LEFT: *Londonderry High School in 1928 represented a high point in the history of girls' education in Londonderry.*

OPPOSITE: *LHS in 1932. From small but dedicated beginnings, girls' education in Londonderry had achieved universal recognition.*

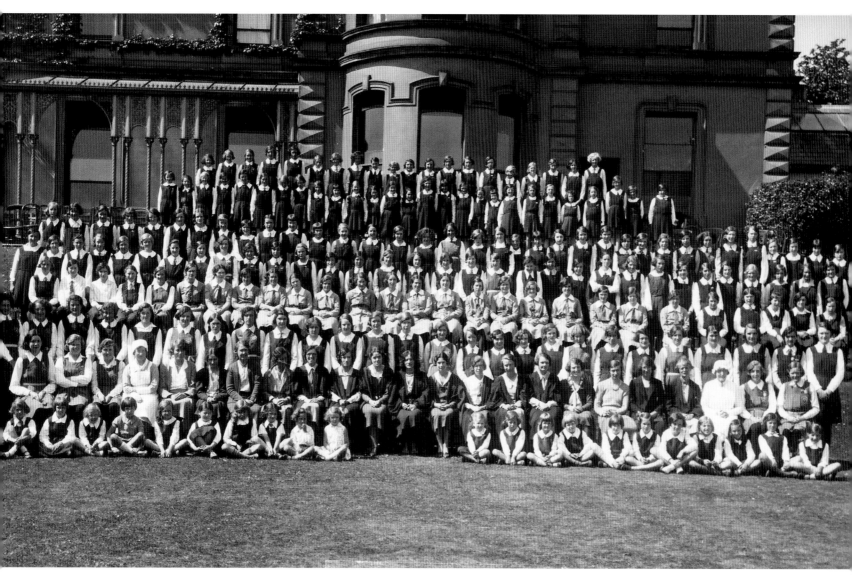

staff posed on the steps of No 18 Crawford Square, at windows and on the pavement outside, some dressed in the fashionable Gibson Girl style of the late 1890s, with full-length skirts, mutton-chop sleeves and straw boaters. The summer vacation lasted from 30 June until 1 September and reports were furnished to parents after Christmas and Easter examinations. There is honourable mention of old girls who have met 'the unprecedented demands for National Service which the War has made upon them'. The booklet records the achievements of former pupils at Cambridge, Oxford and St Andrews and notes that since its foundation in 1877 'pupils of the school have taken forty-two medals and 170 exhibitions'.

The best summary of the Ladies Collegiate/Victoria High School in our archives is a typescript of the interview given by Margaret MacKillip to Mrs Edith Magee. From early childhood she wanted to become a teacher and in 1872, when she was 24, a friend arranged for her to become a teacher in Londonderry Academical Institution. Though without formal qualifications she was clearly a natural and when on 25 March 1877 her father John died in Coleraine, the family, including his widow Jane, came to live in Derry:

Then we started a small school at 24 Great James Street and Sara, with her certificate of the Cambridge Higher Locals, came to start the teaching. We had but one idea to guide us, and that was to teach the same subjects as were taught in the privileged boys' schools.

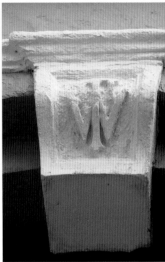

LEFT: *Duncreggan House in 1928. The home of the Tillie family, who had brought prosperity and employment to Londonderry. The site of Londonderry High School from 1930.*

BELOW: *The arms of LHS feature the owl of Minerva, goddess of wisdom, books in which wisdom is to be found, and an embattled tower symbolising the walls of the city.*

She confirmed that Northlands, the 'Housewifery School', was set up in 1908 at the suggestion of and financed by the Department of Agriculture and Technical Instruction, 'to develop a side of Domestic Economy'.

With their ambition to provide a first-class education for girls, they decided that St Lurach's School could be amalgamated with Victoria High School, and bought it in 1899 to form Londonderry High School. The 1923 directory gave little more information than the title, the address in Crawford Square and the name of the headmistress, Sarah MacKillip. It also associated St Lurach's Hostel with the school and gave the warden's name as Miss Phenix. The 1928 entry indicated that the headmistress was Miss R McIlroy MA Sen Mod TCD, and that there was 'a well-qualified staff'. She had taken over the post from her sister Mrs Bailie, who had served for a few years after Miss Sarah died. In 1930, with the growing numbers of pupils, a change of location to Duncreggan

was necessary, and the new headmistress was Mary French McIlroy OBE, who was to serve until 1962, when Miss KM Cowper took over. Duncreggan, the former residence of the late Marshall Tillie, provided the home for Londonderry High School and later for Foyle and Londonderry College.

It is not clear when the motto on the school's crest (Ωσ αει ενωπιον του Θεου – '[behaving] as if ever in the presence of God') was devised but it continued to be an implicit part of the school's ethos. The 1947 Education Act and the greatly increased school population of 'qualified' pupils required more accommodation and further building. The school continued to grow until in the early 1960s under Miss Cowper the total enrolment rose to nearly 400.

With the 'Troubles', cooperation between schools became the rule. For example Denzil Stewart of Londonderry High School and Sean McMahon of St Columb's founded the Inter–

Schools Drama Festival, involving most of the secondary schools of the city. The first festival was held in the Londonderry High School assembly hall with Brian Friel as adjudicator. In 1976 Linda Storey, Londonderry High School head of music, involved schools, primary and secondary from all over the city and beyond, in a spectacular production of Benjamin Britten's *Noyes Fludde*.

In spite of the disruption caused by the Troubles, the school continued to teach and show by the example of staff and pupils that education, cheerfulness in the face of adversity, integrity and right-thinking should eventually succeed. By the time of the amalgamation in 1976, Londonderry High School could look back with pride on more than a century of honourable endeavour and achievement.

ABOVE: *Miss Mary French McIlroy, head of LHS 1930–62.*

ABOVE RIGHT: *Ms Mary K Cowper, head of LHS 1962–73.*

RIGHT: *Duncreggan House today.*

12 REFLECTIONS ON AMALGAMATION (1973–94)

On applying for the post of headmaster in January 1973 I was notified that Miss Cowper, head of the Londonderry High School, had also decided to retire, thus the amalgamation of the two schools became possible. With the reduction of pupil numbers to 600, both boards of governors concluded that the joining of the two schools was essential. To achieve this the Foyle College Act would have to be repealed. Thanks to Sir Robert Porter's unceasing work the required legislation (the Foyle and Londonderry College Act: 1976) was completed in July, two months before the reconstituted school opened.

With my appointment confirmed, and with Miss Christie willingly delaying her retirement for two further years, we faced the many logistical problems that amalgamation posed. Fears of the staff about the future were allayed when the Department of Education agreed to the governors' insistence that no member of staff should lose salary or status. A number of senior staff left, so we had only three departments with joint heads.

The limited financial help from government and no possibility of a new building meant we had to make use of the two existing buildings. Internal changes were necessary and both buildings needed alterations, some of which the Department was able to fund, but not all were ready for the start of the new term on 1 September 1976.

A problem about the name for the new school now arose, and unfortunately the one which was chosen bore all the marks of the ultimate in compromise. With Londonderry High School operating an eight-period day and Foyle a nine-period one some rationalisation was necessary, but the latter provided three breaks in the day allowing staff to move more freely from one campus to the other. Many other procedural differences had to be harmonised; new school rules were drafted; and the house system was revised, with some ancient names jettisoned.

The overwhelming response from parents was positive and the pupils accepted the coeducational changes. There were benefits: years 10 and 11 had been unfocused because GCSE seemed so distant; now Form III pupils had more responsibility, with a 'Leaving Certificate' exam and a 'graduation' ceremony.

The split site made communication more difficult, and while staff had to adapt to the new situation, some members found it too difficult and resigned – a distinct loss to the school. Timetabling to find a solution to these and many other problems required ingenuity and flexibility. I will conclude by paying tribute to those who brought the amalgamation about: staff, not least office staff, governors and especially the chairmen, Professor JL McCracken and John McFarland.

Hugh Gillespie

ABOVE: *A student wearing the uniform of Foyle and Londonderry College post 1976.*

OPPOSITE: *Hugh Wishart Gillespie, headmaster 1973–94.*

RIGHT: *LHS staff in 1968.*

The house system in Foyle appears to date from about 1930. That is the earliest mention of inter-house sport in the school magazines, and the impressive house cup, presented by the Irish Society and still in use today, dates from 1931. At that time there were about 40 boys in each house, which was just about a viable number for competitive activities. There were four houses: Andrews, Lawrence, Montgomery and Springham. These were named after illustrious former pupils and the school's founder: Andrews (Francis Andrews), Lawrence (the Lawrence family – Alexander, Henry, George and John), Montgomery (Sir Robert Montgomery) and Springham (Mathias Springham).

Londonderry High School also had a system of houses, which have their origin about the same time as those in Foyle. It is supported by the existence of a fine bronze circular trophy presented by the School

Governors, with the earliest engraving dating from 1934. The trophy is divided into three sections, one for each house and with a coloured diamond in each house colour. The houses were named after the school's buildings, Duncreggan, Dunseveric and Northlands.

The magazines of both schools record the vibrant competitive system based on a wide range of sporting activities as well as in debating, choir and other competitions. Both trophies are engraved with the names of the victorious houses from 1934 until 1964, when engraved details cease. During that period in Foyle, Lawrence dominated (14) followed by Andrews (5), Montgomery (3) and Springham (2). In Londonderry High School the records show a more even balance, with Dunseveric (11), Northlands (10) and Duncreggan (8).

With amalgamation in 1976, a dilemma arose about preserving the house system. It was decided to retain two houses from each school – Lawrence and Springham from Foyle and Duncreggan and Dunseveric from Londonderry High School. Each house retained its original house colours, except Dunseveric, and these were worn on ties, badges and sports kit: Lawrence (blue), Springham (yellow), Duncreggan (red) and Dunseveric (green, formerly blue). After amalgamation many activities remained within the preserves of the boys or girls but an attempt was made with combined competitions such as house choir and debating. There was some resistance, especially from the boys, and the number of inter-house competitions has dwindled, with the house cup now being awarded solely on the result of sports day performances and confined to the junior pupils and year 11. Today each house has about 200 pupils, and these larger numbers, combined with the difficulties of a split site, have contributed to the lesser status of the house system.

William Lynn

TOP: *LHS House Trophy.*

ABOVE: *Rita McIlroy House Shield (LHS).*

FAR LEFT: *Foyle College House Cup.*

FORMER SCHOOL BADGES

Foyle and Londonderry College Head Boy Badge

Foyle and Londonderry College Head Girl Badge

Foyle and Londonderry College Prefect Badge

Foyle College Badge

Foyle College Prefect Blazer Badge

Foyle College House Prefect Lapel Badge: Andrews House (red), Lawrence House (blue), Montgomery House (green), Springham House (yellow).

Londonderry High School Badges: Dunseveric House (blue), Northlands House (green), Duncreggan House (red).

THE CHANGING CURRICULUM

CURRICULUM, 1800–1945

At the end of the 18th century the study of Classics was the core of the curriculum and a religious as well as a secular programme was clearly intended. Fees in 1814 were £18 for six-months' board and tuition with an additional cost for a French master. A report (August 1832) by the Revd William Knox described in some detail 'the content and purpose of the studies' undertaken there: 'a course of education pursued' at the core of which was a 'Classical Course necessary for entrance into Dublin College'. In addition, a general course of theoretical and practical mathematics was followed, in particular those elements which were requisite for undergraduates of Dublin College. The mathematics course at the diocesan school also included aspects usually adopted in military and naval schools.

OPPOSITE: *Chemistry lesson, Foyle College, c.1920.*

BELOW: *An etching of Foyle College in their prospectus, 1886.*

Included in a 'Course of Commercial Education necessary to qualify a lad for entering a Counting House' were listed 'History, Geography, the Use of the Globes' and English composition. Religious instruction was provided with reading focused on the Bible, Christian history, lectures and the Church catechism. In January 1833 the Revd James Knox iterated that the purpose of the school was 'to dispense to youth a general course of initiatory and manly Education'.

In the *Londonderry Journal* (March 1835) Mr Flanaghan invited 'Parents and Guardians of such young gentlemen as may be desirous of acquiring instruction in dancing at Foyle to signify their intentions'. The *Londonderry Journal* (January 1837) invited the citizens of Derry to attend a debate at the 'College School-Room' on the topic 'Was Caesar a great man?' indicating that the school was merely reaffirming its dedication to classical education! In the 1836 and 1837 examinations excellence was manifested in Latin, Greek and Hebrew, while prizes were awarded for mathematics, English, French, geography, astronomy and bookkeeping, as well as 'Use of the Globes'. Four boys received honours in elocution and a number excelled in their studies of Holy Scripture. In the 1837 list of subjects it was stated: 'Henceforward lectures on Elocution will be delivered on the Tuesdays and Thursdays of each week, and the classes will be instructed in the elementary parts of Botany and Chemistry'. From the mid-19th century the curriculum included Latin, Greek and Hebrew with a strong emphasis on grammar and history. The school also employed a 'gentleman from the continent', who was to teach foreign languages. Foyle included navigation as a subject, and with military mathematics in the

FOYLE COLLEGE

FOYLE COLLEGE–TIME TABLE 1898-9.

curriculum there was no doubt about the destination of many of the boys.

From 1866 the Revd Dr Percy Robinson made it his aim to promote Foyle as a 'church school', but with Maurice Hime's appointment to Foyle in 1877 a noticeable change occurred in the culture of the school. The school chapel was deconsecrated and it became a classroom.

Our School Times (16 September 1879) describes the work of the various classes in Foyle. It focuses on the studies undertaken by all classes in ancient history, Latin and Greek grammar and literature and mathematics. Trigonometry, arithmetic and algebra formed the core, with regular lessons in mental arithmetic. The second half of the 19th century witnessed an increased interest in science, with some of the Foyle staff being actively involved in the Londonderry Scientific Association. Experimental science was taught to about 20 boys in different classes, the teaching directed towards studies of optics, heat, magnetism, electricity, mechanics and inorganic chemistry. Only five or six boys took advantage of the lessons on bookkeeping.

The boys were well grounded in grammar and literature, with lessons also in copy-writing, composition, dictation and English history. By 1878 the school had two trained teachers amongst its staff of six assistant masters. In a noteworthy speech in 1881 Hime, perhaps with limited vision, stated: 'It

is not the business of the state to interfere with the choice of parents and schoolmasters as to the subjects of instruction'.

A former master at the school wrote in the school magazine in 1884:

> *About fifty years ago all that was really taught was classics, and sometimes logic in the upper forms and the '3 Rs' in the lower forms; in the literature of their own country, or in the ordinary mathematics they were usually left in a state of the most utter ignorance.*

Admitting that French was sometimes taught he concluded 'And no one ever dreamt of introducing any of the physical sciences into the school programme'. By December 1884 arrangements had been made for some senior boys to attend science lectures in Magee College.

Hime later stated: 'Foyle will never become a place for cramming boys; we schoolmasters *educate* boys'. Convinced of the value of sporting activities he encouraged the boys to participate and ensured that the facilities were available: in the 1880s boys at Foyle had the luxury of a gymnasium, the opportunity to go rowing on the two school boats, as well of course as participating in the traditional games of cricket and 'football'. The drill sergeant from the Ebrington Barracks was employed to instil in the boys the mysteries of deportment. Only one boy was examined in chemistry in the school's Intermediate Examination in the early 1890s. However, following the amalgamation of 1896 Foyle was able to offer a more balanced course of study. The curriculum was more than the sum of subjects taught and in that regard Foyle offered a wide range of experiences. At the ball alley, boxing between boarders and dayboys was a feature and energetic times were spent participating in paperchases in the Waterside. Maurice Hime noted in 1887 the excellent education provided by Miss McKillip and also Miss Holmes at the Strand House School. If the relationship between the Foyle boys and the girls of Victoria was not yet co-educational it was certainly most cordial according to reminiscences from former pupils.

Following the 1896 amalgamation a staff of eight masters conducted a school day which began at 9am with roll call, Scripture reading and prayers, followed by continuous lessons, each approximately 50 minutes long, until lunch at 12.40. Afternoon lessons began at 1.30 and ended at 3.15. Every Thursday afternoon the last half hour was devoted to religious instruction. In addition to Classics and modern languages, the boys were instructed in mathematics, English and history. Included in the timetable were classes in mechanics, chemistry, magnetism and electricity, and the headmaster took the

university boys for Latin. Part of his teaching timetable was allocated to delivering typewriting to the commercial class. These boys also studied bookkeeping, shorthand and mental arithmetic.

In 1915 Strand House School closed, its girls going mainly to St Lurach's and Victoria High School. World War I, too, was to have a significant effect on social patterns and curricular thinking. By 1917, the year before women's partial emancipation, Victoria High School was able to boast of a well-qualified science mistress and experimental laboratory, with junior girls following courses in elementary physics and chemistry along with botany and physiology. While Latin at that school was considered an important subject and reference was made to the success of students in Greek, it was really at Foyle where Classics still held dominance. Foyle boys consistently performed well in the Intermediate Examination in Classics. While there were some prizes for composition in German, it was Latin and Greek that took the honours. However, the college class-prize lists for the war years and later show awards for success in experimental science but surprisingly German is absent. Curriculum change had come slowly, but in 1921 a new Northern Ireland state would begin to assert its control over educational matters.

FAR RIGHT: *Foyle College scale of fees and list of awards, 1931.*

BELOW: *St Lurach's prize bookplate.*

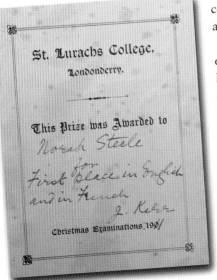

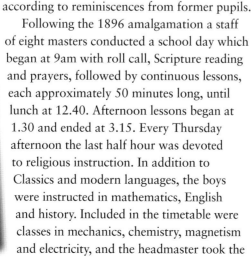

Curriculum, 1945–85

The grammar school years in Foyle began with the 1947 Education Orders of the Stormont administration. This legislation followed on from the arrangements put in place in Westminster and known to all as the Butler Education Act, which expanded the scholarship system of pre-war years into a universal entitlement for state-funded secondary education. Children would be streamed for three types of school: grammar for the most academically adept, technical for those with a vocation to more practical skills and secondary modern for those who did not wish to engage with education at a high level and who wanted a basic education to qualify them for jobs at an early opportunity. Grammar schools selected pupils at 11 on the basis of an examination but whereas before only a minority of pupils were funded, now everyone who passed the exam was entitled to a free academic education.

Foyle prospered under the twin benefits of bright pupils and a guaranteed income. With the latter came the need to accept direction from the Department of Education, but this too had benefits in organising transfer, maintaining standards and providing capital. The theory of the grammar school was that all pupils from any background could 'qualify' for an academic education at schools some of which, like Foyle, had formerly had limited free places and had become the enclaves of those who could pay.

Working-class families could at last inculcate an aspiration in their children that academic success would offer an improved future. By 1952 the next tier of reform was a qualification to permit entry to the professions and university with advanced-level examinations in subjects now chosen by the candidate to match the entry requirements of the courses.

The effect of this on the curriculum was more profound than any of the previous changes over 300 years. The change to the new grammar school system enabled a greater proportion of the population to study the sciences as a route into professional life. Technology was harder to assimilate into the 'academic' curriculum and was only legislated for by the mid-1980s National Curriculum.

FOYLE & LONDONDERRY COLLEGE

PROSPECTUS

More students pursued maths and sciences, and with the amalgamation more girls, too, chose the scientific pathway. This revolution in women's careers was aided by the increasing access, through grammar schools, to a curriculum that was not merely academic but blatantly technocratic.

Curriculum, 1985 to the present

With the introduction of the Common Curriculum in the 1980s, schools were obliged to provide a broad, balanced, relevant, differentiated and progressive curriculum for their pupils. All schools had to ensure access to subjects within a common core: English, mathematics, science, modern foreign languages – while humanities, arts and technical subjects were to be offered as optional.

Classics, especially Latin, were disregarded in the emphasis on a *modern* foreign language, and many grammar schools had only the rudiments of technical subjects. The new examination, General Certificate of Secondary Education (GCSE) was an attempt to set tests for the entire ability range. Ordinary Levels had been taken only by a small number of (largely) grammar school pupils. The Certificate of Secondary Education (CSE) was meant to supply qualifications for the next tier of candidates, with only the least able exempted or un-catered for.

The GCSE was an assessment designed for comprehensive schools catering for the whole ability range. The differing standards persuaded many parents that the 11+ was a 'high-stakes' test. They assumed that secondary schools were under-performing when compared with examination outcomes in grammar schools. The idea that the schools served different groups with different aspirations was lost in league tables.

Lawrence Hill as a school building had what the Department of Education today would call 'deficiencies'. There were no rooms for music or art, for instance, with pupils using the nearby technical college facilities. Biology was only belatedly allocated laboratory space, so the move to Springtown in 1967 allowed some of this to be addressed. After the 1976 amalgamation with Londonderry High School the organisation of the split-site school required some adjustment.

FOYLE COLLEGE LONDONDERRY

OFFICIAL OPENING
OF
THE NEW SCHOOL BUILDINGS
BY
H.R.H. the Duke of Kent
ON
2 May 1968

The Department of Education graciously funded girls' toilets in the boys' school. One benefit of the amalgamated school was a gradual expansion of the curriculum. Geology and economics were introduced to expand the range of A-Levels on offer. Vocational subjects including technical drawing were now taught. Language labs were much in vogue and were sited in both schools until fashions changed and computers took over.

The Common Curriculum gave a more familiar look to the subjects taught and each had to fight for its own allocation of time and content. The pupils now had greater choice at GCSE and up to four subjects could be chosen by each individual, although a strong art or science divide remained. Woodwork, technical drawing and other 'crafts' were now subsumed into Craft, Design and Technology (CDT), which was seen as a mainstay of the 1980s curriculum. This required a dedicated, specialised teaching space. For this purpose in 1997 the Henderson Suite, complete with state-of-the-art facilities for Information and Communication Technology (ICT) and a new library, was built, while music gained its first dedicated room in the history of Foyle.

Duncreggan had already gained a CDT/IT Suite in the 1990s as a result of collaboration among schools, and EU funding was available for projects spread across three national jurisdictions. Foyle entered into a triumvirate with a Donegal school and a school in Hanover and generated a project which required state-of-the-art computing. At this time Foyle's only facility for computing was the Kerr Suite. An upgrade was clearly required and, given the EU primacy in the tri-school project, the Comenius Fund paid for the new suite, which was an extension of the existing CDT classroom block. With the financial support of Lex and Eileen Roulston, a room to accommodate open access to computers for use by the sixth form was established.

At present, the idea of a curriculum which is differentiated to match the aspirations and ability of pupils now dominates the basic provision in all schools. The Entitlement Framework seeks to offer myriad courses at GCSE and A-Level quite beyond the reach of individual schools. Schools are required to offer 24 subjects up to Year 12 (16 years old) and 27 subjects to Year 14 (upper sixth). Now the Foyle Learning Community – comprising all post-primary education providers in the Derry City Council area, theoretically allows for a huge range of qualifications to be offered.

Jack Magill and Jim Heasley

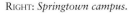

ABOVE: *The Duke and Duchess of Kent open the magnificent Springtown campus in May 1968, beginning a new chapter in Foyle College history.*

RIGHT: *Springtown campus.*

14 THE PREPARATORY SCHOOLS

Preparatory education for pupils under the age of 12 became available at the LAI in 1870. *The Derry Almanac, North-West Directory and General Advertiser* of 1870 described the children's schoolroom as an upper bedroom in the house at East Wall that was also their playground.

Jane H Wright joined the staff of the LAI preparatory school in 1890 and was appointed principal on the amalgamation of LAI and Foyle in 1896. She quickly became very popular, as is clear from the fact that the pupils presented her with two volumes of poetry in December 1892. When her sister Katherine joined her in 1898 they became the guiding spirits of the prep for almost half a century. Jane retired in 1929 and Katherine continued until she had to give up on doctor's orders in 1938. As numbers increased, extra accommodation had to be sought and their boys won many free scholarships to the senior school. Murray Moore, a former pupil said of Katherine: 'Unknown to us we were being educated in greater things than

OPPOSITE: *Foyle College Prep School, June 1929.*

RIGHT: *Jane H Wright (left) and her sister Katherine embodied the spirit and aspirations of the LAI preparatory school for nearly 40 years.*

the three Rs, in whatsoever things are true, whatsoever things are honest, whatsoever things are just'.

Another tribute was paid to the sisters in a letter to the late SD Irons by Colonel HV Glendinning:

> I started my schooling in 1912 under the taller and younger Miss Wright at one end of that immense upper-storey room and was promoted in time to the other end under the other Miss Wright, where I started French. What wonderful women were these two sisters! They taught young Derry all it knew, and were respected, admired and adored by generations of Foyle boys.

Following Katherine Wright's departure in 1938 and with the takeover by the military of Lower Foyle and a portion of Upper Foyle in 1940 the school experienced 'virtual disintegration' (*Our School Times*, December 1940). The attached photograph of the entire student body supplied by and containing the image of Basil Singleton shows how small the prep was in 1945.

Scott Marshall succeeded Miss Wall as head of the Prep in September 1967. He was tasked by Stewart Connolly to raise its profile and attract more pupils to the school. The writing and producing of plays by the principal that were suitable for the age range became a feature of the life of the school. Sports were encouraged and their football teams enjoyed considerable success against other primary schools. There was a flourishing cub pack.

The amalgamation with the Londonderry High School prep brought Foyle pupils to the new buildings at Dunseveric, and Scott Marshall continued as head with assistance from Miss Orr and Mrs Campbell. Mrs Elaine Marshall would eventually become the last principal of the school. There was a most active parents' association, which supported the school in both curricular and extra-curricular ventures, and socially the annual supper dance became a highlight of the school year.

The school grew from about 25 pupils in the mid 1960s to 65 in the late 1980s but when the Department of Education forbade automatic transfer and reduced funding, numbers declined to an unsustainable level. The prep department moved from its Dunseveric site to a three-classroom suite on the ground floor of Springtown in the mid 1990s, freeing up much-needed space for senior pupils on the Duncreggan campus. When in June 2003 the numbers fell to nine boys and girls, the school closed. Elaine Marshall had taught there for almost 30 years until the final dissolution of the school.

As Elaine was happy to note: 'Over the years, more pupils with special needs have come to the school and the fact that we were able to cater for these children's needs is something we are very proud of. Everybody's special needs are catered for here'. Another tribute came from the journalist and writer, Elizabeth Day. Author of two novels and staff member of the *Observer*, she recalls her time at Foyle prep with great warmth and fondness:

I can't begin to explain Foyle Prep to anyone who wasn't there. Words like 'unique', 'special' and 'irreplaceable' are too tired to express a fraction of what Foyle prep was to its pupils, even though the prep was all of these things and so many more. If you want me to count just how many, you'll have to ask Mrs Marshall. I was never very good at Structured Reasoning.

The Londonderry High School preparatory school was instituted in 1935, when it was known as the kindergarten and its first principal was Mabel Colhoun (1905–92), herself an old girl of St Lurach's. Shortly after the acquisition of Duncreggan House the outbuildings were transformed into Dunseveric. Most of the accommodation served as dormitories for the Londonderry High School boarders, while the ground floor became classrooms for both prep and first-form pupils transferred on its completion from Crawford Square. During World War II the prep was given a separate location in Gwyn's Institute, Brooke Park.

With the introduction of the 1947 Education Act there was a significant increase in the school population. The prep school was moved first to 58 Northland Road opposite the school gates and called 'Dunluce'. In 1964 it was sited in the custom-built building opposite the Glen Road but with 84 pupils accommodation was very cramped. Miss Colhoun retired in 1969 and her successor, Editha Riddell (1913–89), an honours graduate in history from London University, had come into teaching late in a career of bewildering variety that included photography, working with MI5 and (at her own insistence) in the Land Army during the war.

MABEL REMINGTON COLHOUN (1905–92)

Mabel Colhoun combined preparatory teaching with local history and archaeology. Born in 1905, she attended Strand House and St Lurach's, where her cousin by marriage was principal. Always interested in education, especially of the very young, she first established a nursery school in her parents' home in Deanfield and was active in the formation of the local branch of the Nursery School Association in 1946.

She was appointed as head of the Londonderry High School preparatory school in 1935 and was a kind and imaginative teacher with a gift for blackboard illustration, especially during 'nature study' lessons, when her accurate 'lightning' sketches of birds and plants added to the effectiveness of the lesson. Small but wiry, she was an indefatigable cyclist, swimmer, hockey player (as a member of the Ulster Rovers team) and turned out for the Londonderry High School staff team in 1959 when she was 54.

The war years saw the surge in Mabel's fieldwork, travelling on self-selected archaeological journeys until she knew the location of every site of ancient interest in Inishowen, specialising in bullauns and stones with cup-marks or other carvings. In 1940 Mabel began to record archaeological sites in the North West, continuing to visit the sites, often by bicycle and later by car, until the late 1970s. She published five papers detailing her journeys in Donegal and Tyrone. A considerable archive of her material is now in the Derry Museum as the Mabel Colhoun Collection, donated by her family. Much of the written work and correspondence relates to her survey of Inishowen, and the majority of newspaper cuttings are related to the history of Donegal and Derry. The nursery materials range from teaching booklets to posters used for teaching purposes in the classroom. Three years after her death on 4 April 1992 the Northwest Archaeological and Historical Society published *The Heritage of Inishowen: Its Archaeology, History and Folklore* (1995), a volume containing most of her archaeological research.

She was also intensely interested in local Derry history, especially of her old school and her new one. An essay using the dates of Derry's four bridges (1790, 1863, 1935, 1983) as a framework gave a fascinating account of the origins and development of Londonderry High School. Other written work included a sketch of the life of MF McIlroy, the headmistress she most admired, a history of Duncreggan House (1990) from its building for the Tillie family until its establishment as the senior school of Foyle and Londonderry College and – typically – a survey of all the trees in the Duncreggan grounds.

15 EXTRA-CURRICULAR ACTIVITIES

The school has a long-established tradition of extra-curricular activity which is an integral part of the its ethos to this day. In earlier centuries, when many of the pupils were boarders, there was a necessity to provide pastimes to occupy them when not in lessons. Today pupils have a wide range of pursuits to choose from in the areas of sport, music and drama.

The earliest activity recorded is chess, which is mentioned in *Our School Times* for September 1878. Dr Maurice Hime knew that some pupils were not natural sportsmen and needed to be provided with activities beyond handball, rugby and cricket. In the magazines there are instructions on how to play chess, together with detailed reports on games, some of which were carried out by correspondence. The Debating Society was inaugurated on 17 February 1882. Detailed reports for the six debates in that series appear in the June magazine. Dr Hime's wife founded a local branch of the Schoolboys' Scripture Union in 1879.

Most of these early activities survive in the present school. During the 1960s and 1970s, the chess club was popular with boys of all ages and there was a tradition of both inter-house and inter-schools competitions. Debating and public speaking have remained popular, and over the years a number of individual pupils have been successful even at a national level. Some activities such as philately have flourished under the enthusiasm of particular members of staff (in this case WJ Walker, who was also responsible for lessons in ballroom dancing) only to decline or cease upon their retirement. Other activities which have followed this path include sailing, fishing, badminton, swimming, rowing, table tennis and scouting. Some activities, such as

the Duke of Edinburgh's Award Scheme and the Bar Mock Trial competition, have been introduced only in recent years, but have become well established and are flourishing.

William Lynn

OPPOSITE: *Foyle students in Paris, 2012.*

RIGHT: *School production of Bugsy Malone, 1999.*

ENTRANCES AND EXITS –
MUSIC AND DRAMA AT FOYLE

The tradition of school music and drama is as old as education itself. It played an important part in classical antiquity, in medieval and renaissance schools, and was a feature of Foyle in its evolution from Free School to its modern form. JS Goodman, a participant on both sides of the footlights, here brings its modern story up to date.

1924–5: Scenes from *The Merchant of Venice*, Sheridan's *The Rivals, A Midsummer's Night Dream* and Dickens's *A Christmas Carol*.

1927–8: Gerald Macnamara's *Thompson in Tír-na-nÓg* and Lady Gregory's *The Workhouse Ward*

1930–1: *Macbeth*

1931–2: *Henry IV Part I*

1932–3: Clemence Dane's *When the Wind Blows*, Scenes from *Twelfth Night* and Lord Dunsany's *A Night at an Inn*

1933–4: Mayor's *Thirty Minutes in a Street*, John Drinkwater's *X=O, A Night of the Trojan War*, JJ Bell's *The Thread of Scarlet* and AA Milne's *The Boy Comes Home*

1934–5: Rudolf Besier's: *The Barretts of Wimpole Street*

1935–6: Bruno Franck's: *The Twelve Thousand* and Laurence Houseman's *Brother Wolf*

1936–7: Shaw's *Captain Brassbound's Conversion*

1937–8: *Henry IV Part I*

1938–9: Shaw's *Pygmalion*.

EARLY DAYS

From this list of pre-war school presentations, remarkable in its variety and scope, I have selected *The Barretts* (1934) to comment upon, mainly because it featured one of Foyle's most famous actors, Noel Willman. Noel went on to be a professional actor, on stage and screen. (He starred in *Dr Zhivago*.) Mr Hall produced the play but Willman was singled out for special praise. 'The longest and heaviest part was that of Elizabeth, and although it is now three months since December and one's enthusiasm must cool when the cause is so far removed, we still think that for beauty, sympathy and entire conviction, Willman's acting was extraordinary'. His brother John played the part of Henrietta and the off-stage support team was not forgotten: 'Mr Harris who, using only a hammer, a few tacks, and an electric bulb or two, can conjure a Victorian drawing room out of half a dozen planks and a few yards of wall-paper' and Mr Lawrence McCann, who, out of a 'cello, a viola, three violins and a piano, produced a most efficient orchestra'.

The willing cooperation of staff and pupils, an essential condition for the success evidenced here, would continue to be characteristic of Foyle productions. During the war years inevitably there was a paucity of performances in school, although in 1942 there was a fundraising Spitfire Concert organised by Forms I and II. At prizegiving in the following year the headmaster in his speech gave us an insight to the importance with which he regarded music at the time: 'Music, I fear, with the existing curriculum, is a matter for the home!'

Four between-the-wars productions from the Foyle College Players: Top Left The Rivals, *1924; Above* The Merchant of Venice, *1925; Right* Journey's End, Pride and Prejudice *c.1930.*

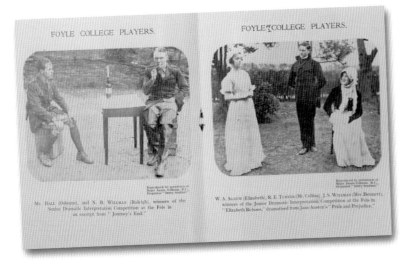

FOYLE COLLEGE PLAYERS.

FOYLE COLLEGE PLAYERS.

Mr. Hall (Osborne), and N. B. Willman (Raleigh), winners of the Senior Dramatic Interpretation Competition at the Feis in an excerpt from "Journey's End."

W. A. Agnew (Elizabeth), R. E. Turner (Mr. Collins), J. S. Willman (Mrs. Bennett), winners of the Junior Dramatic Interpretation Competition at the Feis in "Elizabeth Refuses," dramatised from Jane Austen's "Pride and Prejudice."

THE FOYLE OPERAS

The year 1949 saw the start of the phenomenon known throughout the North West as the Foyle Opera. Much credit for the outstanding series of Gilbert and Sullivan operettas must go to Michael Franklin, organist of St Columb's Cathedral, Derry, who trained the boys to become convincing little maids or *contadine*, and the young men to convert to threatening pirates or roguish *gondolieri*. *HMS Pinafore* was presented in the Apprentice Boys Memorial Hall on 21–23 March 1950. The producer was DCG Craig, who earlier and later was a dedicated director, and Michael Franklin along with T Parker was responsible for the music. The main principals were WT Smith as Sir Joseph Porter, WS Gibbons as Captain Corcoran and DO Coulter as Josephine. In the chorus were names that became synonymous with the school operas of the period: WM Kinghan, WJ Carruthers, EC Coulter, WJ Traill, CD Orr, ES Marshall, A Wilkinson and EW Walker.

Patience, 1952. Gilbert and Sullivan formed a staple of the Foyle Opera's golden years from 1949 to 1956.

The Mikado followed later in that year on 11–14 December 1950, again in the Memorial Hall with the same production team. The title role was played by CD Orr (later to become Dean of Derry), Nanki-Poo by JB Smith and Pooh Bah by LM Dixon. Ko-Ko was DO Coulter and his twin brother EC Coulter played the devious Katisha. Yum Yum was ES Marshall and her little maids were A Wilkinson and WJ Carruthers. Bob Le Clerc reviewed each show and I wish I had the space to quote at greater length, so humorous and elegantly expressed were his views. DO Coulter was singled out: 'When he runs at Springtown he is a rather awkward and galumphing creature, on the stage he moves and dances as lightly and as gracefully as a feather'. On Katisha: 'As a piece of sheer acting it was the best thing in this production. Here was a boy of thirteen who had so thought himself into his part that one felt all Katisha's predatory fierceness, her grim strength of character and at the same time the biting scorn which Gilbert so often felt for his old maids'.

The Gondoliers sailed into the Guildhall on 28 November 1951 and berthed for four nights. The Duke of Plaza-Toro was DO Coulter and his brother (EC) played Guiseppe, one of the *gondolieri*. Marco was played by JB Smith and three of the ladies' chorus included ES Marshall, WJ Carruthers and WJ Temple (now a retired pharmacist) who 'stood out as having a fine voice and an ability to give it vigour'. JS Connolly, later to become headmaster, was heavily involved with the drama and noted that when some original castings developed flaws 'my especial admiration goes to those who without ill-feeling or demur stepped out of parts for which they proved unsuitable'.

Patience was staged in the Guildhall from 2–5 December 1952. Once again the musical direction was in the hands of Franklin and Parker but this time the production was shared by Graham Craig and Stewart Connolly. The parts of the Colonel, Major and the Duke were played by DR Craig, A Wilkinson and WA Caldwell. The poets Bunthorne and Grosvenor were portrayed by DO and EC Coulter. Carruthers, Traill and Marshall, all mentioned previously, played the parts of the Solicitor, Lady Jane and Patience. The orchestra had grown to 18 players, including three boys of the school, R Harte (trumpet) A Payne (tenor horn) and R Millar (double bass).

The Pirates of Penzance was presented in the Guildhall for a four-night run in December 1953.

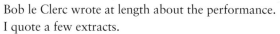

David Coulter (left) and his brother Edmund were stalwarts of the Foyle Opera.

Bob le Clerc wrote at length about the performance. I quote a few extracts.

Vocally AT Hamilton (Mabel) demonstrated emphatically his advanced power and technique, whilst EC Coulter (Frederick) shows he has the making of a very adequate voice. His own assurance and his reassurance of his stage companions were as great as ever. DO Coulter's (Major-General) parts have made him more of an individualist but he has demonstrated in other operas that he can be a first-class partner too. HJ McMorris (Pirate King) impressed not merely by virtue of his stature and valiant singing but by the effective gesture and leadership he gave on the stage.

It should be noted that the orchestra ran to 23 players, most of whom were adults who gave of their time and talent freely. Sadly, some would say, this would not be the case nowadays.

Onwards to December 1954 and in the Guildhall another Gilbert and Sullivan, this time *Ruddigore* – the one where the portraits come to life in the ghost scene. Revd Carson, who was in charge of building the stage, and his team of stage hands were praised highly for the excellent effect. Rose was played by Michael Houston, who incidentally was head-chorister of St Columb's Cathedral. Stewart Connolly in his report mentioned four boys who had finished their sixth and probably their last opera. 'They are Carruthers, Coulter, Fleming and Marshall. They have deserved well of the school, and we shall miss them sadly'. In fact Carruthers and Marshall did not retire but returned for the 1955 production of *HMS Pinafore*. As usual the conductor was Michael Franklin and the production team comprised JH Brockhill, JS Connolly, DCG Craig and H Evans.

The second presentation of *The Gondoliers* took place in the Guildhall from 5–8 December 1956 and in fact it ended a seven-year run but was there 'life after the Foyle Operas?' I felt somewhat cheated landing at

ABOVE: The Pirates of Penzance, *1953*.

BELOW RIGHT: *AT Hamilton as Mabel in* Pirates.

supplied the excellent continuo. The Easter Concert was a combination of music and Sheridan's *The Critic*. Under the tutelage of Mr Brownlow and Mr Addinell there was the visible sign of the birth of the new school orchestra. West was instrumental in organising music tutorials for the pupils and the school was beginning to reap the rewards of his endeavours. The title The Musical and Dramatic Society was replaced by The Foyle Players (in fact it was just going back 30-odd years to the original name).

The Players Report of 1977 noted that the amalgamation of the two drama societies did not go swimmingly: 'It seemed to repel rather than attract new members'. In March of the following year, however the *Belfast Telegraph* noted the 'Polished Pygmalion Performance'. Ingrid Logue was a convincing Eliza, whose elegance was matched by her poise. Professor Higgins (Philip Adams) was well portrayed and balanced by the mildness of Colonel Pickering (Adrian McClay). The Senior Choir by 1978, however, had benefited by being mixed, and it won the John Maultsaid Challenge Cup at the Londonderry Feis. Belinda Story and Billy West were joint Heads of Department following amalgamation, and the impressive Easter Concert that year was testimony

Foyle to find that the era of the Opera was over. For years I had attended the performances and listened to all the backstage gossip and excitement from my brother Victor, who took part in three – and then the school decided to drop them! For staff and pupils they probably took over their lives for much of the school year. It became increasingly difficult to keep the senior boys on board as they prepared for university entrance or further education. We had passed through a golden age with the pupils mentioned above.

Friday, 3 March 1967, was the last working day in Lawrence Hill after 153 years and Springtown opened its doors on 8 March in a building that cost £300,000. Understandably there were no music or drama productions that year. The Easter concert that year was to mark the debut of Billy West as music teacher in Foyle. As we shall see he went on for over 30 years inspiring and guiding pupils with his love and knowledge of music. Very many of his pupils went on to become full-time musicians, a true testament of his dedication to his profession.

Although the amalgamation was some years away, there was collaboration with the Londonderry High School in March 1969 for the staging of *Black Ey'd Susan* directed by Tom Dunn and leading parts played by Haydn Deane, Nicholas Hunter and David Haslett of Foyle and Marilyn Atkinson and Valerie Bainbridge from the High School. Trevor Burnside

to the great work of the newly introduced Music Service of the Western Education and Library Board (WELB). There now was a string orchestra, with horn trios, bassoon solo, Irish pipes, a school band and a madrigal choir. So with pupils such as Sharon Graham, Alan and Rosemary Moore, Stephen and Shaun Gillespie, Christopher Matchett, Trevor Barr, Helen Fulton, Brian Stafford and Nigel Priestley all playing their part in raising the musical profile of the school, Foyle had become a centre of musical excellence, long before 'specialist' schools were thought of. The Tillie Shield (Londonderry Feis) was won in 1979 by a large mixed choir trained by James Goodman.

THE MUSICALS' RETURN

It was only a matter of time before musicals were resurrected, and 1981 saw the return of *HMS Pinafore*, 16 years since the last Gilbert and Sullivan. Patricia Mackey and Mark Haslett played the leading couple with Keith McCracken cast as Dick Deadeye. Alan Rodden, David Middleton, Sharon Craig and Rosemary Moore had principal roles. It was a major achievement to have persuaded most of the 1st XV to don sailor outfits and prance around the stage. The production team comprised Belinda Story, Jim Goodman, Billy West, Gordon Fulton and Hilary McCloy. Fired by the success of *Pinafore* the school undertook to stage *Patience* in February 1982.

When *Ruddigore* was performed in 1983, the *Belfast Telegraph* reported: 'Principals were obviously at ease in their roles, and the typically ludicrous complications of the plot were all the more enjoyable for the clarity and individuality of the characterisation'. In 1984 the Savoy Opera was replaced with Irving Berlin's *Annie Get Your Gun*, and the uninhibited world of show business that it paints stimulated the youthful cast to a lively performance. The sharp-shooting, rough-talking Annie Oakley, played by Hilary Ferris, was the outstanding individual performance. Andrew Love as a smooth Frank Butler was a good foil to Annie's uncouthness and the show business impresarios, ranging from Keith Norris as Charlie Davenport to Peter Campbell as Sitting Bull, brought out all the fun of the story. The teachers responsible for the production were: Jim Goodman, William West, Brian McCay, Hilary McCloy and Helen McCay.

Thanks to Billy West the annual Easter Concert took place as usual, and it was a wonderful platform for the many hugely talented pupils who were receiving tuition through the WELB Music Service. The following names appear regularly during this era: George McCloskey, Ryan Simpson, Martyn Goodman, Lois McBride, Catherine Harper, John McClelland, Jonathan Kennedy, Lucy Montgomery, Donna Marie Kelly, Brenda McCay, Andrew Buchanan, Lynda Matchett, Carol Gibson, Radhika Raj and Brian McFetridge.

One of the best-known Old Boys of Foyle is Percy French, and in April 1986 a concert of his music and dramatic sketches was presented by James N Healy and his assistants in Duncreggan. Percy's two daughters were in attendance and the school choir sang some of his songs, including 'The Mountains of Mourne'. The 1986 musical was *Oliver*, with the experienced production team led by Jim Goodman. Seventeen members of staff were actively involved in the cast, and the orchestra comprised over 80 pupils. Darren Greer as Fagin was singled out as the star of the show: 'This actor is a revelation … a central performance of skill'.

In 1987 with Foyle's reputation in the musical world riding high, the school produced a professional recording entitled 'School of Harmony', It was recorded and edited by Colm Arbuckle (Radio Foyle) and Jim Goodman and featured the orchestra, choirs (senior and junior), instrumental and vocal soloists, ensembles and the Junior Wind Band. In February 1988 Frank Loessers' *Guys and Dolls* was staged and proved to be a popular choice. The principal line-up of Hargan, Greer, Burns and Gregg was probably as strong as any I have worked with. Also featured were significant cameo performances and 'big' numbers: the slick professionalism of 'The Crapshooters' Dance' or 'Luck Be a Lady' and the rousing chorus work in 'Sit Down You're Rocking the Boat' led by the ebullient Nicely-Nicely (Jason Campbell).

The return of *The Mikado* in 1989 proved to be a huge success. Helen Gregg was a commanding Katisha, Michael Harkin a polished Nanki-Poo while Shauna Wilson displayed great serenity in her role as Yum-Yum. David Wright excelled as Ko-Ko and Geoffrey Moore and Alan Henderson suited their respective roles as Pish-Tush and Poo-Bah. Christopher Keys acquitted himself extremely well as the Mikado. Much of the success of *The Mikado* and the concerts was due to the quality of a group of eight pupils who attained Grade 8 standard in their music examinations, all in 1990. That was a record for schools of a similar size in Northern Ireland: Stewart Smith (organ and piano), Jonathan Howe (double bass and piano), Gail Norris (oboe), Serena Crichton, Geoffrey Moore (piano), Carol Gibson (cello), David Birney and Nigel Cairns (flute). Robert Goodman was the brass tutor for the WELB, and his work with the Foyle pupils stimulated a growing interest in jazz, now a major feature in our annual concerts.

Sandy Wilson's *The Boy Friend* was produced in December 1991. Foyle's Polly was Serena Crichton and her beau Tony was played by Alan Henderson. The music highlight of 1992 was the senior choir's success in reaching the finals of the Sainsbury Choir

The Mikado, *1989*.

of the Year Competition. Having won the Northern Ireland heat in Belfast, we were invited to Manchester (Royal Northern College of Music) for the televised quarter-finals. On arrival at Larne the choir was met by a television crew and presenter/composer Howard Goodall to film a documentary about the build-up to the competition. Howard travelled to Manchester on the school coach and so began a friendship which lasted several years.

Later the choir travelled to Limerick for the International Church Choral Festival and started a tradition which lasted for seven years. The display cabinet in Duncreggan houses many beautiful pieces of crystal presented to us as winners. We were often complimented on behaviour and presentation during our stays, and the Mayor of Limerick paid a courtesy visit to Foyle to show appreciation of our contribution to the festival.

With the stagecoach a-rollin' and the guns a-bangin', *Calamity Jane* began its four-night run on 8 December 1993. 'Why you slab-sided, yellow-bellied sons of cowardly coyotes!' These words transported us back in time to the welcome setting of the Golden Garter. 'If you caught all those words you were one-up on me, and I was that thigh-whacking, gun-slinging dame centre stage,' recalled Orla Hasson some time after the show. David Keown, as assistant producer, joined the team and brought much energy and enthusiasm into the project. It has many memorable numbers, including 'Secret Love', 'Deadwood Stage' and 'The Black Hills of Dakota'.

In June 1995 the school played host to the BBC 3 radio programme *Key Questions*. This musical

discussion evening was chaired by Howard Goodall and it was at his insistence that the broadcast should come from Foyle. Our new piano in the assembly hall was christened that evening and the celebrity panel consisted of Una Hunt, concert pianist, Philip Hammond, composer and musical journalist, and Timothy Allen, organist of St Columb's Cathedral.

The choir performed successfully at the Londonderry Feis, the Limerick Festival as well as our own Easter concert. Another Gilbert and Sullivan opera, *The Pirates of Penzance* produced in Duncreggan on 6–9 December 1995 with teacher David Keown playing the Pirate King. Bryan Morgan stole this show with his Major-General's patter song. Jillian Wilson played his daughter Mabel, who fell in love with Frederick (Christopher Wright). Wesley Dunne was nothing short of hilarious as the Sergeant of Police and indeed the performance of the whole police force was purest pantomime.

In 1996 the first engagement of the choir was the biennial Christmas Charity Concert in the Guildhall. Our programme ranged from Joubert's 'Torches, Torches' to Rutter's 'The Shepherds Pipe Carol' and 'Deck the Halls'. In the second half we included a tribute to Havelock Nelson and further livened things up with 'The Rhythm of Life'. Early in the spring term the serious choral business started: Limerick! From an early stage it was clear that we had the makings of an exceptional choir. The group was in top form and won the adjudicators over with 'Lord, Give Thy Holy Spirit' by Tallis, 'God Be In My Head' by Rutter and the very moving song by Stanford, 'When Mary Through the Garden Went'. Then came the Easter

TOP LEFT: The Pirates of Penzance, *1995*.

ABOVE: Calamity Jane, *1993*.

TOP LEFT: *The Hired Man, 1997.*

TOP RIGHT: *Billy West, musical driving force at Foyle 1967–98, at the keyboard in St Columb's Cathedral.*

ABOVE: *Bugsy Malone, 1999.*

Concert, the UTV Choir of the Year competition, a Gala Concert with the Britannia band and the McCafferty Singers, and finally the Londonderry Feis, when the Tillie Shield returned with us once more.

The school renewed its association with Howard Goodall when his musical *The Hired Man* was chosen for the 1997 production. He very kindly sent his personal orchestrations to me (they were not available on hire) and with them this message to the school:

> *I'm absolutely thrilled that Foyle and Londonderry College are doing* The Hired Man. *Ever since I met the choir at the*

Sainsbury's Choir of the Year competition seven years ago, I have had a very soft spot for the place, its excellent people and its admirably high musical standards ... I am only sorry I won't be able to make it over to Derry to see the production.

Set in a mining village and leading up to World War I it required a large cast of villagers, and soldiers. David Keown and Cormac Cosgrove played the brothers John and Jackson with Jillian Wilson, Caitriona Rowe and Rosalind Haslett playing the leading ladies, Emily, Sally and Mary. The pub scenes and union meetings were played out convincingly, particularly by Chris Abel and Richard McRory, and probably the biggest smile on the faces of the audience came when Aonghus Mayes as the vicar pronounced blessing on the proceedings. Later we made our annual visit to Limerick, when not only did we win for the third successive year but we were also invited to make a recording in the University of Limerick Music Faculty. Four girls from Foyle, Sinead Cassidy, Natasha Guthrie, Carolyn McGettigan and Caitriona Rowe auditioned successfully for the Ulster Youth Orchestra in 1998, and in August played at three prestigious concerts in Dublin, Coleraine and Belfast.

After 33 years of teaching in Foyle Billy West retired due to illness in 1998. Anyone associated with music in Derry at this time would have known Billy as organist and choirmaster at St Columb's Cathedral and Christ Church. Many of his pupils became professional musicians: David Jones (director of the Festival Choir, Edinburgh), Dr John McIlroy (organist, Dunfermline Abbey), Trevor Barr (head of music, Warwick School), Mary Bergin (London Symphony Orchestra) and Stewart Smith (head of music, Lisneal College).

Brenda Barron (Mrs O'Somachain) was appointed Head of Music in 1999. Recognised as an outstanding traditional harpist, Brenda was very quick to put her own stamp on the music scene in Foyle.

Bugsy was the show selected for 1999, and the Al Capone setting was very popular with members of the cast. They seemed to take to the Bronx accent and the smoky nightclubs with ease. As David Keown's first production it was a resounding success. In March the Senior Choir was invited by the Merchant Taylors Company to take part in a special Millennium concert in the Barbican Theatre in London. Foyle was asked to prepare some madrigals for the first part of the programme and I felt very proud to have the opportunity to conduct a choir in the Barbican. Limerick followed directly after this and we returned with crystal for the fifth year in succession.

Foot-and-mouth disease in 2000 caused the cancellation of the Limerick Festival and so ended our annual excursions south. An outstanding pupil was Ian Mills, now the organist and choirmaster of St Columb's Cathedral, and he retains strong connections with the school as a part-time teacher and a valued accompanist at school concerts. In the autumn term we sang in Derry's Millennium Forum along with several musical groups including the Britannia Band. The Foyle Jazz Group was formed that year under the watchful eye of Robert Goodman, who is a peripatetic teacher with the WELB and gives of his free time on Tuesday afternoons to work with his jazz enthusiasts.

TOP LEFT: *Foyle Senior Jazz Band.*

ABOVE: *Members of the Foyle Jazz Group.*

LEFT: *Foyle students play at the Christmas concert in Christ Church.*

RIGHT: Annie, *2003.*

BELOW RIGHT: Me and My Girl, *2005. Lee McMullan.*

The 2001 season saw the production of Lerner and Loewe's *My Fair Lady*. Musical numbers include 'Wouldn't It Be Loverly', 'I'm Getting Married in the Morning', 'I've Grown Accustomed To Her Face' and of course 'The Ascot Gavotte'. Katie Patton, a Year-12 pupil, was cast as Eliza Doolittle, and she has recorded some memories of the show.

'I'm a good girl I am,' I cried continuously, going to all the lunch and break-time rehearsals with the rest of the cast, which included Lee Thomas as Professor Henry Higgins, a perfect gentleman in and out of character, Gary Logan as Colonel Pickering, the playboy of the cast, and Michael Poole as Alfred Doolittle, the witty cockney who had a head start on the accent.

The choir, orchestra, band and soloists kept going with Christmas and Easter concerts and the UTV Choir of the Year competition. Mrs Steele has provided outstanding service for many years as the extremely talented and conscientious accompanist for both the Junior and Senior Choirs.

Annie was the 2003 musical and relied heavily on junior pupils as well as the tried and tested talent of Duncreggan. The role of the ginger-headed title character was played by Rachel Stone. Her performance was outstanding, and many tears were shed as she delivered the powerful ballads,

Oliver, *1985. Ryan Dougherty as Fagin.*

'Tomorrow' and 'Maybe'. The orphans' chorus delighted the audience with their rendition of 'Hard Knock Life', and the part of Warbucks was taken by John McClean as the millionaire who discovered that money was not everything. An adjudicator from the Schools' Musical Competition was present and the 'Oscar' nominations included Best Choreography, Vanessa Chapman, Best Musical Director, Jim Goodman, Best Director, David Keown along with pupils Sarah Warnock and Katie Patton.

In 2004 Billy West died and it was decided that the next Spring Concert would be dedicated to his memory. This took place in Christ Church in March 2005 and several former pupils were asked to perform. They were Caroline Millar (mezzo-soprano), Carolyn McGettigan (violin), Ian Mills and Stewart Smith (organ), Gail Quigley (oboe) and Robert Goodman.

Another rags-to-riches story formed the plot for that year's musical, *Me and My Girl*. This was a very stylish production with no expense spared and included such well-known numbers as 'Leaning on the Lamp-post', 'The Sun has Got His Hat On', 'Lambeth Walk' and the title song 'Me and My Girl'. We held concerts in 2006 which were notable for the performances of two junior pupils, Nicky Morton and Louis Fields, who currently hold organ scholarships in St Columb's Cathedral.

Oliver by Lionel Bart was the 2007 production, with the title role going to Dylan Reid. He endured the journey from workhouse through undertakers' parlour to thieves' kitchen with great zest. Ryan Dougherty gave a consummate performance of the miserly Fagin. Following on from the show I conducted the senior choir for the last time before handing the baton to Miss Barr, and the beautiful renditions ranging from Vivaldi to Rutter formed a nice finale.

The 2009 production of *Calamity Jane* is the last to be considered in this survey. The popular Wild West musical was staged in December with Julianna Ayton in the title role and Stephen McFaul, Mícheál O'Kane, Alison Maybin and Lee Cruikshank as supporting principals. Later Mrs O'Somachain accompanied Julianna Ayton and Rachel Longwell to perform at the Merchant Taylors' School Music Showcase in London. The Jazz Band played at the 350th anniversary of Wallingford School (a Merchant Taylor school), the City of Derry Jazz Festival and the Tall Ships Festival. A real team spirit has developed in the band and many ex-pupils return to play whenever they can. Robert's children, Olivia and John Goodman, are committed members.

I have now reached the end of my teaching career in Foyle after 34 years. Many members of my family have happy memories of taking part in Foyle musicals. I was given a tremendous send-off at the Easter concert and invited to lead the company in an arrangement of 'Hey Jude'. As I sang from the piano gradually the Jazz Band joined in, followed by the choirs and orchestra

FOYLE MUSICALS

1949: *HMS Pinafore*
1950: *The Mikado*
1951: *The Gondoliers*
1952: *Patience*
1953: *The Pirates of Penzance*
1954: *Ruddigore*
1955: *HMS Pinafore*
1956: *The Gondoliers*
1957: *The Little Sweep*
1980: *HMS Pinafore*
1981: *Patience*
1982: *Ruddigore*
1983: *Annie Get Your Gun*
1985: *Oliver*
1987: *Guys and Dolls*
1989: *The Mikado*
1991: *The Boy Friend*
1993: *Calamity Jane*
1995: *The Pirates of Penzance*
1997: *The Hired Man*
1999: *Bugsy Malone*
2001: *My Fair Lady*
2003: *Annie*
2005: *Me and My Girl*
2007: *Oliver*
2009: *Calamity Jane*
2011: *We Will Rock You*

and indeed members of the audience. It was very moving, and when I was presented with a painting of Christ Church and other gifts I felt quite overwhelmed. After a lifetime's music-making in Foyle I treasure many happy hours working spent with such good friends and colleagues and enjoying the support and encouragement of my two principals, Hugh Gillespie and Jack Magill. I know that music and drama in Foyle are in safe hands and I look forward to future concerts and the next musical, which I hear is *We Will Rock You*.

Above: We Will Rock You, *2011.*

Left: *Programmes from a range of Foyle Musicals.*

Tours-de-Force –
School Trips and Excursions

It is not entirely fanciful to suggest that the first known school trip was that undertaken by the then headmaster Ellis Walker only days before the beginning of the great siege of 1689 when, seeing trouble brewing, he betook himself to Whitby, where he remained for the duration of the siege. (He returned to the school and then took up an appointment in Drogheda.) However since no pupils were involved in this excursion it can scarcely be claimed as an official school trip.

Little is known of what outings may have taken place during the first two centuries of the school's existence but it is well documented that on finishing their education Foylemen occupied positions of some importance throughout the nascent empire. When we study the old school magazines from the 1870s we begin to get an understanding of what the youth of Foyle were doing in their spare time and during school holidays. We read of expeditions to far-flung destinations such as Ballyliffin or Castlerock to spend a week at camp. Maybe such outings were as logistically difficult as some of the more exotic trips currently undertaken by our students.

These early outings were expected to broaden the pupil's outlook and aid character formation in those who were destined to serve the Empire or take up the reins of a family business. Early in the 20th century travel for those at school seemed to become more fashionable, and trips abroad were undertaken. These outings were evidently not only for cultural development but also to afford students the opportunity to practice languages acquired in the classroom. Accounts of these journeys were reported in the school magazines and written up in the language of the country visited.

The school continued to promote trips throughout the ensuing years and many pupils went abroad under the guidance of school staff. A comment from a daily diary and published in the school magazine stated 'Once the Hitler youth left we had the hotel entirely to ourselves'. I wonder if any of those travelling with the school at that more happy time were to return later under vastly different circumstances?

My first recollection of a Foyle trip as a pupil was when I went to France with a group led by Curzon Mowbray, head of modern languages at the time. Curzon was involved with an enterprise called

Organisation Scolaire Franco-Britannique, whose remit was to take pupils from all over Northern Ireland to stay with French families. Our destination was Compiègne, a small town just north of Paris. The trip lasted for 17 days and cost approximately £60 including spending money. The journey was an adventure in itself. We departed from the Waterside railway station and on arrival at Belfast made our way to the Liverpool boat, where embarkation was still via a gangplank, and settled down for the overnight voyage to Liverpool.

We took the train to London, where we had to change stations to get the boat train to Dover, and onwards to Amiens, and made the final drive to Compiègne by coach, arriving around midnight after a journey of 36 fairly sleepless hours. The actual journey was planned with military precision due entirely to Curzon Mowbray's almost legendary thoroughness. Every morning we had French language classes and most afternoons were spent with the group visiting local landmarks. Evenings and weekends were spent with the host family. I can remember one of the several crises with which Curzon had to deal. A student reported for class on the first morning declaring that he had been given no bedclothes and had spent a cold night lying on top of the bed. It was discovered that the bed had been made in a traditional French fashion so when he was shown how it worked he had many nights of undisturbed rest. The highlight of the trip was undoubtedly the overnight trip to Paris, where a more relaxed atmosphere prevailed and there was much socialising among the students. My involvement on these trips as a student alerted me to the possible pitfalls which might catch an unwary member of staff when I began to organise school trips myself.

At Foyle, the first excursion I led was a ski-trip to Austria. It was held under the auspices of the Western Education and Library Board and involved students from many different schools in the area. Once again it lasted two weeks, was relatively inexpensive, and was an enjoyable experience in which happily no one was injured. A number of years later I was invited by William Lynn to accompany him on a tour to Greece to instil some culture into our students by visiting all the famous classical sites such as Mycenae, Epidaurus and Delphi. Since this tour took place shortly after amalgamation, we had a party of both boys and girls. That said, I recall that some time earlier a mixed party of pupils had gone cruising on the SS *Uganda* (which

ABOVE: *Ski trip to Sannenmoser, Switzerland, 2009.*

Rugby team jet-boating on Sydney harbour, 2011.

Top right: *Staff (with friendly local) in Berlin, 2011.*

later became a hospital ship during the Falklands war), calling in at various locations along the Mediterranean coast. This trip was organized by Belinda Storey, who was accompanied by Ian McCracken and Hazel Cathcart, among others.

Due to double booking our hotel in central Athens could not accommodate us, and for two nights we had

to move to Glyfada in the suburbs. The staff stayed on the very top of the hotel in a room built on the roof and it was certainly a surprise when we heard a tremendous roar of jet engines and found ourselves waving to the pilots of the aircraft coming in to land at Athens airport. On this trip an often retold event occurred. We had gone to eat at a local restaurant near the harbour at Piraeus when we noticed some of our pupils enter and sit at a nearby table. The restaurant was not overly full so we overheard the conversations at neighbouring tables. An Australian couple, who were obviously quite taken by our pupils asked where they hailed from. One of our students answered Drumahoe. When further quizzed as to the location of Drumahoe he replied, 'You know where the bus stops at Altnagelvin, well it's just a wee bit down the hill from that'. The student was mystified at the bemused expression on the Australians' faces.

Glyfada was a place where NATO forces spent their rest and recreation time, and there were some very dubious locations. It was with some concern that we heard that some students had made their way into the 'Pink Pussycat Club'. A member of staff sent to investigate was able to report that no pupils had come to any harm and indeed were very impressed by the warm and caring nature of the girls who had welcomed them in such a friendly fashion and even encouraged them to buy them drinks.

I also recall another tour undertaken in conjunction with William Lynn. This time we set off to visit the classical sights of Italy. It was a large party consisting of two coaches, one filled with senior pupils and the other much more noisy coach filled with juniors. At Stranraer our drivers assured us that they were well used to European conditions. We later discovered that their main means of navigation was by dint of maps printed on paper napkins found in motorway service stations. Not once on the 12-day tour did we arrive on time; indeed on one occasion we were at least ten hours late. I have several very distinct memories of that trip. The first is of a member of staff drifting quietly out into the broad Adriatic in the dead of night in a rowing boat launched by colleagues and secondly on approaching the Vatican a displayed Ulster flag had to be hastily removed by members of staff. I believe that the owner of the flag was subsequently called to the ministry.

I was a very nervous passenger as our two coaches drove through Rome ignoring most of the very few rules observed by the Roman drivers. I clearly recall one coach shielding the other while it did a U-turn in a one-way street which he had entered from the wrong end. There was also a dispute over packed lunches when a hungry party of youths returned from a visit to the Vatican to find that the coach drivers had sold the lunches to passing tourists.

In the early 1980s I decided it was time to make French more relevant to our younger pupils and organized the first Year-10 trip to France. I was very ambitious and organised a trip lasting ten days in three different centres. Once again it was a marathon journey. In order to have the maximum amount of time in France for the least amount of money we went overland. We left at an ungodly hour of the morning and travelled for almost 48 hours before reaching our destination. It must be remembered that this was during the 'Troubles' and fireworks were banned in the shops in Northern Ireland. What could be more alluring for the pupils than buying bangers by the bagful! Pity the poor residents of some French towns who had to endure the re-enactment of the D-Day landings when we hit the beaches of Normandy with our bags full of explosive devices.

Numerous events over the ensuing 30 years spring readily to mind: how for example could one forget losing two girls in Paris! This ranks among the most trying few hours of my life. We had stopped at the Madeleine church in central Paris and had set off to do some shopping in the Galeries Lafayette. When we had regrouped and were preparing to set off for dinner we

discovered that two girls were missing. We waited and waited and staff were dispatched to hunt in local shops to try to locate them while I went to the nearest police station to report them missing. I had not counted on the fact that children go missing every day in Paris and was rather surprised when my anxiety was not matched by that of the local gendarmes. As it began to rain and darkness drew in I finally sent the coach off to our hotel and warned that no one was to phone home in case panic set in.

We continued to scour the area but finally we gave up in despair. I began to formulate how best to break the news to the parents that I had lost their daughters. On arriving back at the hotel I was relieved to be told that the girls were in the local police station and could be picked up at once. When the girls discovered that they were lost they did what I had told them to do and reported to the police. Unfortunately in Paris local police stations did not readily communicate with each other. The two girls were none the worse for their ordeal, and might even have enjoyed it, but they were less than pleased when not allowed out to buy a pizza.

Undaunted by this experience I continued to organise trips to France, and I have enduring memories of all of them. I recall numerous medical emergencies requiring trips to the A and E departments of French hospitals, where students soon came to appreciate the value of our own NHS. Once in our hostel in Caen I was confronted by a stream of water flowing from the shower room to the lift and down the shaft! It transpired that one of our group had bought a

Geology field trip in Donegal, 2010.

RIGHT: *A trip on the Seine, 2012.*

toy boat for a younger brother and had blocked the shower outlet to try it out. When our coach broke down at Bayeux we hired a coach from a local company who were short of drivers. The proprietor, a man in his late 70s came to our aid. He drove us to Paris and enjoyed himself so much he decided to finish the trip with us. His memories of driving in Paris were those of the 1950s and it was once again with trepidation that we proceeded down narrow, dimly lit side streets. Several times we had to bump parked cars out of our way, and once we reversed out of an underpass which was too low for the coach.

Food caused many an embarrassing moment. Even at that stage our pupils' palates were not the most sophisticated. Imagine the look on faces when faced with bowls filled to the brim with prawns freshly cooked in their shells served with a delicious garlic mayonnaise were set on their dinner table. Joy Coskery demonstrated how they were to be tackled and Stan Huey and I ate as many as we could lest cooks take offence at the sight of uneaten prawns.

Many are the stories which I could recount about our trips to France, including the practice of a colleague who encouraged students into their rooms at night by brandishing a bull whip bought from some of the many persistent hawkers. Some future archaeologist will have difficulty explaining the array of confiscated flick knives which I disposed of in the harbour at Le Havre. It is always a pleasure to hear former students recount years later that the school trip remains one of the abiding memories of their time at school.

David Lloyd, a teacher at the Londonderry High School, was a railway fanatic and would organise railway excursions at every available opportunity. One such outing to a rugby international shortly after amalgamation began at a ludicrous hour of the morning at the Waterside station and I remember it simply as a long day. Luckily I did not accept an invitation to go on a similar outing to the Isle of Man. Once again it was a day trip, which took all of the available 24 hours. They went by train to catch the steamer to the Isle of Man, and a special treat for the students was a disco organised on the car deck for the return voyage. In those pre-Zeebrugge days we were all alarmed when the ship began to take water through the car doors as the disco was in full swing. While there was no hint of distress from the students, there were no more trips to the Isle of Man.

Later trips abroad became more regular and indeed more far-flung. Exchanges were arranged with schools from Argentina; these took the form of cultural events and we were treated to songs and dances from South America. The return trip saw Argentines learning some of our unique culture. Touring teams from England and France also graced the pitches at Springtown and latterly rugby tours began departing for Australia. The golden rule still holds: 'What happens on tour stays on tour!'

With the increase in students wishing to study at universities in Britain the Careers Department undertook visits to universities in Scotland and the North East of England. These were popular but very intense visits and on one occasion we visited no fewer than 12 universities in three days. While those trips did encourage students to spread their academic wings, too many of those who went there did not return home.

School trips are unquestionably valuable and I firmly believe that staff enjoy them every bit as much as the students – well almost.

Ken Thatcher

HISTORY OF SCOUTING AT FOYLE

Even during the first decade of the 20th century, when Baden-Powell was running his first experimental camp on Brownsea Island, the boys, accompanied by Old Boys, were running annual summer camps at Ballyliffin and at Shalwy near Killybegs. Their activities included hiking, climbing, swimming and even the shooting of rabbits on the neighbouring dunes to augment their camp food. Reference is made to the discovery of 'neolithic kitchen middens' in the dunes at Ballyliffin, where arrowheads and pottery shards were picked up and brought back to school.

In 1911 a boarder at the Upper School, known only by his initials AVH, with his friend AP Acheson, started a 'recruiting rally' and founded the very first Foyle Scout Troop. There were 32 members divided into four patrols. Acheson became the assistant scoutmaster while a member of staff, 'Bobby' Vance, was appointed scoutmaster. With the permission of RF Dill, the headmaster, they were allocated a club room in the old gym building at Academy Road. Their uniform consisted of blue regulation shirts, khaki hats, scarves, lanyards, belts and garter tabs. They were presented with a troop colour (a Union flag) by the headmaster.

They were registered under the British Scouts Association and their activities included 'Saturday outings' in the local countryside, (which must have attracted the boarders), test-passing, signalling and various games. Scouting was perceived as contributing to the 'development of good citizenship and the inculcation of loyalty and thoughtfulness for others'. In July 1913 they spent their first summer camp at Rossnowlagh, where they were joined by Mr Craig, the Irish Scout Association Secretary. There is a reference to a visit to the city by Sir Robert Baden-Powell in June 1915. The Foyle Troop continued to function throughout the early years of the war, with outings, local weekend camps and church parades. JS Hawthorne, assistant scoutmaster, was presented with a wrist watch by the headmaster, Robert Foster Dill, as a farewell token. In 1917 the scout troop was 'prominent in all kinds of war work' helping in charity entertainment in the city. They were also involved in 'picking sphagnum moss [for use in stanching battle wounds] and setting the rest of the school a good example by cultivating a fair-sized portion of land at the Lower School in which they planted potatoes'.

Apart from a brief reference to the formation of a patrol of boy scouts under the leadership of G Osborne in 1919, the troop seemed to fade into oblivion until the mid 1930s.

A Cub Pack was formed under Miss Ingold about 1927, and occasional references are made to their activities throughout the 1930s, including badge work and attendance at local parades and rallies. In 1927 they won the Ricardo Memorial Medallion at the Feis. In 1933 the Wolf Cub Pack consisted of 20 members under the tutelage of RP Wheeler. Those who reached the upper age limit for cubs joined 5th Londonderry Methodist Scout Group – confirmation that there was no troop at Foyle.

In 1935 the Scout Troop was re-formed and designated 12th Londonderry under the guidance of Norman McClure as scoutmaster and WTR Philpott as group scoutmaster. They recruited 15 boys, appointed patrol leaders and seconds and organised regular weekly meetings. A court of honour consisting of patrol leaders and assistant scoutmasters was held after each activity evening. Their first summer camp was a combined affair with St Augustine's held at Ely Lodge near Belleek in Fermanagh during the summer of 1936. This summer camp, under the leadership of HA McKegney, involved testing, woodcraft, cooking, bathing and hiking, plus camp-fires and other related outdoor activities. On 28 July 1937, the troop travelled by train to Belfast to

KANDERSTEG IN SWITZERLAND

My memory of this camp starts long before the actual journey. Our departure to Heysham or Liverpool was in doubt up until the last moment as there was a dock strike but we got away. We stayed overnight in Baden-Powell House in East London and either going or coming home some of us went to Lord's cricket ground. Next morning we left London for Harwich to join the boat for the Hook of Holland. We had reserved seats from the main line station. We (the scouts) were all there but no scoutmaster! There was no problem as the trains ran frequently but we had to stand. I can still remember the train journey from the Hook of Holland to Basel or Berne in Switzerland through Holland and Germany. Perhaps I imagine it but I think we saw the twin spires of Cologne Cathedral on our journey. I also recall at a stop somewhere in Holland where there was a buffet trolley on the platform, and on asking if we could buy a 'weak Dutch beer' were surprised to be given permission to do so.

We changed trains either in Basel or Berne and we scouts were simply given the time of our connection and let loose. Again I cannot see that happening today. The other thing about our train journey I remember was that our luggage travelled separately and arrived at a siding in Kandersteg to be picked up. I know we stayed at what is now Kandersteg International Scout Centre and indeed that may have been its title back in 1960. I think we cooked for ourselves but in the kitchen. There was a little shop nearby that sold *Apfelsaft* and ring donuts. I remember trips to the Blue Lake, Interlaken, Grindenwald and the Jungfraujoch, the long hikes over snow-covered mountains and glaciers with crevasses, the return journeys being by train.

While I was thinking back to my days in the scouts, two other events which had a profound influence on me were the two Easter weeks spent climbing in Donegal, one at Lough Eske and one at Dunlewey. I remember the group meeting with Dennis Helliwell to learn how to tie the tarbuck and other knots we would need for the rock-climbing segment and to organise provisions. We must have been on climbing walks every day, even completing what became known as the Glover marathon from Muckish through to Errigal. Every time we take friends to Donegal I dine out on that memory. Even my three sons-in-law were impressed. It gave me a lifelong love of mountain walking, and many pleasurable days have been spent in the Mournes, the Donegal Mountains, and the Sperrins, not to mention walking holidays in the Dales and the Lake District. The other event I remember is of a group of us off at Butterlope near Plumbridge, from where we did an overnight hike across the backbone of the Sperrins to be picked up somewhere near Moneyneany or Feeny on the Sunday. Boyd Jack and Biscuit McDaid are the only two of the group I definitely remember being there, but it probably included Derick McCandless and Derek Curtis as well.

I have been blessed with many happy experiences here and abroad since my scout and school days but I greatly value my associations with both Foyle and 12th Londonderry scout troop with a set of standards and values that were not preached into me, but rather learned by example.

Brian Wilson

attend a youth rally at Balmoral, where they met the king and queen. Three members, Ross, Davin and Smith, went on to the World Jamboree in Holland. The troop continued to be very active in the years leading up to the outbreak of war in 1939, holding Summer camps at Auchengillen in Stirlingshire and at Bryn-Bach in Wales. Owing to travel and other restrictions after September 1939 the troop was confined to holding summer camps near the city, such as Ashbrook. The Upper School was taken over by the military authorities which deprived the troop of a base for meetings. Summer camp in 1940 was held at Castlerock.

Troop meetings resumed in 1945 in the Upper School gymnasium with Norman McClure at the helm. Activities included Saturday outings to local woodlands for testing and outdoor work associated with first- and second-class badges. A re-structuring of scouting took place in 1947, with those over 15 being designated Senior Scouts while the term Boy Scout was reserved for those under 15. AS Orr, the troop leader, attended the World Jamboree in Paris, the first since 1938.

The appointment of LHA (Leslie) Smith as scoutmaster in 1949 marked the beginning of a revival which resulted in the troop's flourishing throughout the next two decades. Leslie was a maths teacher with a military background and his enthusiasm for scouting laid the foundations for success. Even the walls of Room 17, where he taught, were bedecked with scouting mementos, including a 'knotting board' which intrigued the non-scouts in our midst. Ably assisted by JE Bigger, the range of scouting activities and the achievements of the troop set the highest of standards for others to follow. Summer camps in the 1950s were held at Crawfordsburn, Rathmullan and Portnablagh. Participation in local events such as the Robert Anderson Flag Competition, the provincial 'Gang Show' in Belfast, the Noble Road Race, badge work, Bob-a-Job Week and local hikes kept everyone busy. The highlight of this decade was the summer camp in 1957 to Oslo and Honefoss, where visits to see the Kon-tiki Raft, the Fram, and Frogner Park added a truly cultural element to the trip. The troop returned to Europe in 1960 with a summer camp in Switzerland at the Kandersteg Scout Chalet.

In 1963 Norman McClure was presented with the Medal of Merit by the chief scout to mark 27 years of service to the troop. His conscientious support since 1935 underpinned the ongoing success of scouting at

Foyle. He could be regarded as one of the founders of scouting in the city. Also in 1963 the troop went on a field trip to Bludenz in Austria, led by LHA Smith and JE Bigger, where they spent an enjoyable camp hiking and climbing in the Alps.

The 1966 summer camp at Lake Langen, south of Oslo, near the Swedish frontier, was a memorable occasion for all. The scout chalet, belonging to the 49th Oslo Troop, was perched on a rock about 50m from the edge of a deep glacial lake with no trace of a beach. One of the pre-conditions for attending this camp was the ability to swim a 'pool length' fully clothed, a standard which was achieved by all, except one boy who shall remain nameless. Food supplies were brought in by boat which was rowed a few miles across the lake to the local village at Bru, a task which was delegated to the ASMs under Ian McCracken. Following the visit to Norway a monthly magazine called the *Speidere Express*, appeared detailing reports and planned activities for the future.

Further re-organisation of the movement took place in 1967, when the senior members of the troop were selected to form a Venture Scout Unit, and the regulation shorts were replaced with full-length trousers. This change deprived the troop and scoutmasters of the invaluable experience of the senior boys, many of whom were Queens Scouts and school prefects. It was designed to allow the development of leadership skills among the junior members and to encourage participation in more adult activities by the seniors.

The unit linked up with the NW Mountaineering Club for weekend hikes and engaged in such activities as go-carting and scuba diving. Meanwhile the young PLs of 12th Londonderry organised local weekend camps in Baronscourt, Muff Glen and Inch Island. Summer camps were held as usual in venues such as St Helier in Jersey and Dhoon Glen in the Isle of Man.

The reports on all three sections of the scout movement at Foyle in 1972 would seem to indicate that cubs, scouts and venture scouts were operating as usual. The cub pack had won the McClure Swimming Shield and taken part in a successful weekend camp at Learmount while the scout troop continued to hold regular meetings at the Springtown campus under the leadership of Des Reilly. However, the editorial comment in our 1972 magazine sums up the state of affairs in the city at the time using the term 'lawlessness'. This impacted on all scout activities

throughout the 1970s and adversely affected the numbers involved in attendance at weekly meetings. It is a tribute to the staff involved that the troop continued to exist throughout this troubled decade.

The Scout Medal of Merit was deservedly awarded to LHA Smith in 1972 for his period of sustained and long service to scouting in the Londonderry area. Despite the best efforts of staff members, including the late CW Colhoun, at the end of the decade the turmoil which pervaded the city brought about the demise of an activity which gave so much pleasure to those involved.

The Chief Scout at the 1929 World Jamboree presented a lasting gift to every represented nation with the words, 'I give to you the Golden Arrow of Peace and Goodwill. Carry it far and wide that all men may know of the Fatherhood of God and the Brotherhood of Man'.

JSM Huey

12th Londonderry Scouts magazine, The Fleur-de-lis *[sic], 1936.*

LONDONDERRY HIGH SCHOOL GUIDES AND BROWNIES (12TH LONDONDERRY)

Notes from the Local Association Minute Books
Although the Londonderry High School Guides and Brownies were formed in March 1928, the guide company was not formally registered with Ulster Guide HQ until 14 June 1928, and the Brownie Pack not until 16 October 1929. Miss Noble was the first guide captain and Miss McIlroy was appointed an official tester for the County Shield Competition in April 1929.

The Foyle swimming baths were used by the guides and Brownies in 1932 and both were commended for their keen interest in badge work in 1934. Londonderry High School premises were used for guide meetings in 1944 (and also by the Sea Rangers), while the grounds were used for Brownie 'Revels'. There are photographs of the official platform party at the revels in 1939 and of a church parade led by Miss Hunt and Miss Pigott going past the Craig Memorial Hall on its way to a service in Christ Church.

Miss Hunt, who had a long association with the guide company and Brownie pack died in April 1949. In 1950 the local association reported that the

Londonderry High School guides were without a guide captain. The guide company closed in 1968–9.

Catherine Gilchrist

I joined the Londonderry High School Guide Company in 1942, when Miss Hunt was captain. We camped every year in the first two weeks in July. The guide hut was at the bottom of the hockey field, and one year we painted the entire outside of it. During the war years we collected waste paper and jam jars in our handcart. As the first Queen's Guide in Londonderry I was chosen to go to the International Girl Guide Camp and Folk Festival, London. We camped in the paddocks behind Hampton Court Palace. Some guides were shown around the apartment of Lady Baden-Powell, the Chief Guide, at the Palace and met her in person. We also met Lord Rowallan, who had succeeded Lord Baden-Powell as Chief Scout.

We marched down the Mall where the then Princess Elizabeth took the salute. We stayed one night in three-tier bunks in old, deep underground wartime shelters.

Hilary McClean

THE ARMY CADET FORCE

Foyle Platoon of the Army Cadet Force (ACF) was founded in September 1951 under the guidance and leadership of George Gillanders. As a pupil in his maths class at the time I thought it diplomatic to be first to sign up! Some 35 years later, I recorded my memories of the Foyle platoon in an article printed in the magazine of the Royal Inniskilling Fusiliers and entitled 'My Goodness, my Greatcoat':

Get fell in! The ivy-clad walls of our old school reverberated to a new sound, loud, shrill and ringing. The great bronze boots of Lord Lawrence, old boy and Viceroy Of India, seemed to quiver in response. A cadet unit was being formed at Foyle and this was the first

day, our first parade. We were the first recruits and our response was more amused than bemused.

Once more, O'Grady says 'Get fell in'. A vague shuffling brought us into an even vaguer line. Captain Gillanders, later to become Colonel, had introduced us to this funny little man, Sergeant O'Grady of the Royal Inniskilling Fusiliers who was appointed to instruct the newly emerging cadet units in Londonderry, Tyrone and Fermanagh. Now it was our turn – grammar school boys; we got off to a bad start; the humour of the situation was too obvious to us.

That was 30 years ago, and we were the founding members of what would become undoubtedly the best cadet platoon in the province. We were mostly fourth formers. Foyle was a boarding school and most of the boarders answered the call – anything to relieve the boring boarding routine. Others drifted along out of curiosity or rumour that parades might be held during school hours. In fact our parades were each Friday after school, when we learned to stand and to decipher more correctly the instructions of our little sergeant, who was becoming less and less funny and more and more respected with time. The idle and some of the curious drifted off, but we remained and became a unit. Our training continued – Squad 'brace up', 'strip', 'assemble', 'naming of parts', 'Watcher Front' – new skills, old stories, new words.

ABOVE: *St Lurach's Guide Company flag.*

RIGHT: *The Duke of Kent with Jack Bogle and the Foyle Platoon ACF at the opening of Springtown, 1968.*

Then the day our uniforms arrived: coarse heavy khaki, buxom tunics, web belts, blanco, battledress, Brasso and button-sticks, bulging bonnets and itchy shirts, but above all and over all, our greatcoats – massive, ground-level archaic relics of some 'retreat from Moscow'. Our first parade in uniform was an occasion of comic frustration: great drawing in of stomachs, a pushing out of chests, tightening of belts, twisting of bonnets ('Its not a beret, it's a bonnet; it's a hackle not a feather; it's a rifle not a gun'). Some were too thin, some too fat, a few fitted in but some were not designed to fit in and then there were all those funny-shaped country boys. With much pressing and cutting, soaking and stretching, ironing and creasing, spitting and polishing, from embryo 'Dad's Army' we became quite smart. Pride replaced mirth and a seeking of perfection supplemented the fun and humour of this new side to our young lives.

Weekend camps soon followed at Magilligan. Field craft that first day, midnight pillow fights and poker (Jack taught the lesson and reaped the rewards). 'Your summer camp is the highlight of the cadets' year,' the CO said – he was right; he still is. We were full-time soldiers for a fortnight. 'By the front quickkk ... march'. Marching from Duncreggan, up the Strand, two miles through the streets of Londonderry in full uniform, boots, gaiters, the lot. A band leading us – we were proud, proud of our smartness, proud of our uniform and our unity. Camp itself, the first of 30, was just great.

Annual camp was a fitting end to a memorable beginning – the years to follow were to bring greater success, more lasting friendships, more exciting memories yet nothing in all those years can replace the fun and humour of those very first days of bonnets, battledress, button-sticks and bugles and – my goodness, my greatcoat.

From 1983 our platoon continued as the 'vanguard' detachment of the 1st Company Batallion, The Royal Irish Regiment. It was then the top battalion in the cadets of Northern Ireland under the guidance of various members of staff (Terry Marshall, Dave McCleery, Robert Astbury) until in 2001, but with the growing numbers of boys and now girls interested in cadets, the school decided to convert to the Combined Cadet Force (CCF). Following this, in addition to the well-established army unit, an air force and, most recently, a navy unit have been established, and all three units are flourishing.

Jack Bogle

ABOVE: *ACF camp, 1950s.*

LEFT: *George Gillanders.*

THE DUKE OF EDINBURGH'S AWARD SCHEME

In 1983 there was no Duke of Edinburgh's Award Scheme established in the school. Prior to Ken Hoyle's departure an attempt to start the scheme had been made which was responded to with enthusiasm by the pupils who enjoyed, amongst other things, camping experiences in the Bluestack Mountains. In the academic year 1984–5, with one year's teaching experience, I set out firmly to establish the award scheme in the school. I started with a total of 24 keen pupils: one Gold Award group, one Silver and two Bronze.

The award aims to inspire, guide and support young people in their self-development and recognise their achievements. Volunteering (service) requires participants to undertake service to an individual or the community, while the skill section aims to develop practical and social skills and personal interests. The physical recreation section is designed to encourage young people to improve in sport, dance or fitness activities. In each of these sections participants must show persistence, commitment and personal development over time. Perhaps the best-known section, the expedition, involves planning, training for and completion of an adventurous journey in the UK or abroad. Our bronze and silver expeditions are carried out in the Sperrins on foot, whereas the gold participants can choose to spend four days hiking in the Derryveagh Mountains, cycling in North Donegal or canoeing on Lough Erne. In addition to the four

FAR RIGHT: *Ingrid Sulllivan with the first recipients of the Duke of Edinburgh awards at St James' Palace, 1986.*

sections, Gold Award participants must complete a four-day residential course working away from home and engaging with others to achieve a positive goal.

The numbers grew rapidly and by 1988 96 pupils were working towards a bronze award, 23 silver and 41 gold. With more staffing required, Dee Hannaway was drafted in to assist with canoeing and hill-walking. In 1996 Trevor Nutt, who had completed his gold award in the school and had just joined the teaching staff, agreed to help out, ably assisted by Ann Watson. Many staff have volunteered their time and the scheme continues to boast high numbers, with approximately 80 pupils working at bronze level, 60 at silver and 60 actively engaged at gold. When pupils complete their gold award they have the choice of receiving their certificate at a presentation in St James's Palace (London) or the Palace of Holyrood House (Edinburgh), and occasionally there is an opportunity to attend a garden party in Hillsborough Castle.

Depite many changes in the last 30 years the enthusiasm, determination and resourcefulness of our pupils and staff remain steadfast. The Duke of Edinburgh's Award Scheme enables young persons to develop their mind, body and soul in a non-competitive yet challenging environment. Its ability to elevate their self-confidence, skills and aspirations should never be underestimated. I am confident that the scheme will continue to play a major part in the life of Foyle students for years to come.

Ingrid Hannaway (née Sullivan)

BAR MOCK AND JUNIOR MAGISTRATES COMPETITIONS

When senior students learned of the alleged assault by a science teacher on a pupil in the laboratory they were of course eager to discover more about the incident. Witness statements were closely examined, preparations were made for the important court date and barristers came into the school to give of their expertise. So it was in the early 1990s that Foyle students first became involved in the Bar Mock Competition, a Citizenship venture where the fictitious cases created by real barristers would be enacted by students throughout the UK in courtroom competition in front of practising judges. In countless cases ranging from the alleged assault by a teacher to charges of theft, drugs, and driving offences, Foyle pupils have taken on the roles of barristers, witnesses and court staff, with every annual competition leading to the regional final in the Belfast Royal Courts of Justice. Although our students always displayed strong mastery of those skills associated with this intense legal competition we have unfortunately not yet secured a place in the national final in England.

It was only a matter of time before we moved towards participation in the Junior Magistrates section of the competition and here interest was intense, with as many as 30 Year-10 pupils being auditioned for the 13 places, which included court artist and court reporter. As in the senior competition pupils gained an insight into the workings of the legal system as well as acquiring skills involving mastery of facts, composure under cross-examination, the ability to pose searching questions and the capacity to present fluently a sustained opening or closing speech for the prosecution or defence case. Ably assisted by many teaching staff over the years, Foyle junior pupils have excelled in the Belfast regional heats and gone on to represent Northern Ireland in the national finals in England on at least four occasions.

These two competitions are now well established in Foyle and are organised by a dedicated core of young staff from a range of subject disciplines. Both pupils and staff are grateful for the continued assistance of barristers in the annual competitions and of course the local court staff in Londonderry, who kindly allow and arrange for our visits there.

Jim Heasley

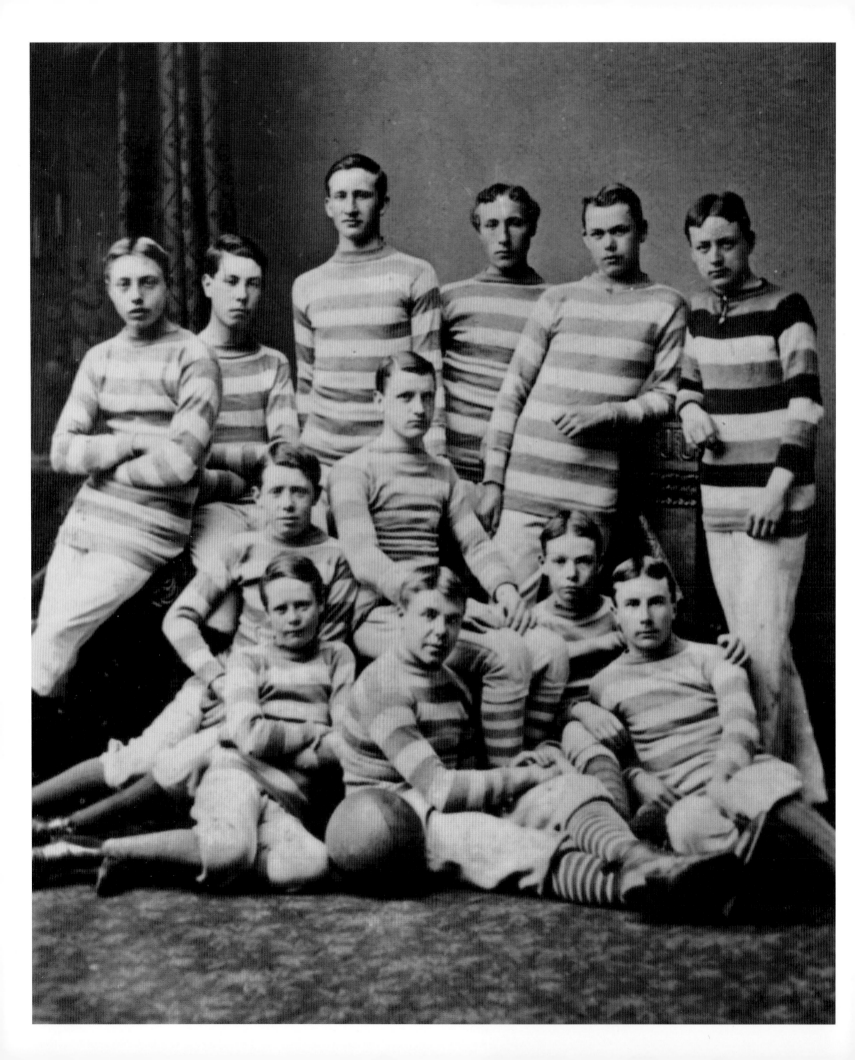

SPORT

RUGBY

The earliest traces of rugby football in Ireland date back to 1848, when some English students at TCD introduced the game to the locals. The Dublin University Football Club was formed in 1854 and so ranks as the second oldest club in the world behind Guy's Hospital of London. The game gradually spread to other centres in Ireland and reached Belfast in the 1860s, with North of Ireland FC being formed in 1868, followed by Queen's College FC in the following year.

Information that some form of the game was played in Foyle in the late 1860s comes from *The Birch* of 30 November 1870, in which a letter to the editor stated that there would be advantages in having definite rules for football, and suggested: 'The committee should get the rules of the principal English and Irish clubs from which they could pick out what rules they thought best.' An old boy writing many years later about his days at school describes a game played behind the school as follows: 'All the boarders had to play, sixty of them, some masters and about ten dayboys. A French master played in a top hat. Dr Moffet, the headmaster (1874–6) kicked the ball if it came his way. Another master M Fasler, a sturdy Swiss, played very well. He charged you head down in your stomach.'

LAI had moved in 1871 to its new school in Haw Lane (Academy Road), and it is a fair assumption that the boys were taking part in the same sort of unorganised mayhem in their field, which was situated between the school and Brooke Park. In 1878 the arrival of two new masters from rugby-playing schools may well have enthused local interest in what was after all a new game. JC Dick came to LAI from RBAI and Maurice C Hime arrived from the Monaghan Diocesan School.

Early copies of *Our School Times* record a draw between Foyle and Monaghan in October 1879, and the April copy of 1880 notes that the Foyle team 'did not have a successful past season. Though the play has vastly improved, the team did not practise hard enough and was very deficient in drop and place kicking'. The laws of the game were subject to local interpretations in the 1870s and 1880s. The number of players in each team was sometimes open to dispute. For example when Ireland first played England in London on 15 February 1875 each team had 20 players. *Our School Times* (May 1881) records that when the Foyle 12 travelled to play Coleraine Academical Institution they were surprised to discover that the home team fielded 15 players. After some discussion Foyle acquired two or three Coleraine players and the result was a draw.

JC Dick almost immediately entered LAI for the Schools Cup in the 1879–80 season and they became finalists in 1881–2. The Ulster Schools Challenge Cup is the oldest trophy competed for by rugby teams in

OPPOSITE: *Foyle College XII, 1878.*

RIGHT: *LAI 1st XV 1878.*

JH MCLAUGHLIN

James Henry McLaughlin was born on 23 April 1864. He entered LAI on 17 October 1870 and 17 Hawkin Street was given as his home address in the school register. With the arrival in 1878 of a new headmaster, JC Dick, from RBAI, games became a part of life at the school. Coached by Dick, the football team soon became a formidable unit, with future Irish internationals Tom Allen, Jimmy 'Cadger' McLaughlin, Tom Taggart and Charlie Tillie in the ranks. McLaughlin left school in 1882 and proceeded to Queen's University in Belfast for a year. He then left for Dublin to the Carmichael School of Medicine, where he studied pharmacy. Returning to Derry after a few years he joined the local club and soon he attracted the attention of the Ulster Selectors and was picked to represent Ulster to play Leinster in November 1885. The Irish Selectors became interested and in the following season, 1886–7, McLaughlin was awarded his first Irish cap.

His first match was against England at Lansdowne Road in Dublin in 5 February 1887. In the previous 24 internationals against the home nations, Ireland had achieved little – one win and one draw – so hopes of a first victory against England were not high. With nine new caps in the Irish team including three LAI boys, McLaughlin played quarter-back (scrum half in the modern game), Charlie Tillie played half-back (now centre or wing) and Stavely Dick played forward. About 4,000 had crammed into the stadium, the biggest crowd ever seen there according to the press. A fourth LAI boy, Tom Taggart, was reserve player for the game, and in an article he wrote later for the school magazine he reports:

Three incidents stand out clearly in my memory. Two were scores from about halfway and McLaughlin started at least one of the movements. The second score was got by Charlie Tillie, an old LAI boy and a scratch 100 yards man. The third incident was altogether McLaughlin. The English centre three-quarter was Fagan, as tall as McLaughlin but more burly. He attempted to round McLaughlin and handed off with the left hand. Jimmy grabbed the hand with both of his and swung Fagan around like the motion of a hammer thrower at the athletic meeting.

Taggart sent a telegram to school: 'McLaughlin the best player in the field'. Ireland had won their first victory over England – two goals to nil. Taggart also notes that McLaughlin played in his bare legs, having forgotten to pack a pair of stockings in his bag before leaving from Derry to Dublin that Saturday morning. This was very unfortunate, for his shins were peeled and later festered. Despite this he played in the next match against Scotland but he was so incapacitated that Ireland practically played with 14 men and so lost the game.

McLaughlin's international career was short, only four matches. He was selected for more, but difficulties with travel and finance forced him to decline. In those days, players had to buy the international jersey, pay the hotel expenses and dinner and only received part of the travelling fare. He then chose to play his rugby with the local club, City of Derry.

McLaughlin died in Australia in 1942. Taggart described him as being over six feet, tall for a scrum half, had a very distinguished figure with fiery red hair and very long arms. As a dribbler he was excelled by none. He was described in Lawrence's *Dublin Football Annual* in the 1880s as 'Always silent and always on the ball'.

Ireland since 1876. LAI's success in reaching the final encouraged Foyle to enter in 1882–3. Games between the two schools were keenly contested and attracted a large number of spectators.

Thomas Taggart, a future Irish international, was a boarder at LAI in the early 1880s. Writing in *Our School Times* in 1935, he recalled some of his early school days. We quote some of his reminiscences:

Woollen knitted caps were worn when playing. They came off easily on contact and a great deal of time was spent recovering them. The game was played with 10 forwards and 5 backs. It was very bad form to pass the ball –

LEFT: *LAI 1st XV 1881.*

LAI rugby team, 1888.

defeated Armagh rather easily before losing in the final against Methody by a single score. This game was played in Derry on Gallagher's field at Rosemount. LAI's star player, Charlie Tillie, suffered a broken collarbone early in the game and with only 14 players, they lost only by a breakaway score in the last minutes.

Such was the strength of LAI's XV in the early 1880s that the first Irish international team to defeat England in 1887 had three LAI Old Boys – JH McLaughlin, CR Tillie and JS Dick (nephew of the headmaster) – playing and T Taggart substitute. Tillie scored one of the tries in the 10–0 victory. TC Allen, another old boy, had earlier played for Ireland in 1885. The Foyle team also had its successes in the 1880s and the *Our School Times* reports that the 1882–3 season was 'most successful.' The school entered the Schools Cup for the first time and reached the semi-final only to be defeated by RBAI, 'having had a number of tries disallowed'! The intense rivalry with LAI led to a complaint after a defeat in the 1886–7 season that 'LAI had played boys who had long since left school'. In March 1886 the United Schools of Foyle, St Columb's and LAI played a match against City of Derry to 'augment the funds of the County Infirmary in front of several hundred spectators.'

Playing for Foyle at this time were FH Miller, RA Yeates and RW Johnston, all of whom were capped for Ireland in the 1880s. After the game against Scotland in 1886, the *Scottish Athletic Journal* reported: 'Millar played a rattling fine forward game, and any time Ireland carried the maul, he was always in the front.' RA Yeates won two Irish caps in 1889 when at Dublin University. After one of his matches, *Sport* magazine commented: 'You could scarcely see Yeates, so fast did he run'. In his obituary (*Our School Times*, September 1894) it was stated: 'He was known throughout Ireland as the neatest and most dangerous half-back that ever donned the green jersey.' Ralph W Johnston was the Foyle captain in 1883–4. He stood six feet two and weighed 14 stone in his schoolboy days. At Trinity he switched from forward to centre three-quarter, gained an extra two stone in weight, and won his three international caps in 1890. He was fondly known by his nickname 'Bosher'.

Also at Foyle in the 1880s were Digby Johns and James McElmunn Wilton. Johns was chosen as first substitute at quarter-back for Ireland in the 1888 internationals but unfortunately did not win

passing was looked upon as pure funk. When the ball went into touch, it belonged to the side that retrieved it first and that side had the throw-in. This rule was changed in 1880 so that when the ball went into touch the throw-in was given to the opponents. But news of this change did not reach Derry until it was announced by a new boarder who happened to be the captain of the team of the Royal Academical Institution of Belfast. Strangely this boy was never considered good enough to play for the Londonderry Academical Institution. In those days only goals counted in the result. A try was originally considered as a try at goal and did not count until it was successfully 'goaled'. Wales defeated Ireland in 1887 by a dropped goal to three tries, and only after that was the system of scoring by points adopted.

Rugby at LAI flourished in the 1880s. The team usually won against Foyle and indeed competed strongly against the adult teams in the city. The school was defeated in successive years by Armagh Royal, then considered to be the strongest school in Ulster in the Cup. They used the tactic of playing three, rather than two, three-quarters, and consequently managed to outscore their opponents. However LAI learned to counter this tactic in the 1881–2 season and so

LEFT: *Foyle College 1st XV, 1896.*

BELOW: *Rugby cap 1907–8.*

a cap. Wilton was regarded as a fine rugby forward at school but his first love was association football. He was capped nine times for Ireland between 1888 and 1893 and elected president of the Irish Football Association between 1914 and 1945. He became the ninth president of FCOBA in 1936-37. Brian O'Brien was elected captain of Foyle for the 1889–90 season. A gifted all-round sportsman excelling in golf and rowing as well as rugby, he won two international rugby caps in 1893.

On joining the Foyle staff MA Dillon, who had been vice-captain of Santry RFC, provided further impetus to rugby in the city. City of Derry won the Irish Provincial Towns Cup on four occasions in five years from the 1888–9 season. The winning teams included boys from Foyle and LAI as well as Dillon and some masters. Foyle fielded a very successful team in the 1891 season, winning nine and drawing two of the 12 games played. In October 1891 in Belfast they defeated RBAI and MCB on successive days by a goal and two tries to nil and by four tries to nil respectively. Coleraine proved an obstacle in several Schools Cup matches but Ulster caps were won by TH Jameson, JC Joyce and L Vereker.

LAI also fielded formidable teams in the 1890s, and were usually too strong for Foyle. Future Irish international TH Stevenson, seven caps (1895–7), captained LAI in successive seasons 1889–90 and 1890–1, as did ST Irwin in 1894–5 and 1895–6. Irwin also played for the Ulster Schools and led his team to a narrow defeat by Methody in the 1896 Schools Cup Final. Sam Irwin won nine Irish caps between 1900 and 1903, was president of the Ulster Branch of the Irish Rugby Football Union (IRFU) 1907–8 and President of the IRFU 1935–6.

Other notable LAI players at this time were ATW Bond, CWL Alexander and RW Jeffares. Bond played on the Irish Triple Crown team of 1894, winning his two caps against Scotland and Wales. Alexander played in Irwin's Cup Final team of 1896, helped Queen's win the Ulster Cup in 1900 and also helped University College Cork win the Munster Cup in 1912. He was elected president of the IRFU in 1909–10. Rupert W Jeffares played on LAI's 1st XV, captained the school's cricket team in 1890 and 1891 and also played for the Ulster Schools cricket XI.

After moving to Dublin, he joined Lansdowne RFC and became its captain, secretary and president. As an international rugby referee he took charge of three games in the seasons 1907–9. He then was appointed assistant secretary of the IRFU 1910–25 and finally Secretary in 1925 until his retirement in 1951. He was president of FCOBA in 1948–49. Others to win representative honours at this time were W Sparrow, WG Byron, JS Myles, EH McIlwaine, M Dillon and M Donnell.

William Sparrow won two international caps at full-back on the Triple Crown-winning team of 1893–4 alongside AT Bond. GG Allen won the first of his nine caps against England in 1896 and captained his country on two occasions. His brother, CE ('Ellie') Allen, also captained Ireland, winning the first of his 21 caps in 1900. 'Ellie' had learnt his rugby at Merchiston Castle School in Edinburgh, whereas GG enjoyed a few years at Foyle (1884–6) before moving to Merchiston. WG ('Billy') Byron played alongside Glynn Allen in the Triple Crown-winning team of 1899 and won 11 Irish caps. J Sproule Myles was chosen to tour Canada with the first Irish touring team in 1899. He had played for LAI and Ulster Schools as a schoolboy. In the first game in Canada he broke a leg and ended his international career. He was president of the FCOBA in 1932–3. EH McIlwaine won two Irish caps in 1895 against Scotland and Wales. MA Dillon was capped a number of times for Ulster and was considered unlucky not to win an Irish cap. Marshall Donnell was selected to play full-back for the Probables on a final Irish trial, and according to Alex Foster was unfortunate not to be selected for the Irish team.

1907-8

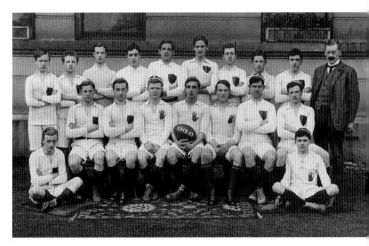

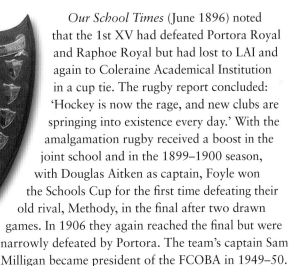

Our School Times (June 1896) noted that the 1st XV had defeated Portora Royal and Raphoe Royal but had lost to LAI and again to Coleraine Academical Institution in a cup tie. The rugby report concluded: 'Hockey is now the rage, and new clubs are springing into existence every day.' With the amalgamation rugby received a boost in the joint school and in the 1899–1900 season, with Douglas Aitken as captain, Foyle won the Schools Cup for the first time defeating their old rival, Methody, in the final after two drawn games. In 1906 they again reached the final but were narrowly defeated by Portora. The team's captain Sam Milligan became president of the FCOBA in 1949–50.

Some lean years followed and an outbreak of 'spotted fever', a form of meningitis, led to matches being cancelled in 1907. On the international scene a trio of Old Boys won 33 Irish caps. With two test appearances in South Africa in 1910 Alex Foster gained his first cap and achieved a total of 17 by 1921. SBB ('Boyd') Campbell appeared on 12 occasions for Ireland including one game against South Africa in 1913. George McConnell gained the first of four caps in 1912. All three played together in the Irish team, captained by Foster, which defeated France on New Year's Day 1912. The Ulster XV, which played South Africa in November 1912, contained four Foyle boys, the three mentioned above and Boyd Campbell's brother, David. He was president of the FCOBA in 1953–4.

ABOVE: *OBA Shield to commemorate Foyle 1st XV (pictured) winning the Schools' Cup in 1900.*

FAR RIGHT: *From the top: Foyle College 1st XV 1906–7; Foyle College 1st XV 1911–12; Foyle College 1st XV 1912–13.*

The Foyle team of 1911–12 was described in *Our School Times* as 'mediocre and handicapped by the paucity of school fixtures'. But that changed when, coached by Alex Foster, the team during the next four seasons was perhaps the most successful in the history of Foyle rugby. In *Our School Times* (June 1917)

131

AR FOSTER

Alexander Roulston Foster, known to all as Alec Foster, was born in William Street, Londonderry, in June 1890. He entered Foyle in September 1903 on the same day incidentally, as William Stavely Ferguson, later Deputy Headmaster of Foyle. He had a distinguished academic career at Queen's University, Belfast, graduating with first class honours in Classics. First of firsts in his year he remained throughout his life a devoted and interested scholar. After graduation, he turned down an appointment in the Colonial Service to take up teaching. He was appointed assistant master at his old school, Foyle, where he taught for some years before joining the staff of Glasgow High School in 1920. He next moved to RBAI before becoming headmaster of Belfast Royal Academy (BRA) in 1923 at the age of 33. An outstanding and popular head, he remained at BRA until 1942, when ill-health compelled him to accept early retirement. He returned to temporary teaching at RBAI during the latter war years.

Alec Foster not only excelled as a gifted schoolmaster and scholar – he was also a talented all round athlete. He was a competent cricketer, good at hockey, rowed for City of Derry and was North West swimming champion. But it was, of course, as a rugby three-quarter that he was best known. Foster captained Foyle 1st XV, Queen's University 1st XV, the Ulster XV and the Irish XV. He was a member of the British touring side to South Africa in 1910 and played in both Tests. Between 1910 and 1921 he was capped 17 times for Ireland, captaining the team on three occasions. He was one of the few international rugby players whose playing career spanned the years of World War I.

He retired as a player in 1921 and within a year he was appointed an Irish selector, and acted in this capacity until the end of the 1924–5 season. The following season, 1925–6, he was elected president of the Ulster Branch of the IRFU.

Alec Foster was proud of his Presbyterian Derry roots and his life was enriched by a liberal and radical philosophy. He was a raconteur, collector and singer of Ulster ballads. He cherished equally his British and Irish background and culture. In his earlier days in Belfast he was a member of the local Wolfe Tone Club. As a 79-year-old, he spoke at a large rally in Dublin on the 10 January 1970 protesting against the South African touring side and its government's Apartheid policy.

Alexander Roulston Foster died on 24 August 1972 in Bantry, County Cork. His son-in-law, Conor Cruise O'Brien, wrote: 'He lived long and many people feel the better and the happier for having known him.'

IN MEMORIAM ALEX FOSTER

We laid him among the stones at Tahilla
In a place that might been Grianan, round, on the top of a hill
Looking over the Kenmare river, studded with islands;
And mourned that we would never hear him praising
The rough gold of the hillside, the warmth of mountain
people.

One day when we had threaded Leitrim
On the string of his travels, leaving its laketorn landscape,
Shimmering through reeds, its green meadows,
He sighed for Kerry, hoped he might live to see it:
He saw Kerry.

Kerry enthralled him, its rich luxuriance
An Ireland he had not known: he unravelled
Tracks over the rocks or through the woods,
Dallied like a child, gathering flowers;
Later, they said, he would not go the road.

He would not go the road. For him the scramble
Over a ditch or knee deep through the grasses,
The richer perfumes of the whins and heather,
A startled hare, a heron on the wing:
Adventure lay beyond the beaten track.

Constantinople, Baghdad and Jerusalem –
This verse is his not mine –
Great names beyond a doubt,
But I, like the Saint, would give them all, if they were mine
For my own house in Derry,
There in the trees, looking down upon the Foyle,
As it slips past green, wooded banks
To the sea at Magilligan.
Perhaps, but when he weighed the richer growth of Kerry
Against the oaks of Derry or the Birdstown Glen
Who knows what, great or small, was in the balance:
Only the pull was always to the men
Who tilled the fields or swept the oar or, later,
Lifted their voices on the tide of song.

His songs were manic music, duck or sash,
Rebel or Rabelaisian, loyal or true,
Or hymn or metric psalm, he knew them all –
Always it was the poetry intrigued him
Homer and Virgil taught him all he knew.

Teaching above all he loved and honoured,
Infinite patience with the dull or slow,
And the swift flight that cut the line asunder –
The Foster try – was part of that technique:
An even mind, in bad times and in good.

And there were bad times, too, that drew him downward
To deeper chasms, where the darkness loomed
So that no song or story brought him comfort;
Only a stiff endurance paved the road
Till music sounded and the day returned.

Leaving him now in Kerry's kind embraces
We leave the greater portion of our lives
Derelict here where the long winds of winter
Will comb Rosdohan's grasses; here, beside
People he loved and who, with others, loved him.

George Hetherington (son-in-law of Alex Foster)

Schools team in 1915 and 1916 and was accompanied in the team by R Young and H Johnston in 1915 and by FG Simmons in 1916.

Many of the boys of these successful pre-war teams were soon to depart for sterner struggles, including JC Fergusson, captain of the 1907–8 and 1908–9 teams, TF McCay, captain of the 1913–14 team and his vice-captain, TS Haslett, Ulster Schools XV 1912–13 and 1913–14. Of the sixteen boys who formed the 1915 Cup winning squad, 11 volunteered for service in World War I.

During the war years adult rugby was dormant in Derry but the game was kept alive in Foyle. Fewer school matches were played and indeed in the 1918–19 season only the Cup game against Coleraine took place, and that was lost. Friendly matches were played against the locally based military regiments. However, many boys were selected to play on the Ulster Schools teams: PG Boyd and JH Eagleson in 1916–17, OW Gilmour and JC Thompson in 1917–18, JM Speer, the school captain, in 1918–19, JW Lusk and CN Porter in 1919–20 and NG Ross and J Cresswell in 1920–1.

Our School Times (April 1924) commented: 'Since the war football has been at a low ebb at Foyle,' and in April 1925: 'Victories few, our defeats many', though CD Henderson did play on the Ulster XV. In December 1931 BS Magee was selected to play on the Ulster senior team against South Africa at Ravenhill. He won further caps in 1932 and 1933. The run of disappointing results continued until 1933–4, when we read that 'the standard of rugby is improving'. Dungannon Royal and Larne Grammar were defeated and drawn matches were played against

Above: Replica OBA shield commemorating Foyle 1st XV (pictured) victory in the Ulster Cup 1914–15.

Right: Portrait of Norman G Ross with his Ireland cap: part of the Ulster schools team in 1920–1, Ross was a member of the Ireland team in 1927.

Professor DB Woodburn wrote, 'Between 1913 and 1917, the 1st XV won more and lost fewer cup matches than any school in Ulster.' Foyle contested three successive Cup Finals in 1912–13, 1913–14 and 1914–15. Campbell and Methody were victors in the first two but Armagh Royal was eventually overcome 5–3 in 1915 and the cup was brought back to Derry for the second time. Later AR Foster recalled: 'Indeed, I do remember that match 50 years ago. It has always reminded me of the Siege of Derry: a long, dogged and seemingly hopeless defence near our own line for most of the game and then at the end a sudden breakaway by wing three-quarter, David "Punch" Cresswell who ran the length of the field from inside our "25" pushing off and out pacing man after man, and finally he grounded the ball over the Armagh goal line for "Dooda" Matthews to kick the winning goal'. He continued, 'a solid team, full of purpose and guts, but the star was the captain AH Matthews. He got his nickname "Dooda" from singing "The Camptown Races – Dooda, Dooda". He was a born leader'. AH Matthews was president of the Old Boys in 1970–1.

The 1915–16 team, captained by Matthews, was described as 'the best school team in Ulster' but due to injuries, was defeated by Campbell College in the semi-final of the Cup. Matthews also captained the Ulster

Norman G. Ross
Member of Irish XV. 1927

Methody and Omagh Christian Brothers. The captain, JLD Mark, won his Ulster cap. This progress was maintained in the season 1934–5: 'The general standard of play has been higher and more matches have been won'. JN McMorris and J Watson made the Ulster schools team, while Hazlett Hunter played on the Ulster senior team against Leinster. A strong team was fielded the following year 1935–6. Only four of the 16 matches played were lost. An exciting cup semi-final match took place at Duncreggan against Methody before a large crowd. The result was a narrow defeat 8–6. The captain WDH McFarland, MR Neely and J Watson progressed to the Ulster Schools team. In 1936–7 DR Marshall won an Ulster School's place.

It was recognised that new playing fields were required because the grounds at Upper Foyle, Duncreggan Road and Brandywell were inadequate. The headmaster, WAC McConnell, invited the FCOBA to launch an appeal fund to acquire suitable grounds. The Springtown property was quickly identified and the 34 acres purchased at a total cost of £3,000. Of the 19 matches played by the 1937–8 team 11 were won. AV Sheppard's team reached the semi-final of the cup but lost 11–0 to RBAI. JG White

was selected to play for the Ulster Schools in the inter-provincial games and went on to represent Cambridge against Oxford in the 1943 Varsity match. The new Springtown grounds were ready for the 1938–9 season. During that year the Medallion XV reached the final of the Shield for the first time. The game was played at Springtown on 31 March 1939 but RBAI proved too strong, winning 11–0.

The outbreak of war in September brought an end to competitive adult rugby in the city and rugby at school marked time also. However, Ulster Schools caps were won by EB Young, GS Lapsley, JA Mooney and RWH Bredin. Senior Ulster caps were gained by MR Neely, J Piggot and WDH McFarland. Indeed, Matthew Neely represented Ireland on four occasions in 1947, the first Foyle representative on the Irish team since Norman Ross won his two caps

Cartoon of Foyle 1st XV 1930–1.

THE MATTHEWS BROTHERS

When RF Dill MA became headmaster of Foyle in 1911, a number of boys who had been pupils at Dungannon Royal School came with him. Among these were three brothers, TM, CCD and AH Matthews, sons of Revd S Matthews of County Wicklow. TM Matthews, the eldest brother, was captain of the 1st XV in 1911–12 and captained the cricket XI in 1912, when he also played for the Ulster Schools XI.

Armour Hamilton Matthews was the most gifted of the brothers. He was a member of the 1st XVs in 1912–16 and was the captain for the last two seasons, which included the cup-winning team of 1914–15. He was also a member of the Ulster Schools XV 1913–16 and captain in 1914–15. Armour was prominent in other school activities and excelled in cricket. He played on the school's 1st XI in 1912–16 and was captain in the last two seasons. He also played for the Ulster Schools' team in 1914–16 and was its captain in the last season. He also captained the school's hockey team in his final year at school.

He entered the medical school of TCD in 1916. Because of increasing deafness he switched to dentistry and qualified at the Royal College of Surgeons, Ireland in 1920. Acting on medical advice he then emigrated to South Africa where he practised as a dentist and oral surgeon in Johannesburg until his retirement. In South Africa he

was also a keen and successful golfer and on several occasions was the leading amateur in the South African open championship. AH Matthews LDS RCS was president of FCOBA in 1970.

Dr TM Matthews, who was in general medical practice in Witwatersrand, was drowned with his wife while on honeymoon in the late 1920s, and CCD Matthews, who was an engineer in Johannesburg, was killed by a train about the same time.

Foyle 1st XV 1911–12.

in 1927. WD Haig McFarland played on the QUB 1st XV (1938–40) and had two trials for the Irish XV.

The 1946–7 team, captained by Noel Henderson and coached by Mr JS Connolly, turned out to be the strongest XV for some years. Due to the severe winter, only one match was played after Christmas and that was against Methody in the semi-final of the Schools Cup. It was played at Springtown but ended in defeat 5–3, the only loss of the season. A member of this team, WJA Armstrong, writing 65 years later, in 2012, recalled the deep disappointment of this defeat: 'Earlier that season we had defeated Methodist College by nine points to three … and there was one controversial decision in the semi-final. During a ruck almost on the Methody line, we believed we had scored but the referee gave a scrum and not a try.' The next few years were not particularly successful for the 1st XV despite the efforts of its talented captain, AJ Rankin. The Ulster Schools selectors recognised his ability by selecting him for the 1948–9 and 1949–50 provincial teams. The Medallion side was rather more successful and reached the semi-final of the Shield in 1948. A highlight of 1948 was the visit of the 1st XV of Ellesmore College, Shropshire in the autumn.

AG (Adrian) Kennedy entered Foyle in 1944, played for 1st XV in 1948–9 and was selected for Ulster Schools in 1949–50 season. At Queen's University he played on the 1st XV from 1952–5, touring British Columbia and California in 1953 in the company of Noel Henderson and Jack Kyle. He represented Ulster from 1953 to 1956, played in the memorable 5–5 draw with the New Zealand All Blacks in January 1954 and played for Ireland against France in January 1956. A subsequent serious injury curtailed his international career. He was elected president of the FCOBA 1995–6.

Senior Ulster caps were won by DH McNally and JC Lapsley in the 1956–7 season. JF McNamee won nine Ulster caps in the years 1959–61 and was selected to play in the Irish trial in 1961. His brother Basil, perhaps better known as a cricketer, also played for Ulster against Munster in 1964 and in 1968 JM Lee represented Ulster against Lancashire. The 1957–8 school team, with WJ Wallace as captain, reached the semi-final of the cup only to be narrowly defeated 3–0 by a strong Annadale Grammar School team, who went on to win the cup. DM Reilly represented Ulster Schools in the inter-provincial games that season. KG Goodall's appearance coincided with the end of a lean period. He played for his school, Ulster Schools, City of Derry, Newcastle University, Ulster, Barbarians and Ireland, winning 19 caps (1967–70). He was selected for the Irish tour to Australia in 1967 and the Lions tour to South Africa in 1968. His close friend, Albert Sherrard, was a regular on the Ulster Schools team in 1965–7 and gained an Ulster Senior cap in 1969 when selected to play against Leinster.

ABOVE: *Ulster Schools rugby cap, 1932–3.*

RIGHT TOP TO BOTTOM: *Foyle 1st teams 1934, 1935–6, 1936–7, 1938.*

NOEL JOSEPH HENDERSON

Noel Henderson, a son of James Henderson, Drumahoe, Londonderry, was born on 10 August 1928 and entered Foyle in 1942. In second form, Henderson was introduced to 1st XV rugby on 15 January 1944. The team coach was JS Connolly, and he wrote in the school magazine, *Foyle Times*, in March 1944 'Henderson promises very well. He is strong, has football sense, makes up his mind where he wants to go and goes there without stopping to apologise to the injured en route. And the bigger the match the more coolly and confidently he plays.' This was the first of four successive years on the 1st XV.

The following year Mr Connolly wrote: 'He is reasonably fast in a run, very fast over a short distance, kicks very well, handles very well, has a good swerve and a powerful hand-off and is as strong as a horse'. Connolly's third-year comments are: 'He has all the essentials – good hands, powerful kick, speed, great strength and determination but he would try to run head first through a brick wall.' Henderson captained the team in his final year, 1946–7, the year of the phenomenally severe winter, when only one match was played after Christmas. This was the only defeat of the year and it was against Methody in the semi-final of the Schools Cup. Noel was awarded his Ulster Schools Cap during the year.

Mr Connolly again writes glowingly in the school magazine, April 1947. 'He has everything a centre needs – weight, great strength, almost incredible stamina, determination, speed, safe hands, a powerful kick, an eye for an opening, judgement and a shattering tackle. He is unperturbable, unselfish, a sportsman to this last inch and ounce, and the best school boy captain I have yet seen.'

Noel Henderson graduated BSc at Queen's University in 1951. He was an inspiring leader and captained not only Foyle and Queen's but also the NIFC, Ulster, the Barbarians and Ireland. In an international career spanning ten years, he won 40 caps and captained the Irish XV on 11 occasions. He made his debut in Ireland's Triple Crown-winning side of 1949 and he played in one Test Match on the British and Irish Tour of Australia and New Zealand in 1950. For business reasons he was unable to play for the Lions in the 1955 tour of South Africa, though he was expected to be selected. One of the highlights of his career happened in Dublin in 1958, when he led Ireland to a 9–6 win over Australia, the home team's first win over a major touring side – and he scored the winning try.

Following his retirement from international rugby he was an Ulster and Ireland selector, President of the Ulster Branch in 1976–7 and President of the IRFU in 1990–1. In 1993 he was honoured by the Rugby Writers of Ireland when he was presented with a Hall of Fame Award. Not only did Noel excel at rugby but he also won five Irish International Badminton Caps. As a schoolboy he represented Ulster Schools against Leinster in the Shot Put. He also enjoyed a good game of soccer and round of golf. Off the field he was a fine singer and raconteur. He was elected president of the FCOBA in 1993–4.

Noel Henderson died on 27 August 1997. A fitting memorial to him is the Henderson building at Springtown, which houses the departments of Craft, Design, Technology and Information Technology as well as the new Junior School library. Mrs Henderson performed the opening ceremony in November 1997.

His brother-in-law Jack Kyle, who travelled with Noel on the 1950 Lions Tour, writes: 'I was home from Africa a short time before Noel's death and my daughter and I were in his room talking to him, when he quoted what may sound trite, but has a great deal of truth and meaning in the words:

It is easy to smile and be happy
When life goes along like a song
But the man worthwhile is the man who can smile
When everything goes dreadfully wrong.

A great character who will be sadly missed.'

Foyle College 1st XV 1946–7. In the white shirt is the captain, Noel Joseph Henderson.

There were few successful school teams in the early and mid-1970s. The 1977–8 team showed improvement and promise, winning 13 of the 21 matches played. Their season ended on a high with a two-match tour to England, where they defeated St Michael's School, Leeds, and Silcoates Grammar, Wakefield. Success continued in the seasons 1978–80. The 1979–80 team again contested the semi-final of the cup but lost out to Campbell College 11–3. Highly enjoyable tours to Edinburgh, Newark and Loughborough brought these seasons to a close.

Marshall Kilgore was next to win Ulster School recognition in seasons 1983–5. A strong team was produced in 1986–7 with Keith Gallick the captain. The team again reached the semi-final of the cup and he was selected to play in the final Irish Schoolboy trial. Stan Huey considers this team to be the strongest he ever coached and believes that but for the introduction of the age restriction imposed during the season, his team would probably have won the cup that year. Members of this team, Keith Gallick, Ian Orr, Stephen Smyth and Neil Stewart, went on to represent Ulster at senior level.

David Martin was selected to play for the Ulster Schools in the following season (1987–8) and consequently earned a tour to Zimbabwe. Graeme Keys was a regular Ulster Schools member in the 1989–90 season. Stan Huey managed a successful Ulster Schools tour to South Africa in 1995 and some South African schools paid return visits to Northern Ireland in the late 1990s. Foyle hosted Michelhouse College, Natal and the Paul Roos Gymnasium, Stellenbosch in 1997 and 1998.

Barker College, Buenos Aires, Argentina, and Trinity College, Toronto, were welcome visitors in 1999–2000 and in February 2002. Waverly College, Sydney played a match at Springtown. In July 2002, 33 boys under Stan Huey, Gerald McCarter and Captain Andrew Walker set off on a three-and-a-half-week rugby world tour, stopping at Singapore to play a match and do some sightseeing organised by Keith Maguire. With stops in Sydney, Melbourne, Auckland, Rotorua and Fiji, it was undoubtedly the trip of a lifetime.

Peter McFeely and Richard Peoples represented the Ulster Schools in 2002–3 and Peter had the honour of captaining the side. Graham Murphy was the school's representative on the Ulster team the following year. Gerald McCarter, head of rugby at Foyle, had the honour of being invited by the IRFU to coach the Irish Under-18 team. Richard McCarter was selected to play for the Ulster Under-19, Ulster Under-20 and Ireland Under-19 teams in the same season. He also played on the Irish team in the World Cup Under-19 tournament in Paris. The 2003–4 team on tour handsomely defeated Northampton Boys Grammar School. The Northampton coach graciously acknowledged Foyle as the most complete school team he had seen in 20 years. S Mallon was a regular member of the Ulster senior team at this time.

ABOVE: *RA McGuire Shield for rugby. Played annually between the School and DFC.*

RIGHT: *Foyle 1st teams. Top to bottom: 1949–50, 1958–9, 1959–60, 1962.*

In 2005, 42 boys and four members of the rugby staff, Mr McCarter, Mr Gault, Mr Taylor and Mr Menown, set off to Australia and New Zealand. The trip was hugely enjoyable despite playing some very formidable opponents. The opportunity to kayak, snorkel, jet-ski and water-ski in Fiji was a bonus. On returning home four of the tourists gained representative honours. Richard Brady and Christopher Warnock played on the Ulster Under-19 team while Jack Caithness and David Funston were selected for the Under-18 XV.

During 2006–7 the Girls Rugby XV, captained by Rachel Fleming, showed their flair and enthusiasm for the game by winning the Schools Cup at Ravenhill in the spring. David Funston and Andrew Semple again won representative Ulster honours at Under-18 level, while Simon Cairns gained a place on the Under-19 team. Paul McFeely, Tom Patton, Andrew Semple and John Burns secured places on the Ulster Schools Under-18 and Under-19 teams in 2007–8.

KENNETH GEORGE GOODALL

Ken Goodall was born in Leeds in 1947 and entered Foyle in September 1958. His rugby career began in Form II, when he played as centre in the school's Under-13 team. He captained the Under-14 team, again playing in the centre. In 1961–2, he played in the same position for the Medallion Under-15 XV. The master-in-charge and coach of the team, Jack Bogle, suggested he should move to play in the forwards, as a wing-forward. As an immediate success Jack noted Goodall as 'the outstanding forward' in his end-of-season report. He played in the 1st XV for the three seasons from 1963 and was chosen to represent the Ulster Schools XV during his last two years at school. He was recognised as 'the outstanding player of the team' in the press reports.

When Goodall entered Newcastle University in 1965 to study chemical engineering he continued to play rugby with his student colleagues in the university team, and occasionally flew home to play for the City of Derry in important league games. Goodall's father was a Yorkshire man and Ken was qualified to play for England. However his ambition was to play for Ireland, and he declined the offer of an English trial. His loyalty to his adopted country was soon rewarded when he was chosen to play for Ireland against Australia in January 1967 in Dublin, at the age of 19. This was to be the first of his 19 consecutive international cups, three of them earned on winning teams against Australia.

Goodall was invited to tour with the Lions to South Africa in 1968, but could not go because of university examination commitments. However, midway through the tour, a substitute was required and Goodall was invited to join the tourists. A broken thumb and finger sustained in his first match meant an early return home. His final game and perhaps his greatest in the green jersey of Ireland was against an unbeaten Welsh team in March 1970 in Dublin. His winning try on that

occasion will long be remembered. Soon after, *Rugby World* magazine judged him to be their international player of the year.

After this match, Goodall announced he was joining the professional code, Rugby League, with Workington Town, accepting a teaching post in a local school. He quickly established himself as a favourite with the local supporters, scoring twice on his debut match, including a spectacular sprint of 70 yards to the try line. Back and knee injuries forced a premature retirement in 1974 after three seasons and he returned home. Harry Edgar, the editor of the *Rugby League Journal*, wrote: 'Goodall was a popular figure in West Cumbria, remembered as a excellent sportsman and a fine schoolteacher. He was an immensely talented rugby player and there is no doubt that, had injury not intervened, he could have become a truly great player in Rugby League – he was a natural for the game'.

He was also an honorary life member of the City of Derry Rugby Football Club (CDRFC).

Ken Goodall died on 17 August 2006 and his obituary in the *The Irish Times* stated: 'in terms of great Irish rugby players, the City of Derry, Ulster, Ireland and Lions number eight would rub shoulders with the best that this country could muster'.

Foyle 1st XV 1963.

Another exotic tour took place in 2008 to Dubai and Australia. In 2008–9 John Burns was selected for the Ulster Academy squad – a richly deserved honour. In 2009–10 the school XV, captained by Aaron Patterson, won the Schools Bowl competition for the third time in five years and David Murdock with Nick Donnell were selected for the Ulster Under-19 squad. In 2011, 40 boys and four staff, G McCarter, N Taylor, R Menown and D Barnett, set off on the fourh Australian tour in ten years. Sydney, Surfers' Paradise, Cairns and the Sunshine Coast were the destinations this time. The 1st XV won three of the five matches played – another memorable tour for all concerned.

TOP: *Foyle and Londonderry College 1st XV 2010–11.*

FAR RIGHT: *John Burns, Tom Patton, Paul McFeely, Andrew Semple: all selected for Ulster schools 2007–8.*

BELOW: *Rugby captains board, Springtown.*

Foyle's contribution to Irish rugby has certainly been significant. It can boast of three presidents of the IRFU, Professor CWL Alexander (1909-10), Sir Samuel T Irwin (1935–6) and NJ Henderson (1990–1). Seven Presidents of the Ulster Branch of the Irish Union have been Old Boys of the school, namely Sir Samuel Irwin (1907–8), Professor SBB Campbell (1920–1), AR Foster (1925–6), NJ Henderson (1976–7), WA Caldwell (1979–80), J Murray (1997–8) and JSM Huey (2006–7).

Of Old Boys of LAI or Foyle, 26 have been Irish international players and one an international referee. Three of these stalwarts: Alex Foster, Noel Henderson and Ken Goodall were British and Irish Lions. Glynn Allen, Alex Foster and Noel Henderson have captained the Irish XVs. Alex, Noel and JC Lapsley have been Irish selectors. JC Lapsley, an Ulster player and Irish trialist, was also a popular and successful coach of Stranmillis College. He was president of the FCOBA in 1989–90. Jim Piggot played for Ulster in the inter-provincials and against the Australian tourists in 1948. He was president of the FCOBA in 1963–4. Scott Kelso won six caps for the US Eagles and was chosen for their tour of England in 1977. Professor Kelso was president of the FCOBA in 2008–9. BWG Mooney and JC Fergusson were regulars on the London Irish XV in their playing days. In recent years Richard McCarter has been honoured by being selected for the famous Barbarian XV on two occasions.

Ken Gamble

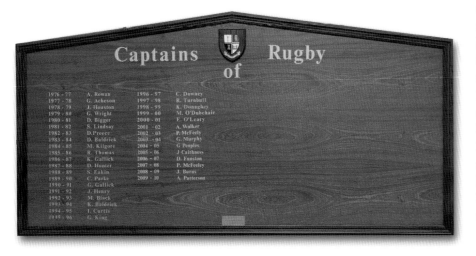

Captains of Rugby

1976 - 77	A. Rowan	1996 - 97	C. Downey
1977 - 78	G. Acheson	1997 - 98	R. Turnbull
1978 - 79	J. Houston	1998 - 99	K. Donaghey
1979 - 80	G. Wright	1999 - 00	M. O'Dubchair
1980 - 81	D. Bigger	2000 - 01	E. O'Leary
1981 - 82	S. Lindsay	2001 - 02	A. Walker
1982 - 83	D.Preece	2002 - 03	P. McFeely
1983 - 84	D. Baldrick	2003 - 04	G. Murphy
1984 - 85	M. Kilgore	2004 - 05	G. Peoples
1985 - 86	R. Thomas	2005 - 06	J Caithness
1986 - 87	K. Gallick	2006 - 07	D. Funston
1987 - 88	D. Hunter	2007 - 08	P. McFeeley
1988 - 89	S. Eakin	2008 - 09	J. Burns
1989 - 90	C. Parke	2009 - 10	A. Patterson
1990 - 91	G. Gallick		
1991 - 92	J. Henry		
1992 - 93	M. Black		
1993 - 94	N. Baldrick		
1994 - 95	I. Curtis		
1995 - 96	G. King		

ABOVE: *LAI Cricket XI, 1880 (left) and LAI Cricket XI, 1884 (right).*

BELOW: *Cricket Cap, 1889.*

CRICKET
1870–1980

There is little evidence of any organised cricket being played by Foyle or LAI before the arrival of new headmasters MC Hime and JC Dick in 1878. Dick arrived from Belfast and was recognised as an accomplished cricketer. Very few matches are recorded before this date, the earliest being a game between LAI and Foyle in June 1870, and another noted when LAI played Ramelton in 1873.

H Stewart is the first recorded captain of Foyle in 1875 and AS McVicker in 1879 is the first LAI captain we can trace. TS McCausland Stewart, the 1880 Foyle captain, recollects in a letter to *Our School Times* some years later that playing against Claudy he made 100 not out on a ground 'with only the pitch mown'. He further comments that he was allowed to keep the bat after the match.

A rental of £20 was agreed in 1878 for Foyle to share a field at Pennyburn with the North West of Ireland cricket club. Early games were played against the local clubs: Strabane, Newtownstewart, Omagh Wanderers and Sion Mills. In 1881 inter-school matches were arranged with Coleraine and Portora. The 1881 and 1882 Foyle teams were undefeated. No cricket was played in 1883, as the Pennyburn ground was 'ploughed up'. The Garrison field in the Waterside was obtained for the 1884 and 1885 seasons, and games were played against Dungiven, Alexander CC of Limavady, Strabane,

Edenballymore, St Columb's College, Wanderers, the Garrison and St Columb's Court.

The May 1886 edition of *Our School Times* records: 'After some difficulty, the cricket club has succeeded in obtaining a fine field at Pennyburn.' However, the rent of £25 per annum was considered to be 'very expensive'. After a petition from the masters and boys for some help, the Irish Society agreed to consider the matter, and in 1887 contributed £15 towards the rental of the field.

Cricket was becoming increasingly popular at Foyle in the later 1880s and matches were played against new opponents: Buncrana, Ardmore, Ebrington, Manorcunningham, Strabane Rovers, the RIC, the GPO and Derry Asylum. The rivalry with LAI was intense, and displeasure was expressed when LAI cancelled a game in 1889. In 1894 a game was lost against Alla 1st XI, Claudy, due to the 'sneak underarm bowling of an opponent'! Inter-school matches were rarely played towards the end of the 19th century but a few games were played against Coleraine Academical Institution, Raphoe Royal, Portora Royal and LAI.

Apathy and a lack of interest in school sports seem to characterise the first decade of the 20th century. However, good weather and the enthusiasm of Mr Samuels and the captain EJ Williams led to an upturn in fortunes in 1909. Five of the seven matches played were won and the other two drawn. The highlight was the

TOP: *Foyle College cricket cap.*

RIGHT: *Top to bottom: LAI 1st XIs 1887, 1891, 1911.*

away victory over Coleraine Academical Institution, with Williams taking 12 wickets for 35 runs over the two innings and scoring 29 not out in the second innings.

Successful teams were fielded 1910–13. C Glover was selected to play for the Ulster Schools in 1911 and the school magazine noted that 'the cricket XI was near the top among Irish schools.' The 1911 captain, SH Andrews' was considered to be perhaps the best all-rounder Foyle ever had. All school matches were won in 1913. Both opening bowlers, TAH Orr and TS Haslett, played on the Ulster Schools XI. The 1914 captain TS Haslett had a superb season, the highlight being his 106 not out against Dungannon Royal and capturing five wickets for seven runs in the same match. AH Matthews played on the Ulster Schools XI in 1914–6 and captained Ulster in 1916. GL Craig and OW Gilmour were chosen to represent Ulster in 1917 and 1918 respectively.

The 1923 team proved to be very successful under the captaincy of AH Montgomery, the future president of the Irish Cricket Union. The opening bowlers Montgomery and CD Henderson were particularly impressive, with the former's eight wickets for 18 runs against Portora being the season's highlight. Henderson was captain for the next two seasons and returned fine figures of six for 15 against Coleraine and four for seven against Methody. Only one defeat was suffered in 1925. JL Rankin and T Orr, both future Irish Badminton internationals, were also talented cricketers and captained Foyle in 1926 and 1930 respectively. Rankin took six wickets for ten runs in a match against Methody and Orr seven for 17 against Coleraine. The 1932 team with COS Thomas as captain had a good record with GD Smyth taking seven wickets for 18 and again seven for 42 in wins against Coleraine and Methody.

JN McMorris was captain of the successful 1935 team, which won all its school matches except the drawn game in Belfast against RBAI. AR Killen was the pick of the bowlers and was man of the match against Coleraine, with six wickets for four runs. Killen captained the team in 1936 and was selected to play for the Ulster Schools XI. Victor Anderson, having played on the team for the previous three seasons, was the chosen captain in 1938. Mr NL Sampson, the coach, noted he was 'the outstanding member of the successful team'. JT Craig emerged as an excellent left arm bowler and promising batsman.

In ten overs he took eight wickets for 13 runs against BRA. He took six wickets for four runs against Coleraine and was top scorer with 62 runs, and also had five wickets for two runs against Dungannon.

TS Semple captained the 1939 team and won his Ulster cap against Leinster. An opening bowler, his best figures were eight wickets for 26 runs against Portora. NJ Dunn opened the bowling with Semple and contributed to the demolition of Methody by taking six wickets for seven runs and was top scorer with 32 runs. Only one school match was lost during the season.

Fewer school matches were played during the war years, but there were many fine individual performances. In 1940 TF Riddall captured five Dungannon wickets for nine runs. In 1942 JB Taylor scored 101 runs not out against Dungannon and EC McKerr had a good innings of 75 not out against a Navy XI. Also in 1942 GS Lapsley took eight wickets for seven runs against Dungannon, JB Taylor seven for seven against Portora and TR Brown four for one against Campbell. In 1943 Brown further tormented Campbell with his left arm slow bowling taking four wickets for ten, and also captured five Portora wickets for six runs. EC McKerr had six for eight against Campbell and BHE Roberts six for 17 against Methody. DW Lapsley bowled six wickets for 24 against Campbell in 1944. JC Lapsley had six Campbell wickets for 23 runs in 1946 and EB Wilson seven for 15 against Coleraine also in 1946. Few games were played in 1947 due to bad weather. However the Coleraine game created a little family controversy. DA Bigger bowled five wickets for seven runs before opening the batting with brother Edgar. David succeeded in running out Edgar before proceeding to top score and win the match. Peace has now been restored. Ulster schools caps were gained by Riddall in 1940, Mc Kerr in 1943 and by JC Lapsley in 1947.

Successes were scarce in the 1948 and 1949 seasons, with batting below the usual standards. There were fine bowling figures from W Warke in 1948 and 1949. In 1948 he took 51 wickets in the season, averaging 5.2 runs per wicket. JR Patterson captured 46 wickets at a cost of 5.6 runs per wicket. Warke and Patterson did 80 per cent of the bowling during the summer. The 1950s proved to be a highly successful decade for cricket in the school. The 1950 team captained by MDL Eakin suffered only two

TOP TO BOTTOM: *Foyle College 1st XI 1922; 1930; 1935.*

defeats in the 12 matches played. JE Millar had a score of 103 and also topped the batting averages. AW Roulston was the leading bowler, taking 50 wickets at an average of 5.6 runs per wicket. Ten of the 13 games played in 1951 were won. JR Patterson had a brilliant season, capturing 65 wickets at an average of 3.8 runs per wicket. Patterson was captain in 1952 and despite his taking eight Coleraine wickets for 23 runs, the game was lost due to a batting collapse. MA Dunlop had a golden spell of bowling mid-season, when he took 22 wickets for 41 runs in only four matches.

J McCandless was the outstanding player in 1953. He topped both the batting and bowling averages.

His best score was 102 not out and averaged 31 runs for the season. In the bowling department he had the magnificent score of 83 wickets, averaging 4.4 runs per wicket for the season. His best spell was six wickets for one run against Limavady Grammar. McCandless captained the 1954 team, and with the McNamee brothers, Derek and Basil, from Donemana, in superb form, another outstanding season was enjoyed. Thirteen of the 14 matches were won. JF (Derek) McNamee was the leading batsman, with a season's average of 32.6 runs per innings, and the bowling honours were shared by McCandless with 51 wickets at a cost of 4.9 runs per wicket and FP Huey, who took 50 wickets at 5.1 runs per wicket. JF McNamee and McCandless were both selected to represent the Ulster Schools against Leinster and against the Leprechauns.

The cricket XI was not defeated by another school during the next two years, 1955 and 1956. The outstanding players were the McNamee brothers, with Derek captain both seasons. Basil headed the batting averages in 1955 with 34.5 runs per innings and scored a century not out against Ballymena. BJ Stanage opened the bowling and captured 32 wickets, averaging 6.3 runs. Basil's batting in 1956 was even more remarkable, when he again scored a century not out and averaged 49.5 runs per innings. Derek also

had a high average of 38.9 runs. VR Eakin was best bowler, taking 50 wickets at a cost of 6.7 runs each. Derek was again selected for the Ulster Schools both years, making it three in a row 1954–6. Basil played for the Ulster Schools and the Irish Schools both seasons and in 1956 scored 77 in the first innings and 54 in the second playing for the Irish team against a strong Leprechaun XI.

The 1958 team, with VR Eakin as captain, had another good season despite the wet summer. Only two matches were lost and Eakin and W Quinn were selected to represent the Ulster Schools. Quinn was also chosen for the Schools of Ireland team. Success continued in 1959 with Quinn as captain. He again headed the batting averages and won his place again on both the Ulster and Irish teams. WS Colhoun, who opened the bowling, took 50 wickets, averaging 5.1 runs, and was also selected for the Ulster team. A few average seasons followed but PJ Hamilton's achievement in May 1962 against Campbell College in Belfast must be highlighted. A slow left arm spinner, he captured all ten Campbell wickets in 18 overs at a cost of 51 runs. However, an inept batting display by Foyle resulted in defeat.

Outstanding teams emerged in 1963 and 1964 with WSF Young captain in 1963 and JSL Mitchell

CLOCKWISE FROM THE TOP LEFT:
Foyle 1st XI 1955; 1956;
1963; 1964.

the 1964 skipper. The 1963 team lost only one game during the year – and that to a strong Old Boys selection. Mitchell and WL Cunningham were chosen to represent both the Ulster Schools and the Schools of Ireland teams. Cunningham captained the Ulster side. Mitchell scored two centuries and three half centuries during the season and had the magnificent average of 49.6 runs per innings. Cunningham also hit a fine century against Belfast Royal Academy in Belfast and headed the bowling averages with 35 wickets at 7.1 runs per wicket. RJ Magowan hit two half centuries in the season and averaged 25.1 runs per innings. Lowry Cunningham recalls playing RBAI in Belfast with the openers Mitchell and Magowan in fine form. After a number of lost cricket balls due to some hard hitting, Mr Mowbray the Foyle coach and umpire whispered to Stan Mitchell: 'Easy on the sixes – they are now using our cricket balls!'

Despite the cold damp summer, 1964 proved to be equally successful. Mitchell and Cunningham again played for both the Ulster and Irish Schools and Cunningham captained both teams. Mitchell scored 114 runs for the Ulster side against Leinster and against the Welsh he scored 36 and 32 in the two innings giving an average of 50.4 in the season's representative matches. Cunningham's bowling was again impressive – he took seven wickets for one run against Dungannon and seven for seven against Limavady. Mr Mowbray in his end of season critique in the school magazine wrote: 'Cunningham is one of the most gifted all-rounders in schools' cricket.'

JAS Kelso was selected for the Ulster Schools in 1965 and the captain D Rankin headed the bowling averages with 41 wickets costing 6.6 runs each. His best was five wickets for none against Belfast High. Rankin was again captain the following year and was chosen to play on the Ulster side against the Leprechauns. He headed the school's averages in both bowling and batting with 34 wickets at 4.7 per wicket and 23.1 runs per innings respectively.

The 1967 team had only a mediocre season, the highlight being the 124 runs scored by the captain, J Canning, against Cork Grammar School. The summer of 1968 was warm and dry and the captain TI Rankin was chosen to play on both the Ulster and Irish schools' team. He averaged 38.0 runs per innings during the year. JIS Lapsley headed the bowling by taking 44 wickets at an average of 8.5 runs. Rankin was again chosen to captain the 1969 team when only

Foyle College 1st XI 1973.

one game was lost. SM McSparron averaged 49 runs per innings and scored a fine century. Both Rankin and McSparron were chosen for the Ulster and Irish sides, with Rankin captain of the Irish team. Lapsley was again the pick of the bowlers; his best figures were seven wickets for 39 against RBAI. After many successful years Mr Mowbray decided to retire at the end of the season. A tribute to him in the *Foyle College Times* stated: 'Foyle is now one of the leading cricket schools in Ulster and Ireland'. Mr J Magowan and Mr I McCracken bravely took up the challenge of replacing Mr Mowbray.

The outstanding cricketer of the early 1970s was undoubtedly WSH Wilson. He played on the 1st XI for four successive years and was captain 1971–3. His first year was 1970. The team did not have a particularly successful season but the young Wilson took 46 wickets at nine runs per wicket and also headed the batting averages. A strong team emerged in 1971 with Wilson as captain. No inter-school match was lost. Wilson took eight Ballymena wickets for 22 runs and had a season's total of 54 wickets at an average cost of 8.5 runs. AW Baird was selected to play for the Ulster Schools and the wicket keeper, JP Rowan, for the Ireland Under-19 XI. The excessive rain in May and June 1972 together with the civil unrest throughout the province deprived the cricket XI of many opportunities to enjoy the game. Only ten school matches were played and the team was undefeated. Three boys, Wilson, Rowan and Baird, were selected to play on the Ulster and Irish Schools teams.

A new and inexperienced team turned out in 1973, with only two of the previous year's team playing.

Nevertheless, with William Wilson in charge again, the team played some top-class cricket, and both Wilson and Gerald McCarter scoring centuries. Wilson headed the batting averages, scoring 511 runs at an average of 34, and McCarter made 468 runs averaging 31.2 runs per innings. Wilson, McCarter and WJ Semple were rewarded with Ulster caps and Wilson and McCarter with Irish caps.

The 1974 team was young and enthusiastic but victories were few. WJ Semple again played on the Ulster team and DWE McKerr was selected but was unable to play. McKerr headed both the battling and bowling averages, with an excellent seven wickets for ten runs against Ballymena being his best performance. In 1975 RJ Wray scored 122 against Portora and WJ Semple again was chosen to represent the Ulster Schools. Both Semple and Wray captured over 50 wickets during the year at an average of approximately ten runs per wicket. 1976 and 1977 were rather lean years euphemistically described as 'seasons of transition'. The 1979 team with Colin Jeffrey as captain was defeated only twice in 22 matches. Jeffrey scored 586 runs in the season and the team reached the final of the Belfast Telegraph Cup but was defeated by Down High School. Jeffrey and Ian Anthony played on the Ulster Schools XI and Jeffrey was selected to tour Canada with the Irish Under-19 team.

In 1980 Graeme Wright scored 111 against BRA. Michael Bruce and David Stafford were chosen to play on the Ulster Schools team.

The following Old Boys of Foyle were Presidents of Cricket Ireland:

1968   Dr AH Montgomery
1982   Mr DW Todd
2005   Mr JSL Mitchell
2010   Dr BT McNamee

Ken Gamble

1980–2011

From 1980 Foyle's fortunes in cricket have varied widely, with the 1980s and the 2000s successful decades during which the Schools Cup was won on three occasions, while the 1990s were not so rewarding.

In 1982, with John Magowan and Ian McCracken in charge, the 1st XI first went on tour to the Chester area and this tour became a very enjoyable end-of-term trip which motivated the players. In 1983 the 1st XI won the AIB Ulster Schools Cup for the first

time under the captaincy of Michael Bruce. Foyle had a five-wicket victory over Ballymena Academy, with Keith McCrory playing a significant role. He, Marshall Kilgore and Stephen Smyth became synonymous with Foyle cricket. After the cup victory in 1983 Gerald McCarter took over from John Magowan, who had been in charge of 1st XI cricket for 13 seasons and for whom the cup victory was a fitting tribute.

This success continued with Ian and Gerald in 1984 and 1985, with a sequence of three cup wins in a row. In 1984 we defeated Campbell College when we batted first, achieving 179–5 in 30 overs, with Alan Henderson (58) and Keith McCrory (50) being our main scorers. Then came a stand between George Walker (25 not out) and third former Stephen Smyth

145

LEFT: *Kyle Hamilton and Steven Clarke, selected for the Irish Schools cricket team.*

BOTTOM LEFT: *Foyle students Graham Crown and Graeme McCarter, respectively selected for the Irish Schools soccer team and the Ireland cricket team.*

We did not again win the Schools Cup until 2003, when Alan Duddy led Foyle to a memorable victory over Strabane Grammar School at Eglinton Cricket Club. In 1987 we lost to Ballymena Academy in the final by six wickets but later won the McCullough Cup against Regent House in a match played at Campbell College.

The 1987 season was remarkable as Stephen Smyth broke virtually every batting record there was to break. He scored 1,026 runs in total, breaking Marshall Kilgore's previous record of 714 runs in a season. He hit five centuries and four 50s, scoring his 100s against Campbell College and MCB. These records are still unbroken.

1990 was to be our last really successful season. Although the team did not win the cup they won all four games on tour in Chester for the first time. In these years we produced some fine individual performances but we lacked the depth to be a forceful team. In 1989 our seconds won the Duke of Abercorn Cup (the premier competition for 2nd XIs), winning again in 1990, 1991 and 1992, but losing it in 1993. This great achievement is very much due to Norman Taylor, who has given a huge amount of time and expertise to school sport. In 1998 Ian McCracken retired as cricket coach and from the school staff. A new era dawned when David Keown joined Gerald McCarter to supervise the 1st XI.

After several frustrating seasons we were not really successful again until 2003. Ian Donaghey captained the side in 1999 and 2000 and we began to improve. David Fleming took over from him and in 2001 we won the Gordon McCullough Cup again, defeating Down High School by 15 runs. By 2002 we had improved further but suffered narrow defeats in the semi-final of the Schools Cup and in the final of the McCullough Cup. David Fleming, David Robb and Salman Qureshi represented Ulster Schools and Nicky Cooke, who had played for Ulster the previous season, was still with us.

The Ulster Bank Schools Cup returned to Foyle in June 2003 when in an exciting final we defeated a strong Strabane GS team by seven wickets. Batting first Strabane scored 168–7 with Nicky Cooke (3–34) and Nigel McClay (2–33) the pick of the bowlers. Steven Campbell and Alan Duddy got us off to a good start, putting on 55, and then Nicky Cooke and Duddy continued to score freely. Nicky scored 51 not

(22 not out). Campbell College quickly lost three wickets for 15 runs and were eventually all out for 112.

The 1985 season brought a double cup success. On Monday, 24 June, we defeated Friends School, Lisburn at their ground to win the Gordon McCullough Memorial Cup for the first time. On the next day we returned to Lisburn to play Bangor Grammar School in the Schools Cup Final at Wallace Park. Foyle batted first and scored 171–5 in the 30 overs. Keith McCrory became the first player to score three 50s in three finals and George Walker hit a quick 53 not-out. The Bangor openers put on 80 for the first wicket, and with one ball left and McCrory bowling, Bangor needed six to win. He bowled a bye to the boundary, Bangor got four runs and we had won by two runs. With two cups in two days and three Schools Cup wins in a row, we set off happily on tour to Chester the next day.

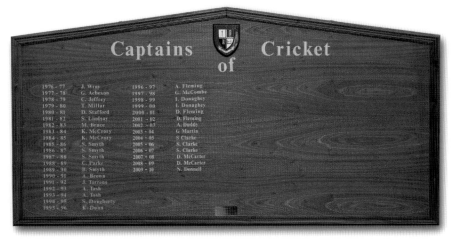

Foyle 1st XI win Schools' Cup 2011 and Captains of Cricket board at Springtown.

1976 - 77	J. Wray	1996 - 97	A. Fleming
1977 - 78	G. Acheson	1997 - 98	G. McCombe
1978 - 79	C. Jeffrey	1998 - 99	I. Donaghey
1979 - 80	T. Millar	1999 - 00	I. Donaghey
1980 - 81	D. Stafford	2000 - 01	D. Fleming
1981 - 82	S. Lindsay	2001 - 02	D. Fleming
1982 - 83	M. Bruce	2002 - 03	A. Duddy
1983 - 84	K. McCrory	2003 - 04	G. Martin
1984 - 85	K. McCrory	2004 - 05	S. Clarke
1985 - 86	S. Smyth	2005 - 06	S. Clarke
1986 - 87	S. Smyth	2006 - 07	S. Clarke
1987 - 88	S. Smyth	2007 - 08	D. McCarter
1988 - 89	C. Parke	2008 - 09	D. McCarter
1989 - 90	B. Smyth	2009 - 10	N. Donnell
1990 - 91	A. Brown		
1991 - 92	J. Torrens		
1992 - 93	A. Tosh		
1993 - 94	A. Tosh		
1994 - 95	S. Dougherty		
1995 - 96	K. Dunn		

out, hit the winning runs and gave us a memorable seven-wicket victory.

2004 was a lean season but we identified potential in the junior teams. Steven Clarke and Dean and Graeme McCarter would bring glory days to Foyle again. Steven Clarke became captain in 2005 and also captained the Schools of Ireland in 2007 following in the footsteps of Keith McCrory and Lowry Cunningham. David Keown recorded in the 2007–8 School Magazine: 'Since 2000 Foyle have played in six semi-finals in the Schools Cup and won only one.' It would be 2009 before we broke our losing habit.

Dean McCarter replaced Steven as captain in 2008 and we lost another semi-final to RBAI, which incredibly involved a tie at Springtown. Both sides scored 262–8, with Graeme McCarter scoring 102. We went to Belfast for the replay but lost again! With

a talented squad, including David Keown and Gerald McCarter, our early net sessions took place to instil team sprit. The year 2009 was extremely successful and in a great Ulster Bank cup final played at Bready CC we avenged our two semi-final defeats by RBAI, who had now become out main rivals. In the 2009 Ulster Bank Cup final we scored a convincing win over them. Dean McCarter quickly got 54 and then in a fourth-wicket partnership of 109 in 11 overs, Aaron Kitson and Graeme McCarter swung the game our way. Aaron scored 57 and Graeme finished 67 not out. RBAI began well but Mark Porter's bowling took its toll of the RBAI batsmen. At 4.10pm we took the last wicket and Inst were all out for 179.

Four of our players, Dean and Graeme McCarter, Mark Porter and Nick Donnell, were included in the Ulster Schools team. Dean and Nick were also selected for the Schools of Ireland and Graeme, at the age of 16, for the Ireland Under-19 World Cup Qualifying Tournament in Canada. Nick Donnell took over as captain with a core of six remaining players and a number of promising newcomers.

We defeated Methody in the semi-final at Springtown in mid-June. We batted first and scored 183–9 with David Murdock (50) and Jack Glenn (47) being our top scorers. With skipper Nick Donnell bowling and taking 3 for 20 Methody were all out for 115. Next we met Sullivan Upper School in the final. They won the toss, batted and made 75 without loss after 16 overs. Then our spinners, Marc Fleming (3–24) and Jack Glenn (3–32) had a major impact and Sullivan finished on 143–9. Our spin duo in a fine stand of 126 saw us home in style by nine wickets. Jack was 73 not out and Marc 41 not out. The boys then went on tour next day and Nick Donnell's team repeated the success of Brian Smyth's 1990 players winning all four tour games.

Four of our players were chosen for the Ulster side. Nick Donnell was made captain the team and was organised by Graeme McCarter, Marc Fleming and Jack Glenn. Graeme McCarter was captain for the 2011 season and with the loss of some of the Nick Donnell team in the semi final against Regent House we did not perform and bowed out.

As well as the many fine players we had between 1980 and 2011, we had also had some excellent scorers: Trevor Lucy, Frank Lampen and Claire Magowan.

GR McCarter

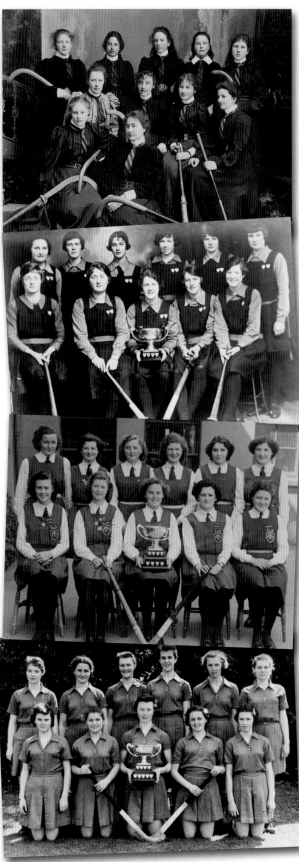

HOCKEY

Women's Hockey in Ireland

The first recorded mention of a competitive women's hockey match was on 1 April 1896 in the *Belfast News-Letter*. The match played the previous day between Methody and City of Derry Hockey Club, which the latter won 1–0. City of Derry became the first ever winner of the Ulster Shield 1896–7. Victoria High School, the forerunner of Londonderry High School, won the Ulster Shield 1901–2 when clubs and schools competed together.

The Schools Cup Competition, which started in 1907, was dominated by Belfast schools until Londonderry High School reached the final in three successive seasons in the 1950s. The first year, 1951–2, Londonderry High School was defeated by BRA, the next year they beat St Dominic's High School and then in the 1953–4 final beat Ballymena Academy. Five of this successful team were selected for the Ulster Schools squad for the inter-provincial tournament that year. That same season 1953–4 Londonderry High School also won the Junior School Cup (Under-14), winning two Ulster major competitions in the same year.

Londonderry High School 2nd XI also shared the spoils of the McDowell Cup 1960–1 with St Dominic's HS.

Rosemary (Templeton) McDowell

RIGHT: *FLC Schools Hockey Cup winners, 1982.*

BELOW RIGHT: *Hockey at Duncreggan.*

Hockey in Londonderry High School and Foyle and Londonderry College

In March 1972 I was a newly fledged PE teacher under the headship of Miss Cowper and later Miss Christie. A sense of tradition permeated the very fabric of the buildings and emanated from the many sporting photographs that adorned the walls of Dalriada House. How the styles and equipment have changed over the years! The 1954 cup-winning wore knee-length pleated tunics, aertex blouses and black canvas hockey boots with very little padding to protect those delicate ankles – how far removed from the modern kit of 'skorts' (shorts that look like a skirt), lycra open-necked tops and all the protective wear in use today. Goalkeepers wear body armour, helmets and high hand protectors made from very light materials so that they can dive and throw themselves around the goal mouth!

The biggest changes I have observed are the different playing surfaces, stick-head shape and the ever-changing rules. Gone is the iconic bully-off; 'Ground sticks, ground sticks, ground sticks' has been replaced by a mere 'centre pass' which has to go backwards! No more off-sides nor 'roll-in 16-yard hits', 'sticks' or 'turning'! The latest rule is that you can quickly pass the ball to yourself when awarded a free hit!

LONDONDERRY HIGH SCHOOL: HOCKEY INTERNATIONALS

Catherine Brown

(Londonderry High School June 1950)

Trained as PE Teacher in England.

Returned to Northern Ireland after completing her studies.

Taught PE in Regent House School, Newtownards 1953–8.

Joined Ards Ladies Hockey Club in 1953.

Represented Ulster and Ireland (caps).

Went to live in USA in 1958.

Sandra Millar (née Wylie)

(Londonderry High School 1956–8)

Trained as PE teacher at Ulster College of Physical Education, Jordanstown.

Taught PE in Belfast Royal Academy 1967–9.

Taught PE in Regent house 1969–72.

Joined Pegasus LHC.

Represented Ulster and Ireland (caps).

Went to live in Scotland (Edinburgh).

Derry girls win the cup

HOCKEY

Two goals by centre-forward Pamela Chittick in the first half and a magnificent display of defensive work by Foyle and Londonderry in the second half gave the North West side a 2-0 victory over holders St. Dominic's in yesterday's Senior Schools Cup hockey final at Shaw's Bridge.

The opening minutes of the game saw both attacks testing the opposing defence. St. Dominic's had a goal disallowed in the fifth minute, while Foyle and Londonderry counter-attacked down the left, forcing a series of penalty corners, but the Belfast side cleared their lines.

In the 15th minute, a fast break from defence saw

Fiona Kennedy free hit was deflected into the back of the net by Pamela for a second goal.

The second half saw St. Dominic's dominate the play, with the North West side able to make only spasmodic raids into their opponents' half. Brilliant goalkeeping by Shauna Kelly and sterling work by the defence kept the eager forwards out.

At times, it appeared that the Belfast side must score, so much pressure did they mount, but the Foyle and Londonderry defence held firm to win the coveted

North West girls 'Foyle' St. Dominic's

Foyle and Londonderry schools' skipper Gillian Barr holds aloft the Ulster Women's Hockey Union Senior Schoolgirls' Cup after her team had defated holders and favourites St. Dominic's 2-0 in yesterday's final at Shaw's Bridge. **See match report page 29.**

A section of the large contingent of supporters who travelled from Londonderry with the Foyle hockey team.

When I returned after maternity leave in 1979 the headmaster, Hugh Gillespie, told me that it was time to put hockey back on the map. We quite literally needed a level playing field in every sense and so in 1980 a new hard shale pitch replaced the bumpy grass at Duncreggan. Peggy McCloskie, a former games teacher and later secretary at Londonderry High School, opened the new pitch, enabling the girls to play a much faster skill-based game. Thus we were able to win the Senior Schools Cup in 1982 against St Dominic's, captained by Gillian Barr – the same school that the 1954 team had beaten in their final.

From the mid 1990s we had the use of a hard pitch at Springtown for the Junior girls and also an Astroturf pitch at Magee University. The building of the sports hall also allowed for simulated 'Astroturf' practice when it was too dark or the weather inclement. Having these new facilities to teach and coach and with the ever-changing skills required for Astroturf hockey the girls were enabled to reach two consecutive Senior Cup finals in 1996 against Portadown, captained by Kathryn Huey, and in 1997 against Enniskillen, captained by Ella King.

The school could now compete with the best in Ulster, as they proved by winning the Shield in 2006 against Grosvenor, captained by Emma Sproule, and the Under-14 XL, coached by Kerry Eakin and captained by Camilla Lyttle, reached the Junior Cup final – and that for the first time! After a tour to Barcelona, I 'hung up my boots and whistle' in 2006 and happily left the organisation of the game to Kerry Eakin, who then went on to produce the third cup-winning team in 2009.

In order to write about my experiences of teaching and coaching hockey, I located my hockey archive, which contained all the photographs, newspaper cuttings, albums, cards, letters, hockey speeches, endless lists of team talks, strategies and practices, as well as poems, songs and even telegrams. I also have three black lab books in which I kept a handwritten record of every team member, dates, opposition, results, goal scores, special hockey award winners and representative data – a collection covering 34 years (1972–2006). How lovely to realise that my predictions about 'Promising Form I Players' were confirmed five or six years later when they became 1st and 2nd XI players.

Also in my 'lab books' were the names of the many wonderful members of staff who gave up their own time to coach teams and umpire for me.

LEFT: *Newspaper clippings of victorious cup winning hockey team, 1982 and Gillian Barr with Ulster Schools Cup hockey, 1982.*

ABOVE: *FLC 1st XI hockey, 2006.*

ABOVE RIGHT: *FLC 1st XI hockey, 2011.*

BELOW: *Captains of Hockey board at Springtown.*

1970–80: Ken Thatcher, Rosaleen Partridge (McKinney), Christine Burns (née Kennedy), Ian McCracken and Valerie Lyttle

1980–90: Jim Heasley, Kenny Given, Nicola McBride, Nick Quaile and John McNee

1990–2000: Kerry Eakin, Susan McCaul, Nick Argent, Beverley Gillen (née McClay), Jackie Allen, Sarah Guthrie and Melodie Leonard.

These staff along with others who travelled, supported, organised buses at finals and celebrations dinners, sewed numbers on shirts, bandaged cuts or took videos, joined the ground staff, office staff, caretakers, canteen staff, pupils and parents to

make up team hockey. We worked together and continued the great tradition of Londonderry High School hockey.

Over my 34 years, past pupils, staff and friends of the school have generously donated trophies for hockey which are presented annually and appropriately span Junior and Senior hockey achievements.

As I recall the emotions that hockey alone can create, I remember the shrieks of delight, the three cheers for the opposition, singsongs in the minibus, half-time team talks, huddles before the match and bloodied knees and elbows afterwards. I remember, too, the pleasure when a much-rehearsed 'set piece' or penalty corner routine was successful and also the sadness when the Form I girls would meet me in the car park and gather round like bees to a honey pot to discover they were not selected for the Form I tournament in Coleraine. Their faces said it. However, I smiled on recalling the annual 'Old Girls' matches played at Christmas when friendships were rekindled over mince pies and chocolates. I am filled with pride at the way all of the girls and their captains (especially Kathryn Huey) were magnanimous both in victory and defeat.

I can only sum up by saying: belonging to a team, whether in sport or in any walk of life, is a character-building and life-enhancing experience; I wouldn't change it for the world. I am so proud to have been a member of both the Londonderry High School and Foyle and Londonderry College staff teams. I hope I shall long be able to support the school hockey.

HG McCloy (1972–2006)

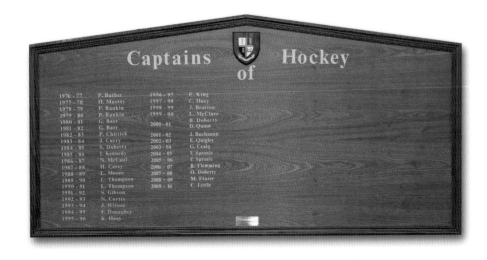

TALENTED PLAYERS

Pamela Chittick: (Prolific goal scorer: 31 goals in one session, including two winning goals in 1982 Cup Final) Captained team in 1983 and won Schools Plate; Played for Ulster School Girls (1983); Ulster Under-21 (1983–5); Ulster Senior 'B' 1986; Ulster Senior 'A' (1987–96); Ulster Indoor (1992); Still playing for Ards Ladies

Gillian Barr: Captained School Team (1980–1); Captained winning cup team (1981–2); Ulster Schoolgirls (1983); Ulster Under-21 (1983–4)

Fiona Kennedy: Member of cup-winning team (1982)

Vivienne McCleary: Ulster Under-21 (1983)

Louise Cummings: Played for Ulster 'B' Schoolgirls

Judith Wilson: Played for Ulster 'B' Schoolgirls

Emma Sproule: Captain of 2006 Shield-winning team

Jill Kennedy: Came to us from Strabane High in lower sixth and captained Ulster Schools 2006–7

Ones who got away (All final trials but not selected): Kathryn Huey, Sarah McDaid and Lizzie Jordan

The most talented player from my 34 years at Foyle: Megan Frazer

Since taking over from Hilary Foyle hockey achievements have been as follows:

2005–6: Hilary's final year. Emma Sproule captained the 1st XI to victory in the Senior School Shield against Portadown College.

2006–7: Retained the Senior Shield, beating BRA in the final – captain Rachel Fleming.

2007–8: Reached the semi-finals of the Schools 'Cup', lost to Royal School Armagh after extra time. Winners of the Derry and Antrim League.

2008–9: Winners of the Senior Schools' Cup – beating Armagh in the semi-final and Ballymena Academy in the final. Lost in the final of the Kate Russell All-Ireland in extra time to Colaiste Lognaid (Galway).

2009–10: Winners of the Derry and Antrim League.

CAPTAINS

2007–8:	Olivia Doherty
2008–9:	Megan Frazer
2009–10:	Camilla Lyttle

TOURS

2006:	Barcelona
2007:	Edinburgh
2008:	Edinburgh
2009:	Holland
2010:	London

REPRESENTATIVE HONOURS

2005–6	Emma Sproule:	Ulster Under-18B
2009–10	Camilla Lyttle:	Ulster Under-18B
2006–9	Megan Frazer:	Ulster Under-16,
		Ulster Under-18 co-captain,
		Ulster Under-21,
		Senior Ulster,
		Ireland Under-18,
		Ireland Under-21,
		Senior Ireland –
		all Megan's achievements while at school.

Megan Frazer is considered to be one of the best ever school girls to have played in Ulster. She is now in her second year of a sports scholarship at the University of Maryland. I think Hilary will agree that Megan is the best ever player to have attended Foyle and Londonderry College. There have been no notable successes at Junior level since the Under-14 team reached the Junior Cup Final in 1995! Perhaps the future will change this.

Kerry Eakin

FAR LEFT: *Ulster Schools Hockey: Jill Kennedy and Megan Frazer, 2009.*

LEFT: *Megan Frazer in action.*

ATHLETICS

In the late 19th century paper chases were organised for the boys, with the trail often being laid by a member of the local garrison. *Our School Times* in 1880 records a sports day where participants competed in such events as throwing the weight or the cricket ball, running, jumping and, for the younger boys, the egg and ladle, three-legged and sack races. Sports Days became social occasions, with the 1911 event being held at the Brandywell. From the turn of the 20th century Foyle competed with most other Ulster schools.

In the 1960s athletics still played a significant role in school life. As a member of the school athletic team in the mid-to-late 1960s I recall meets taking place on Saturdays at venues such as Portora, Magherafelt, Ballymena, Belfast and locally at Springtown and Brandywell. Mid-week meetings were held with local teams such as the Oak Leaf Athletic Club and others with local factories. The weather always seemed to be sunny and the sky blue. With the standard of competition fierce and the commitment total, maybe 40 or 50 headed off on a coach to away matches. Indeed there were many talented athletes who represented the school at Ulster level in the 1960s.

On my returning to teach my preferred option in the summer term was to help with athletics, which then had a reduced profile. Throwing events were becoming too dangerous and the risk of a pupil's being impaled on a misdirected javelin

seemed too great. Nevertheless, being able to throw a lethal weapon appealed to many, and in the 1970s and 1980s we had several excellent exponents of the art, some of whom went on to represent Ulster and Ireland Schools. The girls were keen throwers and we had several medal winners at Ulster level. Dean S Mahon was an excellent thrower of the javelin and went on to win an Irish Schools title in the event. When one of the students was asked by the local athletics club to compete as a hammer thrower and I knew nothing about the discipline I borrowed a book from the library. I then experimented with a short piece of rope, an old sock and a shot until I learned how to do it. In the early 1980s we took a team to Dublin to compete in the All-Ireland School Championship, where we finished second in the senior event. Athletics is now mostly confined to Sports Day, but there is still that ferociously competitive streak manifested by the young competitors on the day.

Ken Thatcher

SWIMMING

The school has a long tradition of competitive swimming and associated aquatic sports. This dates back to the foundation of LAI in 1871. John Clarke Dick, who became headmaster in 1878, was a keen and accomplished sportsman and did much to promote a range of sports by providing the best possible facilities for these in the new school. The completion of a gymnasium in 1888 was soon followed by two new ball courts and an indoor swimming pool – the first for a school in Ireland. The cost of these was supplemented by the proceeds of a bazaar, raising almost £2,000 and additional subscriptions by the Irish Society. By the time LAI amalgamated with Foyle College in 1896, the swimming races were well established and the school was competing against other schools, notably Coleraine, RBAI, Portora and later St Columb's College. The swimming races were held over two nights and attracted large numbers of spectators; it was regarded as a major sporting and social occasion and was covered by the local press. Apart from the full range of races in all styles of swimming, there were diving competitions and water polo. During the war years there were inter-school squadron races and the pool at Academy Road was availed of by the girls from Victoria High School in Crawford Square.

By 1958 plans were advanced for the completion of a municipal pool at William Street and by this time the roof of the pool at Foyle was a cause for such concern that it was closed and the school itself closed shortly afterwards. The school had an especially strong competitive team in 1958–9 including EK Beatty, JG Connolly, CL Clarke, JA Wilson, SH Colgan and JDR Connolly. They were most ably coached by RG Cayless, the school's PE master. The opening of the city baths provided an even better venue for teaching pupils and holding galas. The more extensive viewing gallery accommodated the whole school and some parents as spectators and added to the sense of occasion. When Cayless retired he was succeeded by Roy Seddon, who took a special interest in swimming and continued the tradition of the galas.

The loss of the school pool meant that practice times were curtailed, with only Monday afternoons available at William Street for that purpose. Significant swimming successes in the 1960s included MD Harrison (Ulster Schools Breast Stroke Champion), TK Drought (Ulster Schools Back Stroke Champion), JRW Henderson, JJ Allen and DK Browne. TK Drought was selected to train for the Empire Games in Jamaica in 1966. Emerging talent included RG Addinell, JC Warnock, HJH Deane, KT Thatcher, BT McElhinney, RW Holman, JW Elder and DD Bratton. In 1965 JS Allen and PL Delahaye featured in the Ulster Schools Diving Championships, with JS Allen becoming northwest champion. TK Drought represented Ulster in the Inter Provincial and Irish Schools Championships.

In the 1970s an additional large pool was opened at Templemore Sports Complex, and from that time junior pupils have their weekly swimming lessons at that venue. By this time the school swimming gala had become a thing of the past, but a number of pupils belong to City of Derry Swimming Club, which meets in the William Street baths on Friday evenings, and the best of these compete in inter-schools galas. Some of the most successful of these at the present time are Christine Hamilton, Sarah Hamilton, Rachel Adair and Alex McCorkell.

William Lynn

THE FENCING CLUB

Although there is some record of fencing being taught in the past in both Foyle and Londonderry High School, the revival of this sport was initiated by the new headmaster, Jack Magill, after his appointment in 1994. The Fencing Club was started again in 1996. The headmaster had represented both Northern Ireland and Ireland in his fencing career, was selected for a number of World Cup and World Championships

Foyle College Fencing team, 1998.

Owen McConnell and David Burnside with Gregory Campbell, the minister of sport for Northern Ireland, at Stormont.

and was captain of the Northern Ireland medal-winning team at Commonwealth Championships. The club met two nights a week, with a membership of 20 first- and second-year pupils.

As the club developed and expanded it was felt that a full-time professional coach should be appointed and Mike Westgate, duly appeared in January 2000. He had had experience as a coach to Northern Ireland, Great Britain and Ireland at Olympic, World Cup and World Championship level. The club now meets four times a week and fencing is part of the school physical education programme.

The fencers had immediate successes in Northern Ireland in 1996 and travelled to England and Scotland for competitions. In 1996 Mark Adair became the first Foyle and Londonderry College fencer to be selected for the Northern Ireland junior team for the Schools Quadrangular. The following year seven fencers were selected, and until the end of the tournament in 2006 41 Foyle and Londonderry College fencers represented Northern Ireland at junior level. Mark Adair, David Jackson and Gareth Sykes were selected for the Northern Ireland senior team for the 2002 Commonwealth Championships in Australia. They were joined by Steven Fenwick, Andrew Fenwick and David Downey for the 2006 Commonwealth Championships, and these three also represented Northern Ireland at the 2003 Junior Commonwealth Championships in India.

In 1999 Emma Sykes and Mark Adair were selected by Great Britain for European Cadet tournaments. Mark became the first home-based fencer to be selected for the Cadet World Championships. He was also selected for the Great Britain épée team for the 2000 Championships in USA. The following year Michael Watt was selected for the Championships. From 2002 until 2011 Andrew Fenwick (épée), Steven Fenwick (sabre), David Downey (sabre), David Burnside (épée), Owen McConnell (épée), Raisa Greer (épée) and Niamh Spence (sabre) have represented Ireland at Cadet and/or Junior World and European Championships. David Jackson, Gareth Sykes, Lee Kitson and Claire McMinn have been selected by Great Britain for European Cadet Tournaments and James Nicholl, David Connolly, Richard Magee, Eimile McSorley, Lucia McCafferty, Anna Jackson and Niamh Spence by Ireland for European Cadet Tournaments. Andrew Fenwick won a bronze medal in a World Cup event in Portugal and finished 11th in the Junior World Championships in 2007.

Foyle and Londonderry College fencers have dominated Northern Ireland épée and sabre events both at junior and senior level. They have also won a number of major national titles. Steven Fenwick won the Irish National Senior Sabre Championship in 2002 and followed this with the British Youth (Under-16) 2003, British Cadet 2004 and British Junior 2005 titles. Andrew Fenwick won the British Cadet épée title in 2003, British Junior in 2005. David Downey was Irish Senior sabre champion in 2003 and 2007. David Burnside won the Irish Senior épée title in 2009 and the British Public Schools Championship in 2010.

In 2006 the UK School Games was introduced, involving 11 different sports. Since 2006 23 Foyle and Londonderry College fencers have been selected for the Northern Ireland team for this event. The fencers have been very successful. David Burnside with two individual bronze medals and two team silver medals, Owen McConnell one individual bronze medal and three team silver medals, David O'Donnell, Lee Kitson and James Nicholl all with two team silver medals and Andrew Pollock with one team silver medal.

Jack Magill has presented a cup for fencing that will be awarded to the outstanding fencer in Year 14 at the annual prize night – a fitting tribute to his personal contribution to fencing in the school.

Mike Westgate

FOYLE COLLEGE,
LONDONDERRY.

FINAL REPORT FOR YEAR

Name Robert Bg8.   Age
No. in Form 77   Place

Form	SUBJECT	1st Term	2nd Term	3rd Term	PROGRESS
		60	66	82	
		65	80	72	
English					89
History					
Geography					
Latin			67		
Greek			68	66	
French					60
German					
Mathematics					
Arithmetic			57		
Algebra					
Geometry					

FOYLE

This Certific
B. H. G
in lieu of Fir
by him in Form IV.

Prize Funds were given this year by
boys themselves to deserving objects
war effort.

FOYLE

Christmas, 1936.

F. C. Ch. C

His good deed for

17 FOYLE LIVES

GEORGE FARQUHAR (?1677–1707)

George Farquhar, the last and most decorous of the Restoration dramatists, was a pupil at the Free School, and his studies were interrupted by the siege, which ended in August 1689. It is likely that he was born in Derry in 1677, where his mother had sought 'superior medical assistance', and he was the son of John Farquhar, the curate of Liscooley, near Castlefinn, County Donegal. He was about eight or nine years of age at first attendance and may have played some part in the defence of the city.

Many years later, shortly after George's death, Margaret Pennell, his widow, petitioned Queen Anne, claiming that he had fought on the Williamite side at the Boyne. He may indeed have been there in 1690; there were drummer boys not much older than he. On his return to school he composed 'A Pindarick on the Death of General Schomberg Killed at the Boyne'. Then he was a sizar at Trinity College, Dublin, in 1694 – effectively a college servant, allowed to attend lectures. He left Trinity after an accusation of blasphemy, having remarked about Christ's walking on the water that a man born to be hanged need not fear drowning. He worked for a year for a Dublin bookseller before trying his hand at acting, joining the Smock Alley company in 1696.

Following the accidental stabbing of a fellow actor during a performance that career was cut short, and it was as a playwright with the script of *Love in a Bottle* that he went to London in 1697. The play was a Drury Lane success the following year and his character of Roebuck, 'an Irish gentleman of a wild roving temperament, newly come to London' may have had elements of self-portrait. *The Constant Couple* (1699), about a Restoration rake who underneath is kind, uxorious and highly moral, was so popular that he

wrote *Sir Harry Wildair* (1701), another play featuring his popular hero.

Other important works are *The Twin Rivals* (1702) and *The Recruiting Officer* (1704), that has the ultimate 'breeches' part so much flaunted later by Peg Woffington (1714–60) and based upon his experiences in Holland as a lieutenant in the army. The former play has an Irish servant, Teague, who rescues his feckless master and was a type of effective stage-Irish character, cleverer than their superiors, much used later by another Ulsterman, Charles Macklin (1699–1797). Teague's recipe for survival is typical of Farquhar's wit: 'By eating, dear joy, fen I can get it and by sleeping when I can get none; 'tish the fashion of Ireland'.

OPPOSITE: *A collection of memorabilia from Foyle College's archive.*

Convinced that she was rich Farquhar married Margaret Pennell, ten years his senior but all she brought to the union was three children by her former husband. He bore her no ill-will and she bore him two daughters. Though ill with tuberculosis he worked steadily at his best and last work, *The Beaux' Stratagem* (1707) now part of the classical repertoire, which was presented with great success as he lay dying.

CHARLES MACKLIN (*c.*1697–1797)

Little is known of the earliest years of Charles Macklin, David Garrick's great rival in 18th-century London theatre. He was born McLaughlin, perhaps in Derry but more probably in Culdaff. His precise date of birth has never been established, but as he was believed to have been 100 when he died in 1797, his birth year is taken as 1697. He is thought to have attended the Free School until some years after his father's death in 1704, when on his mother's marriage to Luke O'Meally, a prosperous tavern keeper in Werburgh Street in Dublin, he was transferred to a school at Island Bridge. There he was taught by a man called Nicholson, whose treatment caused in him a lifelong hatred of the Scots.

He began acting playing Monimia, the female lead in a school production of *The Orphan* by Thomas

Mr MACKLIN in the Character of SHYLOCK
Act 4.^ Scene 2.^

Otway (1652–85), a singular piece of miscasting since he was big and burly. At age 17 he ran away from home, having stolen money from his mother, and became a strolling player in the west of England, where he gradually lost his brogue and, despairing of attempts at pronouncing his name properly, shortened it to Macklin. He became an established member of the Theatre Royal company at Drury Lane when he was 33, with a reputation firmly established as a hard drinker and great lover. He was known too for his ungovernable temper; once in a quarrel over a wig he killed a fellow actor. Found guilty of manslaughter and sentenced to be branded, he appeared that night to tremendous applause on Drury Lane stage, the branding carried out with a cold iron.

He continued to dominate the theatre of London and Dublin for 50 years, and his greatest part was Shylock, first played in 1741. His performance brought out the pathos and dignity in a character usually played for low comedy. The couplet: 'This the Jew/That Shakespeare drew' that expressed popular approval is usually credited to Alexander Pope but it is unlikely that the invalid poet who died in 1744 ever saw the performance. In general Macklin introduced a 'naturalness' to acting that at the time was regarded as revolutionary. He wrote ten plays including *Love à-la-Mode* (1759), *The True Born Irishman* (1762) on which Brian Friel based his play *The London Vertigo* (1990) and *The Man of the World* (1781). Married to an Irish actress Ann Grace and after her death to Elizabeth Jones who was the same age as his daughter in both cases after long cohabitation, he was also assumed to have lived in a *ménage-à-trois* with Garrick and Peg Woffington. Failing memory caused him to retire from the stage in 1789 and he died eight years later on 11 July 1797.

SIR HENRY LAWRENCE (1806–57) AND SIR JOHN LAWRENCE (1811–79)

Alexander, George, Henry and John, four of seven sons of Alexander Lawrence of Coleraine, who would later like their father find careers in the India of the Raj, were once pupils of Foyle. Their mother was Letitia Knox from County Donegal, and since her brother, the Revd James Knox, was headmaster it seemed logical to place her boys under his avuncular care. Alexander Junior became a general in the Madras cavalry, and George a lieutenant-general in the Bengal army, so Henry and John were destined

RIGHT: *Major General Alexander Lawrence, 1803–68, attended Foyle 1815–18. He was the oldest of the Lawrence brothers.*

BELOW RIGHT: *The crest of Foyle College.*

BELOW: *Last recorded words of Henry Lawrence, 18 February 1926.*

facilities in the hill stations for them and before he died of wounds at Lucknow he asked that these 'Lawrence Asylums', as they were known, become the responsibility of the government. His mien throughout the long siege was summed up in the words 'No surrender', that had greeted James II at Bishop Gate on 18 April 1689 and were afterwards incorporated in his old school's motto as: 'Ne umquam cesseris'. His last recorded words were characteristically self-effacing: 'Let there be no fuss about me; let me be buried with the men'.

Meanwhile his younger brother John's star was in the ascendant. He was one of 25 old boys of Foyle who found careers in India, in the army and the Indian civil service. He joined the East India Company in 1818 but soon transferred to the civil service. During his time in Delhi he did what he could to prevent the exploitation of people by their oppressive rulers. He identified closely with their native culture, and as commissioner and later lieutenant-governor of the Punjab brought about many reforms in the fields of

to play an important part in the development and political character of their adopted sub-continent.

Henry was destined to die in July 1857 during the Indian Mutiny at the heroic defence of Lucknow, where he made himself responsible for the safety of the 1,800 mainly European people who had sought shelter there. He had been born in Sri Lanka but his parents had no hesitation in sending him back to their native country for a sound education with his uncle James. Between 1828 and 1848 he fought in many of the endemic wars that afflicted the fragmented Orient of the time: in Burma in 1828, in the first Afghan War (1838) and the two Sikh wars of 1845 and 1848. In spite of this necessary military service he was essentially a peacemaker, sincerely believing that *Pax Britannica* was the only solution to the sprawling country's political ills. He was particularly concerned with the condition of the children of the 'other ranks' British soldiers; the mortality rate among these children was unacceptably high and their education was neglected. He set up schools and hospital

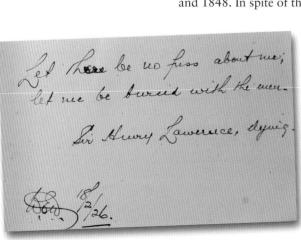

irrigation, railways, urban sanitation, famine relief and defence. Florence Nightingale (1820–1910), the famous 'Lady with the Lamp' of Scutari, was a noted collaborator in his crusade for improved sanitation in the Indian Army, the professional training of nurses and the public health of the people. Though invalided she kept up a vigorous and effective correspondence with him while also continuing to lobby in parliament.

His concern for the plight of the people made him impatient with the many local rulers who were slow to accept his structural and political reforms. In this matter he disagreed with his brother Henry, who preferred a non-intrusive, purely advisory stance. Lord Dalhousie (1812–60), the governor-general, backed John and re-appointed Henry to the minor post of agent in Rajputana. The sense of demotion and exile was felt most bitterly by Henry especially as John climbed steadily to reach the supreme rank of governor-general in 1863, with the title of 1st Baron Lawrence of the Punjab and Grately, though Henry did not live to see that accolade.

Like his father and older brother, John found a wife in County Donegal. Harriet Hamilton must have known that she was accepting as a husband a notorious workaholic who was never known to take a holiday. Such was his reputation that three statues of him were cast in bronze, two placed in London and the third in Calcutta (Kalkota). One of the two London pieces was sent to Lahore and after the convulsions of independence was removed from its plinth and ended in a scrap heap missing its right hand and a sword once held in the left. It was acquired by the Foyle Old Boys Association and journeyed via Karachi to London where its missing bits were restored. Now decently weathered it stands in the Springtown grounds, the fustian clothes and the symbolic supremacy of the pen over the sword making an appropriate mute comment on the character of its subject. He is also remembered as the bearer to London of the Koh-I-Noor diamond, which was presented to Queen Victoria in 1850 by Lord Dalhousie on behalf of the East India Company, to commemorate the 250th anniversary of its foundation by Elizabeth I.

TOP LEFT: *Lord John Lawrence.*

ABOVE: *Statue of Lord John Lawrence at Springtown.*

PERCY FRENCH (1854–1920)

Even today Percy French is celebrated as the lyricist who gave the world such perennials as 'Abdulla Bulbul Ameer' (1877), 'Phil the Fluther's Ball' (1889), 'Shlathery's Mounted Fut' (1889) 'The Mountains of Mourne (1896), 'Eileen Oge' (1903) and 'Come Back, Paddy Reilly, to Ballyjamesduff' (1912). In all he wrote 81 songs, poems and parodies, the songs usually set by his partner Houston Collison (1864–1920). Audiences all over these islands from 1888 until close to his death in 1920 flocked to see a small man with a drooping moustache who played the banjo to accompany his songs, which were sentimental and mildly satirical. He was also a talented water-colourist and his lightning pictures done with chalk were given away to lucky members of the audience. He had the extra trick of doing 'double pictures', turning the canvas on his easel upside down to reveal an entirely different picture, often of the house. And as an encore he did 'smoke-pictures' on plates, merely using the smoke from a candle.

He was born on 1 May 1854 at Clooneyquin, ten miles from the town of Roscommon, and used his second forename Percy (his mother's maiden name)

only when he began his stage career. At Foyle (1870–2) he was known as Willie to his friends and Gulielmus to his headmaster and kinsman, the Revd William Percy Robinson in the inscription on the book *Sound* by John Tyndall, won as a prize for mathematics in June 1872. He had been sent to the school because of its reputation in the subject and by that means successfully entered Trinity College that year. He graduated BA CE in 1881 after a very pleasant eight-year sojourn, having passed, as he phrased it, 'on a cable of cram'. Appointed Inspector of Drains for County Cavan he developed his skills as a painter, met the original of 'Phil the Fluter' and fell in love with Ettie Armitage-Moore, whom he married in 1890. Her death in childbirth and that of their baby in 1891 was a bitter blow that he sublimated by frantic involvement in the travelling entertainment that made his reputation.

While at Foyle he became friendly with Sir John Ross, who afterwards became Lord Chancellor of Ireland. Together they produced a school magazine, believed to be the first such in Ireland, called rather pointedly *The Birch* and later *The Foyle Monthly*. The Foyle connection did not end there. He taught art there for a term *c.*1885 while still an undergraduate at Trinity and was remembered by Frances McClintock, the daughter of Maurice Hime, the headmaster, as having poor class control but as giving her mother water-colours of the school that he had painted during his stay there. Before that he had visited the school as a popular performer at concerts there in June and November 1882 and again in May 1884.

French married Helen May Shelden in 1894 and they had three daughters: Molly, Ettie and Joan; those last two visited Foyle in April 1986 to attend a special concert in their father's honour. He died on tour on 24 January 1922.

JB BURY (1861–1927)

John Bagnell Bury was born on 18 October 1861 in Clontibret, County Monaghan, the son of the Church of Ireland rector. As a boy he showed great promise as a scholar and was one of the boarders who came to Foyle with Maurice Hime in January 1878. Hime knew Robert Yelverton Tyrell, the head of Classics at TCD, and he persuaded him to come to Derry precisely to assess this talent. The boy of ten could not be puzzled in Greek grammar and vocabulary and he was marked by the TCD establishment as 'one for

LEFT: *JB Bury.*

the *Cambridge Ancient History*. Oddly for a man whose first published work was *A Study in Byzantine History* he later dismissed the term 'Byzantine', stating magisterially: 'No "Byzantine Empire" ever existed; the Roman Empire did not come to an end until 1453'– the date of the fall of Constantinople to the Ottoman Turks. Two books on philosophy, *Freedom of Thought* (1914) and *The Idea of Progress* (1920), caused controversy because of their perceived rejection of Christianity, but his revival of the TCD literary journal, *Kottabos*, originally founded by Tyrrell, was generally popular, The Greek word meant a drinks party in which young men in the midst of a philosophical discussion would break to throw wine dregs at a set target as a form of divination.

MARGARET COUSINS (1878–1954)

Margaret 'Gretta' Gillespie was born on 7 November 1878 at the Crescent, Boyle, County Roscommon, to a prosperous Methodist family. She was awarded a scholarship to Victoria High School and afterwards graduated B Mus from the Royal University. In 1903 she married James Cousins, a self-educated Belfast intellectual who became one of the minor figures of the Irish Literary Renaissance. She was a founder of the militant Irish Women's Franchise League in 1908, became its treasurer and was chosen as one of six Irish delegates to the Parliament of Women in London in 1910. She organised the Irish lecture tour of Christabel Pankhurst and chaired the meeting when Sylvia Pankhurst addressed a 'Votes for Women' meeting in Derry. Admitting to breaking windows in Dublin Castle she was jailed for a month in Tullamore and later that same year was given six months in Holloway for throwing stones at 10 Downing Street, experiences she described as a 'living death'. A theosophist since 1908 it seemed logical for her and her husband to emigrate to India in 1915 when they had perceived that women in Ireland were unlikely to be granted the franchise.

One year later she was the only non-Indian member of the Women's University at Poonah, and was one of the founders of the Indian Women's Association in 1917. She became the first headmistress of the National Girls School at Bangalore (1919–20) and in 1923 became the first woman magistrate ever appointed in the Indian subcontinent. Her days of civil disobedience were not past, however. In 1932 as one of the legal establishment she addressed a proscribed meeting in Madras to object to the British

us!' His brilliant career continued there, including a collaboration with John Pentland Mahaffy, then professor of ancient history, in an edition of Euripides' tragedy *Hippolytus*, while still an undergraduate. He secured a double first in 1882 and was made a fellow in 1885, at the age of 24.

Already he was noted for an absorption in research and that was his chief reason for accepting the chair of modern history in 1893. On his election to the Regius professorship of Greek in 1898 he continued to hold the earlier position. He relinquished both chairs when offered the Regius chair of Modern History at Cambridge in 1902. Here he eventually agreed to monitor the work of the medievalist Steven Runciman, best known for his *History of the Crusades*. He later remarked that he had been Bury's 'first and only pupil'. Bury remained at Cambridge until his death in 1927 in Rome, where he was buried. His health began to deteriorate when he was in his early 50s, characterised by intermittent eye-trouble.

He published many works of scholarship, including a demythologised life of St Patrick, a scholarly edition of Edward Gibbons' *The Decline and Fall of the Roman Empire* and a work that linked his two Trinity disciplines of history and classics *A History of Greece* and later in his work as senior editor of

incorporating special powers into the penal code. She was imprisoned for a year in Vellore Women's Jail, during which she went on hunger strike to protest against the imprisonment of Mahatma Gandhi. Incarceration by the British never harmed an Irish person's reputation and after independence in 1947 she was recognised by the new state as a significant contributor to Indian freedom. She left parliament after an accident in 1943 that left her paralysed, and several state officials including Pandit Nehru, the prime minister sent her a total of 15,000 rupees to assist her in her recovery. In 1950 she and her husband published a joint autobiography, *We Two Together,* that told the story of two remarkable lives and of a significant contribution to women's independence and to the freedom of her adopted country. She predeceased James by two years on 11 March 1954 in Adyar, Madras, and is buried there.

Forty years later in September 1994 in response to an invitation by Derry physician Dr Keith Munroe, Margaret Cousins' grandnephew, and Mrs Shobana Ranade, the current head of the All-India Women's Conference that Cousins had founded, paid a visit to Ireland to unveil a plaque in her memory in her native town and also gave an address to the sixth formers of Foyle and Londonderry College.

RIGHT: *Margaret Cousins.*

SIR ARTHUR MORSE KBC CBE LLD (1892–1967)

Arthur Morse was born in County Tipperary on 25 April 1892, the second son of Digby Scott Morse, who was a manager with the Bank of Ireland according to the Irish Census of 1901. At that time Arthur was eight years old and he appears to have been educated at home before being sent to Foyle, as the census also shows that there was a governess living in the home at that time in Mount Bellew, Galway. According to the school's records he entered Foyle on 4 September 1906 as pupil number 4,762. There is little or no record of his academic achievements and according to his own report, when I had lunch with him in May 1961, he ran away from the school by jumping through a window. He still had fond memories of the school and made a visit in his later years. With his help numerous Old Boys, including Clarence Walker, Paul Huey, Roy Gault, Tommy Campbell, Freddy Williamson and myself found positions in the bank. He would entertain to lunch in the manager's room new recruits from his old school prior to their being posted to Hong Kong.

Arthur Morse went to the Far East about 1913 and served in various offices throughout the region with furlough back to the United Kingdom every five years.

By 1941 Morse found himself in management in the Hong Kong and Shanghai Bank in London. He was 47 and evidently the right person to take charge in a crisis. On 13 December Morse received a cable from the Colonial Office indicating that Sir Vandeleur Grayburn, the chief manager, has asked for an Order in Council transferring the bank's head office to London and his appointment as acting general manager if the bank should fall into the hands of the Japanese.

Morse wrote: 'I arranged a conference on Monday with the Colonial Office at which it was concluded that to leave control in Hong Kong till the colony was in the hands of the enemy would mean a temporary freezing of the bank's assets, especially in America'. The result of that meeting was that he was authorised to take control and on 16 December he instructed all offices not to take any further instructions from Hong Kong. He then sought to ensure that the transfer to London, authorised by the Colonial Office, precluded the possibility of the bank's assets being frozen in America and called on the governor of the Bank of England, Montagu Norman, to inform him of the

position. Norman was concerned that the action already taken might not be legally sound and advised that the British government should make a public announcement of the transfer.

Morse arranged that announcement through the Colonial Office and the Order in Council was issued on 13 January 1943. One of Morse's duties in London was to keep in touch with the bank staff and their relatives interned by the Japanese in Hong Kong and other countries in the Far East. Morse returned to Hong Kong in early 1946 and reopened the head office in accordance with an Order in Council dated 15 May 1946 and at a general meeting in June he was confirmed as chief manager and elected a director and chairman. He then took key actions to restore the colony to normal.

Morse remained reasonably optimistic about the situation in China, although that changed dramatically when the Communists took control and the bank was forced to close all its branches in that country except the one in Shanghai. In a speech at a later shareholders meeting he stated: 'We see a revolution in progress of development'. But he was hesitant to express any opinion except to say that as the Communists must industrialise China if she is to hold her own in the modern world and she will need the services of worldwide banks.

Arthur Morse should be regarded as the founder of today's bank, now probably the biggest in the world, and although the bank lost its Chinese branches the reconstruction of industry in Hong Kong paid the bank well and its assets rose from £94m to £220m. He retired as chief manager in March 1953 and became

chairman of the London committee of the bank. His services to the community were recognised by the honorary degree of LLD from Hong Kong University in 1940, when he was its treasurer, his CBE in 1944 for his management of the Far Eastern Relief Fund, which he founded to look after families in England whose men were interned by the Japanese, and his knighthood in 1949 for his restoration work in Hong Kong. Sir Arthur Morse died on 13 May 1967 and a memorial service was held in St John's Cathedral, Hong Kong, on 8 June 1967.

SR Stewart

WILLIAM STAVELEY FERGUSON BA (1894–1972)

WS Ferguson, son of Revd Samuel Ferguson, was born at Mile End, Caw, on 27 July 1894 and became a pupil of the Foyle preparatory department in September 1903. In the main school he was awarded exhibitions in Classics in the junior, middle and senior grades of the Intermediate Education Board for Ireland. In 1912 he entered QUB with an entrance scholarship in Classics and obtained the Blayney Exhibition in June 1914. In October 1915 he won the Porter Scholarship, graduating in June 1916 with an honours BA in Classics.

In September he joined the staff of the Wolverley Grammar School, Kidderminster, and stayed until 1920. Returning to Foyle as the Classics master he would spend the rest of his career there until his retirement in 1957. After 1945, with the school organised into departments, he became head of the Classics department and from 1952 was the vice-principal. From February 1961 he served as a governor of the school.

It came as no surprise, considering his absorption in Foyle history, that he was a foundation member of FCOBA when it was set up in 1928. He served as a committee member and later treasurer. From 1933 he was the joint secretary of the association and when Alan Roberts joined him in 1953 they, along with George Gillanders ran it for the next 20 years. During that time 27 dinners, and lunches were organised in Derry, Belfast and London. He minuted all committee meetings with infinite care and perused newspapers, university libraries and other sources for information relating to the school and its Old Boys. When the Lawrence statue became available in Lahore in 1959, he persevered with the negotiations until it was successfully transferred to Lawrence Hill in March 1962. In 1960–1 he was the president of the FCOBA.

Throughout his life Will assiduously assembled archival material relevant to the history of Derry and the school. He collected maps and letters, and built registers of Foyle pupils who attended TCD from 1683. He published a major work on grammar school education in Ireland before 1800 and contributed articles to the school magazine. After his retirement he was the Honorary City Archivist and worked with Alan Roberts to publish many articles relating to Foyle. Alan later came into possession of Will's archival material of the school and he added to it during his lifetime. The school now has both archives, and they have been used extensively in order to prepare this manuscript of the history of the school. It is no exaggeration to claim that without his work and that of Alan this history of Foyle would have been a more paltry and less comprehensive affair. There is also a WS Ferguson Archive in PRONI, and part of it was used when *Maps and Views of Derry 1600–1914: A Catalogue by WS Ferguson* was published jointly by the Royal Irish Academy and Derry City Council in 2005. WS Ferguson died on 31 July 1972, after a lifetime of service to our school.

TOP RIGHT: Garden Green, *1962, by Norah McGuinness (c.1901–80).*

RIGHT: *William Staveley Ferguson.*

NORAH McGUINNESS DLITT HRHA (1901–80)

Norah McGuinness was born in Derry on 7 November 1901, the daughter of a coal merchant and shipowner, and was educated at Victoria High School, 18 Crawford Square. She showed artistic promise while still at school and her first life classes were taken at Derry Technical School. At 18 she began study at the Metropolitan School of Art in Dublin, where her teachers were Patrick Tuohy, Oswald Reeves and Harry Clarke. It was through Clarke that she got in 1926 her first design commission, to illustrate *A Sentimental Journey* by Lawrence Sterne. Book illustration became something of a specialty and she was praised by such authors as Elizabeth Bowen, whose monograph on the Shelbourne Hotel she wittily illustrated in 1951. Her pictures for Yeats's *Red Hanrahan and the Secret Rose* (1927) so pleased the mage that he wrote to her: 'I like their powerful simplicity ... you have done me great service and I thank you'. Another author whose work she visually interpreted was Maria Edgeworth, author of *Castle Rackrent*.

She led a Bohemian life (in a decorously Irish way) in Dublin in the 1920s and became an important figure in the literary and theatrical life of the city, easily accessible from her cottage in Wicklow. She designed sets for the Abbey and the Peacock productions of Yeats's *Deirdre* and *The Importance of Being Earnest*. Acquaintance and later friendship with such major artistic figures as Mainie Jellett, Evie Hone and Mary Swanzy followed, and on Jellett's advice she went to study in Paris under Andre l'Hote in 1929. By then her three-year-old marriage to Geoffrey Phibbs, a poet whose pen-name was Geoffrey Taylor, had ended in divorce. During the 1930s she travelled in Egypt and India and worked in London and New York, before returning to Dublin in 1939. Her output of watercolours and gouaches was prodigious – in 1968 her retrospective in the Douglas Hyde Gallery in Dublin had more than 100 items – and with her interest in theatrical costume she was the designer of sales windows for Altman's in New York and Brown Thomas in Grafton Street in Dublin for 30 years.

One of the founders of the Irish Exhibition of Living Art, she succeeded Jellett as president in 1944 and with Nano Reid she represented Ireland at the Venice Biennale in 1950. At the first appearance of her work at the Royal Hibernian Academy in 1924 Norah was granted the status of honorary member (HRHA) in 1957 but resigned in 1969. In 1977 she received an Honorary DLitt from TCD. Her work may be found in all the major Irish public collections including the Hugh Lane Gallery, Dublin, the National Gallery of Ireland, the Crawford in Cork and the Ulster Museum in Belfast. She died in a Dublin hospital on 22 November 1980.

MINA HOLMES CHRISTIE (1909–2001)

Miss Christie – it seems almost disrespectful to refer to her in any other way – was the last headmistress of Londonderry High School, serving from 1973 when Miss Cowper retired until the amalgamation with Foyle in 1976 (though near to retiring age she was persuaded to stay until the planned conflation should take place). She did this out of a sense of duty but also as the person best placed to ensure that the tradition and ethos of Londonderry High School should be continued under the new dispensation. These values she helped sustain and so contributed to a successful union of what had seemed serious, if not irreconcilable, differences.

She had come to Duncreggan as boarding mistress in 1951 after years as a missionary in Damascus, the

ABOVE: *Miss Christie with Mrs Price-Owen and Senior Girls, 1975.*

LEFT: *Landscape painted by Miss MacKillip.*

experiences of which greatly imbued her remainder life. (Her excellence in her other subject, French, was acquired while her father worked for the Presbyterian Church in Nimes.) She insisted on near-perfect French accents from her language students, and tried to inculcate the same pupil involvement in Scripture, as

RE was known in those days. An automobile accident had left her with only one working eye, which had the effect of increasing attention from her often daunted pupils. She had a simple trick of inviting the members of her French classes to bring with them hand mirrors (of which even the first years had no lack) so that they could understand the full anatomical and physiological aspects of speech and accent.

She had a wide range of extra-scholastic interests, including the rearing of goats and dogs. She was an amateur of china and silver, and effortlessly and unobtrusively indicated the existence of a private elegance of taste and appreciation of the finer things of life – an important part of true education. The Northern Ireland 'Troubles' were at their height during her headship but typically, as part of a coffee morning for charity held in the school, one of the items that produced a mixture of delight and awe was her presentation of a large number of table place-settings using her own vast store of antique silver and china.

On retirement she went to live with her sister Betty in the family home at Burren, near Ballynahinch, County Down. Betty became ill, having suffered a stroke, and Mina nursed her for ten years until she died. She herself suffered grievously from osteoporosis but her mind was sharp and active until her death on 2 February 2001.

NOEL WILLMAN (1918–88)

Noel Bath Willman was born in Derry on 4 August 1918, the son of Romain Willman, a native of Alsace, and who owned and ran the leading gentlemen's hairdresser in the town. He entered Foyle in 1929 and made his acting debut in December 1934 as Elizabeth Barrett, in Rudolph Besier's West End hit *The Barretts of Wimpole Street* (1930), which told the story of the dramatic wooing of the invalid poet by Robert Browning, and of their elopement in spite of the strong opposition of her father. The play ran for three nights and it became clear even then that his was a remarkable talent. The editorial in *Our School Times* printed at Easter 1935 noted that: 'The longest and heaviest part was that of Elizabeth, and although it is now three months since December and one's enthusiasm must cool when the cause is so far removed, we still think that for beauty, sympathy and entire conviction, Willman's acting was extraordinary'. That reputation was reinforced by his performance as Raleigh, the idealistic young lieutenant, in an excerpt from the anti-war play *Journey's End* (1928) by RC Sherriff that won him first prize at Londonderry Feis.

After graduation from RADA he was in repertory with the Old Vic Company in London, The Playhouse in Liverpool and in Stratford. His prestigious stage debut was as Hamlet at the Lyceum Theatre in London, but his almost feline delicacy and capacity for menace were better seen in such roles as Claudius in the same play, Judge Brack, Hedda Gabler's nemesis and Don Pedro in *Much Ado about Nothing*. His finest acting was seen as the Interrogator in *The Prisoner* by Brigid Boland in 1954, playing opposite Alec Guinness. In addition he made more than 20 film appearances with performances that mingled a grisly humour with an unease that was chilling. He appeared often on television, never giving an undistinguished performance.

As a stage director he was equally successful, and in Robert Bolt he found an ideal collaborator, directing his play *A Man for All Seasons* (1960) in London in 1960 and winning a Tony Award for its direction on Broadway in 1962. He made his home in New York but returned regularly to Europe for stage, film and television work, both as actor and director. He died at home in New York of a heart attack on Christmas Eve, 1988, in his 71st year.

Rod Steiger, Noel Willman, Omar Sharif in Dr Zhivago *(1965).*

Alan Roberts (1924–2012)

David Alan Eccles Roberts was born in Derry in June 1924 and became a pupil of Foyle preparatory school in September 1930. His apparently idyllic sojourn there he later celebrated in a tribute in 1988 to Katherine Wright, the prep's remarkable principal. Gifted both intellectually and physically, he had a brilliant academic and sporting career at Foyle. Winner of the Lieutenant JH Barr memorial prize for Classics in 1941, he was captain of the school the following year and was awarded the Lawrence Memorial Medal. He gained colours for cricket and rugby before proceeding to TCD to study English and Spanish.

In 1943, when just 19, he decided to leave the safety of academe for involvement in World War II as a non-commissioned officer with the Royal Marines. He became a member of the 30th Assault Group Royal Marine Commandos that operated behind enemy lines before and after D-day. It was a period of his life about which it was difficult to draw him and those who knew him in later life as a genial, witty, helpful university librarian found it impossible to imagine this alternative lifestyle. After VE day he was seconded to the Education Corps and became a qualified instructor

in the Forces Educational and Vocational Training scheme until his demob in 1946, when he returned to TCD.

The wholesome balance of physical and mental activity continued; he graduated in 1950 with a Moderatorship in modern literature and completed his MA in 1958. While an undergraduate he was a member of the university cricket club and captain of the 2nd XI in 1949. His fluency in Spanish was used to good effect during the years 1951–3, when he worked as assistant export manager for the firm of Clark and Sons, Upperlands, County Derry. Returning to Derry he became a director and company secretary of the family firm of motor engineers located in Foyle Street. When the firm ceased to trade in 1967 he joined the library of the New University of Ulster at Magee. He remained there until his retirement in 1984.

After his return home Alan continued his involvement in rugby and cricket – captain of the City of Derry 1st XV (1954–5) and permanent vice-president as well as membership of the cricket club. Even dearer was his other passion, FCOBA. Much of his leisure time was dedicated to Association affairs, acting as honorary treasurer for many years and combining with WS Ferguson and GC Gillanders to organise the annual dinners at home and other Old Boy luncheons in Belfast and London. He shared with Ferguson an absorption in the past history of Foyle and of the several strands that went eventually to make up Londonderry High School. Like Ferguson he was jealously protective of any scrap of the school's archival material and contributed historical essays to the association's journal. Together they compiled the invaluable *Old Boys' Chronicle*. Because of this assiduous concern many important elements of the school's history that might otherwise have been lost were preserved for posterity. Alan, like Ferguson, though now sadly silenced, must be regarded as a leading contributor to the present volume. He died on 15 March 2012 and is buried in Ballyoan cemetery.

Hazel Cathcart Helliwell (1928–88)

Hazel Storey was born in Monasterevin, County Kildare, in 1928 and educated in Celbridge in the same county. Aware of the relative obscurity of her place of birth, she derived a wry pleasure after the autumn of 1975 when Monasterevin acquired a certain notoriety because of the Teide Herrema kidnapping.

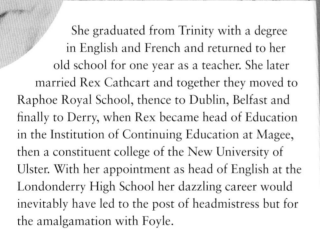

Hazel Cathcart Helliwell. Trees in the grounds of Duncreggan were labelled in her memory.

She graduated from Trinity with a degree in English and French and returned to her old school for one year as a teacher. She later married Rex Cathcart and together they moved to Raphoe Royal School, thence to Dublin, Belfast and finally to Derry, when Rex became head of Education in the Institution of Continuing Education at Magee, then a constituent college of the New University of Ulster. With her appointment as head of English at the Londonderry High School her dazzling career would inevitably have led to the post of headmistress but for the amalgamation with Foyle.

Her years at Londonderry High School were characterised by wit, kindness, grace and high efficiency. Her love of literature and drama was patent, and her particular interest was characteristically in the works of Jane Austen, relishing the clear-eyed worldview of her favourite author. She made many visits to the Royal Shakespeare Theatre at Stratford and to the West End, enamoured of the glamour but retaining a wise and critical scepticism, which she could use to devastating effect. As an expert at the cryptic crosswords of the *Guardian* and *Times*, she survived many rounds of the fiendishly difficult radio quiz *Ask Me Another*. She fought and won a battle with cancer, an experience that deepened her store of empathy with those in trouble and made her a ready resource of comfort or salutary advice for pupils and fellow staff members alike.

After amalgamation her management skills greatly helped overcome the teething problems of the coeducational school and her marriage in 1987 to fellow English teacher Denis Helliwell seemed strikingly appropriate. Her sudden and tragic death in a car accident on 19 November 1988 left her husband, three children and her many friends of both town and gown shocked and bewildered. Her memory is preserved in the labelling of the trees in the grounds of Duncreggan and in the hearts of those who loved her.

AMANDA BURTON (1956–)
Amanda Burton was born on 10 October 1956, the youngest of four sisters in Balloughry, County Derry, in the schoolhouse where her father was principal. She was a pupil at Londonderry High School from 1968 to 1975 and then went to study acting at the Manchester Metropolitan School of Theatre. Her first part was as

Eva Birthistle (1974–)

Eva Birthistle moved to Derry in 1988 and attended Foyle and Londonderry College for three years. On completing her GCSE she went to the Northwest Institute of Further Education to do a B Tech in performing arts. It was under the tuition of Gordon Fulton that her love of acting was born. She then went back to Dublin to continue studying her craft. After training at the Gaiety School of Acting she got her first TV role on the long established show *Glenroe*. For the next five years Eva worked on numerous Irish feature films including *Borstal Boy*, *All Souls' Day* and *The American*.

In 2001 she moved to London and has worked steadily in TV and film ever since. In 2004 she starred in Ken Loach's *Ae Fond Kiss* and for her performance received a joint win with Kate Winslet at the London Critics Film Circle Awards and an Irish Film and Television award. She has since worked with a large number of esteemed directors and actors: Neil Jordan, Peter Greenaway, Liam Neeson, Olivia Williams and many more, earning her awards and nominations along the way. This year she can be seen starring in the thriller *Case Sensitive* for ITV, *Amber* for RTE and the Irish comedy feature *Life's a Breeze* starring Pat Shortt and Fionnuala Flanagan.

Eliza Doolittle in an excerpt from *Pygmalion* for an Inter-schools Drama Festival, and there then followed a memorable performance as Lady Macbeth in the St Columb's College production for 1975. She was at the Metropolitan for three years and while there married her first husband Jonathan Hartley, a theatre technician.

She became the best-known character in the gritty Channel 4 Liverpool-based drama series *Brookside*, in which she played the accountant Heather Black. After four years she asked to be written out of the series and appeared in a number of individual television dramas such as *Minder*, *Morse* and *Van Der Valk*, and as Michael Elphick's Irish boss Margaret Daly in *Boon*. In 1989 she married Sven Arnstein and had two daughters Phoebe (b.1989) and Bríd (b.1991). They were divorced in 2004. She continued her career as Dr Beth Glover in *Peak Practice* (1993–5) and as everybody's favourite pathologist Professor Sam Ryan in *Silent Witness* (1996–2004). Most recently she appeared as Karen Fisher, the new headmistress in *Waterloo Road*, but in 2011 confounded producers and public alike by leaving after 30 highly popular editions.

FOYLE AND THE PROVISION OF MEDICAL CARE IN DERRY AND DONEGAL

Since the 18th century, a significant number of our pupils entered the medical profession and some had distinguished careers in many parts of the world, where they worked in the services, the colonial administration, academia and more recently in the NHS. For example, of 77 pupils who came to Foyle in 1917, 13 would become medically qualified and two would become professors, CHG Macafee (QUB) and ACT Campbell (Manchester). In this piece we have focused mainly on the provision of medical care locally and looked at the contribution of doctors who were our former pupils.

Prior to the establishment of the NHS most doctors worked from home and some surgery was carried out in nursing homes. In 1810 the City and County Hospital opened as a general hospital on the Northland Road. By 1829 the asylum on the Strand Road became available while in the Waterside in 1840 the Workhouse and Fever Hospital provided care for patients with fevers and infectious diseases. Later it would be known as St Columb's Hospital for Chest Diseases, sited then in St Columb's Park, and it would eventually transfer to a site at Gransha Hospital. In 1894 in Bridge Street, Dr Donaldson and Dr Hunter opened an Ear, Nose and Throat Hospital which later became the Eye, Ear, Nose and Throat Hospital when it moved to the Northland Road with services in Ophthalmology provided by Dr Killen. In 1927 Dr 'Lex' Johnston opened a laboratory in his house at Bayview Terrace and would provide a pathology service for the doctors of Derry and Donegal.

Demands on the City and County Hospital continued to increase, and by the 1930s the hospital board knew it needed to expand. With plans to provide a new obstetric unit, a children's ward and a surgical unit, by 1939 the board had collected £45,000. During World War II the hospital valiantly continued to cope with the demand from both civilian and naval casualties. In 1945 a delegation that included Dr Johnston met the minister of health, Mr Grant, hoping he would agree to their plans for an expansion. They could hardly believe their luck when the go-ahead was given for the building of a completely new general hospital on a 50-acre site. This, the first large general and maternity hospital built after the advent of the NHS and initially an 11-storey building, was Altnagelvin Hospital, which would admit its first patients on 1 February 1960 with remarkably little ceremony. Dr Johnston wrote: 'One day we were all working at the City and County and the next we were working at Altnagelvin'. Soon afterwards the Eye, Nose, Ear and Throat hospital would move to this site.

At the same time, provision for psychiatric services was being put in place, with Gransha Hospital being built in five stages from 1957. This was the first new psychiatric hospital to be built in the UK after the war. During that next decade all patients were transferred from the old asylum, with Dr Donald Dawson and Dr Raymond Haire leading the way for the changes which also put community services in place. Since then Altnagelvin and Gransha Hospital have provided care to the citizens of Derry and Donegal, and over the years there has been continuing development of medical services on both sites.

Altnagelvin Hospital.

18

REMINISCENCES OF SCHOOL LIFE

LONG LONG AGO
[excerpted from *Foyle College Times* (FCT)
Spring 1976 (Vol. 38)]

In September 1916 I entered Foyle as a boarder and due to the education I received and the fun of being alive then, I still have pleasant memories of the events of the subsequent two years.

Foyle in my time was in two parts known to us as the Upper and Lower Schools, this terminology being an account of their respective heights above the river and not to any question of importance, or proximity to heaven. The Upper, on Academy Road, comprised living quarters for the boarders and some masters, while the Lower was where the formal education took place, and was seldom, if ever, entered by masters or pupils except during teaching hours. Understandably, therefore, my remarks will be mostly about the Upper School, though the Lower was more important academically speaking.

The Upper School comprised three separate buildings, namely a large three-storey house used for sleeping and eating, one of two storeys known as the gymnasium building and an indoor swimming pool between them, arranged in such a way as to form three sides of a rectangle used as a yard. The open ground incorporated in the school area consisted of a garden or landscape strip between the house and the road and a sizeable grass field at the back intended for games. It was surrounded by a high wall but unfortunately had a very steep slope.

The headmaster and his wife had living accommodation at the far end of the house, while the rest of that building was devoted to the resident masters and the boarders. The masters had single bed-sits and the 60 boys slept in dormitories on the second and third floors. There were seven dormitories, some

with as many as 14 beds. Food was an obsession and difficult to obtain because of the German blockade. Breakfast at 8am was porridge, bread and 'marge' and dinner at 1pm might be of anything, but always meagre, uninviting and mostly of potatoes with very little, if any meat and that of doubtful origin. Tea was at 6pm, often with bread only, the bread being khaki coloured and frequently laced with pieces of string or similar foreign matter. At 9pm before retiring, we had bread again, this time soaked in dripping, and some sort of drink. Fortunately there were some weekly-boarders, mostly from Donegal, and they brought back after their weekends some of the scarce foods, which they generously shared with friends. The lack of decent food and the shortage of adequate heating – it seemed always cold – were the most unpleasant aspects of boarding life in those days.

Mr RF Dill, the headmaster, though capable in several ways was somewhat remote from the other masters and the boys. Though living at the Upper, he was seldom seen except at dinner in the dining-room or when there was a 'crisis'. On such occasions he would descend in a violent temper, followed by his wife trying to calm him down. Mrs Dill was a charming and cultured lady, sharing great popularity with Bella, the head of the kitchen and domestic staff, because they both sided with the boys in any confrontation.

There were three other masters resident at the Upper, namely Messrs Threfall, Davidson and Scott. Mr Threfall, known as 'Mushy', was a very old and portly gentleman. He took some German classes in his room, which he seldom left. Mr James Davidson was the maths master and the strictest disciplinarian in the school. He was an excellent teacher and very loyal to the school where he remained until retirement.

OPPOSITE: *Staff and pupil spectators at the semi-final of Ulster Schools Cup (rugby) at Ravenhill, 1980.*

He had a very good nature, with a sense of humour. Mr Bob Scott, the English master who was better able to mix with the boys and was very well liked, stayed only about a couple of years, then left to become headmaster of St Andrew's College, Dublin.

Rain, hail or snow, we walked in crocodile twice a day to and from the Lower School, i.e. down in the morning, up and down at midday for dinner and up after school, always with a master in attendance – a boring business, only relieved by a glimpse of waving and smiling 'Skinnies' (the Victoria High School girls) as we threaded our way through the passage to Crawford Square. School started at 9am when the headmaster read briefly from Scripture and prayed. In the autumn of 1916 he announced the appointment of prefects for the first time, two from the dayboys and two from the boarders. Prefects could wear a special metal badge on their caps and had the authority to give 'lines'. This power was very seldom used and never by the dayboy prefects. The boarding prefects had the wonderful privilege of going out of the school premises without permission in spare periods.

The Lower School building was somewhat run down and down-at-heel. The masters included Messrs Foster, Samuels (the 'Goat', on account of his beard), Galbraith, Bland and Mercier ('Tarts', a Frenchman). Alec Foster, who efficiently coached the Foyle team and taught Latin left in 1917 to become headmaster of BRA. Samuels taught geometry and algebra, rode a motor-bike and caught fish in his spare time. Galbraith (chemistry) and Bland (various subjects) were highly thought of. 'Tarts' was a character, very pleasant withal, outstanding in his passion for behaving as he thought the British behaved. The building also accommodated a primary school with its schedule so arranged that its protégés could never be contaminated by us.

Sport then meant rugby and cricket, which were the only games played against other schools. The overriding consideration was success in the Ulster Schools Rugby Cup competition, in which Foyle had recently reached the final several times, winning in 1915 under the captaincy of AH Matthews.

Other activities in 1918 included an attempt to restart a rowing club on the river, a resuscitation of the Athletics Day at Brandywell, and the organisation of a public concert in one of the city halls, the artists being pupils and friends, and especially soldiers from the barracks at Waterside, who very generously took over a large part of the programme.

The school has changed vastly and improved in many ways but I hope I may be forgiven for saying that I am glad my time at Foyle was during the days of long, long ago.

OW Gilmour
[Colonel Oswald W Gilmour MA was a pupil at Foyle 1916–18. He was president of FCOBA (1971–2)]

FOUR GENERATIONS

After reading the recent former pupils' magazine, I was inspired to record a few details of both my own experiences at Londonderry High School and that of my four sons and three grandsons plus one granddaughter at Foyle and Londonderry College.

As a recently returned evacuee during the war years I was enrolled in January 1945. My entrance exam was conducted at Miss McIlroy's desk in her private office all on my own! At 11 years old it was intimidating. I enjoyed the following six years (actually rising to the dizzy heights of becoming a prefect). My future career was influenced by coming first in Northern Ireland in Domestic Science exam. (I also spent a year between at Northlands.) So I proceeded to Belfast College, where I became head girl. After qualifying as Domestic Science teacher I taught for 14 years, interrupted by the birth of my four sons. They all attended Foyle and followed on to university. The eldest son, John became an engineer (Edinburgh University), Richard an archaeologist (Sheffield

OW Gilmour.

A HUNDRED YEARS AGO IT WAS NOT EASY TO GET AN EDUCATION

The story of my uncle Dr David Glenn Roulston is an example of the lengths a student went to to get his education:

David Glenn Roulston was born at Creeve, Carrigans, County Donegal in 1897 and travelled by pony and trap into the Model School and to Foyle on the Killea road before it was paved. The ten miles to the city are nothing today but it was then difficult with no public transportation and the surface being too rough even for a bicycle. He stayed four nights each week in Londonderry with family friends.

David started at Queen's University when only 16 and graduated with a medical degree before he was 21. David went to England following graduation and started a medical practice with a fellow Queen's graduate. In 1940 he got out of his sick bed to help neighbours following the bombing of homes in his neighbourhood and died a few days later of pneumonia. David's schooling was paid for by John James Glenn, brother of his grandmother Mary Glenn.

Alex W Roulston

University), Andrew media, TV and films (Stirling University) and Mark, who went into business.

John worked both in Norway and Indonesia as field engineer for a number of years until he took over his late father's business. John married Asrim from Reykjavik, having met as students at Edinburgh University. Their son is John B McClean. Richard was the adventurer. Having worked on archaeological digs for a number of years he proceeded on his adventures around the world. Andrew was film director for Paul Wieland both in London and Hollywood, US. He later became media representative for Europe. He married Sarah and they have three children. Mark married Wendy and live north of Barcelona in the 'Bay of Roses'. Mark works at property business in Spain.

Richard (the adventurer) was hard to keep up with. He cycled France (north to south) and Spain (north to south). The Himalayas were next. He and his friend travelled up and down that area and raised money for the local hospice. Richard then, forever on the go, travelled Africa (north to south, east and west) – 15,000 miles *solo* on a mountain bike! He passed through 22 countries in Africa, climbed five mountains en route and bungeed over Victoria Falls. He swam with sharks (in a cage) at South Africa. He met up with pygmies, who took him for a meal (monkey stew). They shot monkeys with bow and arrows (poison-tipped). He was chased on the bike by wild dogs. While climbing Kilimanjaro, his rucksack was taken at night from outside his small tent by a hyena. He lost warm clothes and food. These are only a few of the things that happened in Africa. He survived it all have undergone hunger and danger at times.

Richard then announced he was going to climb Mount McKinley (highest mountain in North America). He flew to Alaska and joined a party of ten. They were almost at the summit when a snow blizzard came on so they had to stay put in a tent until it abated, one week later. However, they continued on and made the summit of 20,000 feet with a temperature of –40°C at the top. Richard built himself a lovely chalet home in Briacon, France some 3,000 feet up in the Alps (near to a ski slope). We had lovely holidays in September 2009 with him. The scenery is magnificent.

When John, my eldest son was at Foyle, I heard on the radio one morning about a new Outward Bound course. We mentioned it to the headmaster and John was the very first pupil to go on the very adventurous course, which he thoroughly enjoyed. Many other boys took part in the following years, including Richard, who was sent to the Black Forest, Germany. (I wonder does the course still exist?) Richard had the honour of being presented to Queen Elizabeth who asked him all about his wonderful journey through Africa on a bike. Prince Philip also joined in and asked lots of questions.

On to the next generation. My grandson John B (2004) as head boy excelled at Foyle and after four years at Oxford gained a first-class honour degree in maths and physics. His last post was in Amsterdam with the European Space Programme. He now has a position with Rolls Royce. Keen on music, JB was a member of the Oxford orchestra and choir. At present there are three more of my grandchildren at Foyle. Counting my aunt that makes four generations at Foyle (and Londonderry High School) in total!

I wish the new school every success in the future, keeping up its excellent reputation in education.

Hilary (Selfridge) McClean

THE FOYLE BOYS AT THOMSON MCLINTOCK AND CO. IN GLASGOW IN THE 1940s AND 1950s

In the days before careers counselling at Foyle, the headmaster Mr McConnell sent the following students to Thomson McLintock and Co. (TML) Chartered Accountants, in Glasgow: Harry Best (1943), Brian Roberts (Alan's brother) (1946), Alexander Roulston (1951), Blair Smith (1952), Billy Regan (1953), Gavin Kelly and Tom Rankin in 1957.

Initially we travelled from Londonderry to Glasgow overnight in the Burns and Laird boat. It took 12 hours and we usually sat up all night as there were few bunks. Gavin's father worked for Burns and Laird and he usually got one of the two-person berth cabins. Often there were live cattle in the hold of the ship and between their roaring all night and some drunken Irishmen, we did not get much sleep. In later years we flew to Belfast and took the train to Londonderry. In Glasgow we lived in digs. In 1951 I paid £2 per week for lodging, which included breakfast, dinner and laundry.

Harry Best came back to Belfast and worked in public accounting. Brian Roberts joined the Dunlop Rubber Company in 1954 and remained with the group for 18 years, mainly in Brazil, as finance director, but also with spells in India and Malaysia. Brian retired in 1988 after a further 17 years in Brazil with Reckitt and Colman, as *Contador Gerente*.

I emigrated in 1960 to Canada, joined Johnson and Johnson (JNJ) and spent 33 years with them in Canada, Brazil and USA, the last eight years as worldwide corporate controller. Blair Smith stayed in Glasgow and became a tax partner with TML, which later merged to become part of the international accounting firm KPMG.

Gavin Kelly spent a few years in industry before returning to the accounting profession in 1980 and starting his own practice in Merseyside, England. Gavin is still working and two of his sons have joined him. Tom Rankin spent 29 years in Glasgow, 14 with TML and 15 with Yarrow Shipbuilders, the last nine as Financial Director. Tom then had 13 years in Belfast with Short Brothers finishing his active working life as VP treasurer and secretary of the Belfast subsidiary of Bombardier. We had a great start to our education at Foyle and the accountancy training in Scotland prepared us well for our future careers. Brian, Blair, Tom and I are enjoying retirement in England, Scotland, Ireland and the United States respectively.

Alex W Roulston

FOYLE, 1945–51

My father took me to see Mr McConnell, the headmaster, at the Academy Road (Upper School) on the morning the school opened in August 1945. Afterwards I was escorted to Mr Craig's classroom for the second period. My classmates had started that morning down at Lawrence Hill (Lower School), so I waited outside the door as it was locked. Shortly along came Mr Craig with his torn gown flowing behind, and without a good morning he took out his key and tried to open the door. Then he hit me across the side of the head and said 'who stuck putty on my key hole?' The putty was hard and it took some time to remove it with a penknife.

The armed forces had used the Lower School facility during the war and had just handed it back to the school that summer. We had many classes that first year at both facilities and walked through Crawford Square as we moved between them. This gave us an opportunity to wave to the high school girls at Northlands. The Lower School building was in bad shape, with holes in the wall, and badly needed a coat of paint that first year.

Many of the staff had joined up during the war and in 1945 had not yet returned, so we had teachers who

had retired before the war, back teaching temporarily. Mr Davison was our mathematics teacher and I thought he was very old. On the first day he came into class with great difficulty, sat at his desk and put a large flask of coffee on it. The desk was on a small platform, and he never left his chair during class and sat sipping his coffee. He started the first day by asking us to stand in turn and give our name. When it was my turn, he asked if I was the son of John Roulston, a farmer near Carrigians. When I confirmed that I was, he told us about a great doubles badminton match he had played with my father many years before.

The janitor, who we called Sergeant, had been in World War I. He was really ancient and stood in the middle of the gym with a rope and had us run around the room in a circle. If he thought a pupil was 'slacking', he hit him with the rope to make him go faster. We did not change shoes or clothes to take gym, and went to the next class a little sweaty and no doubt smelly (hopefully no one noticed the unpleasant odour).

The boarders lived at the Upper School, and that was where we had lunch every day. I soon learned that if I ate quickly and got back in line (if I was not caught) I would get a second helping. The usual diet was mince meat, potatoes and vegetables. The boarders were small in number, many coming from Donegal, and had the use of an indoor swimming pool at the Upper School.

There were no school buses in those days, and the day boys travelled by public bus, some from as far as Sion Mills (20 miles). We usually walked along the quay from the bus station on the Strand road to the Lower School, and on one occasion there was a large mound of Indian corn piled up on the quay with rats running through it. To this day I will not eat that vegetable which Americans think is delicious.

Mr Craig, whom we called Ikey Moe, was our form master that first year, and it was necessary to have a form captain. There was a vote and we conspired to vote for the biggest clown in the class. Weeks later Mr Craig announced that I was elected captain (he must have felt guilty for blaming me for putting putty in the key hole). I was never told what the duties of the captain were! In the first summer term Mr Craig took us out for cricket and I was having some success, bowling everyone out (most had not played cricket

ABOVE: *AW Roulston.*

BELOW: *DCG Craig.*

THE PLUS FACTOR

Londonderry High School was a school that had the plus factor. By that I mean the education there was more than about passing exams, important as that is. We had elocution lessons with Miss Plaskitt and I still remember reciting excerpts from *The Gondoliers* about the Duke of Plaza Toro. There was an emphasis on courtesy, such as standing up when the teacher came into the room. You were not allowed to walk on the grass or cycle through the grounds. This applied even to the staff. I can still visualise Miss Park and Mrs Greep wheeling their bicycles past Duncreggan. Prior to the annual dance with Foyle we had a talk from Miss McIlroy about how to behave. You were not to sit on the boys' knees!

Miss McIlroy was a great influence on the school. We respected her greatly. I am sure those who went to Londonderry High School will remember her sweeping on to the platform for morning assembly with her gown falling off her shoulders and her greeting: 'Good morning, girls'. She married a Frenchman, Monsieur Loullier, while I was at school. When she came to assembly after her marriage we gave her three cheers. My friend, however, instead of saying. 'Hip hip hurrah!', said 'Hip hip Loullier!' We were fortunate in those days that the headmistress had time to teach, and I still remember her French classes, when we were in fourth and sixth forms. There is so much that I am grateful to her for, such as her wise advice when I wanted to stop Latin. If she had allowed me to stop Latin I would never have been able to go to Trinity College, Dublin. The irony of it is that I taught Latin when I first started teaching in Limavady Grammar School – also I would not have met my husband if I had not gone to TCD!

World War II was still on when I went to Londonderry High School, and the boarders were in Greenfield, Strabane. We were used to the staff travelling to Strabane. Some of our lessons were in the huts, cold in winter and too hot in summer. I can remember the only male member of staff, Captain Douglas, who taught Latin. We often wondered how he felt in the staff room surrounded by females! His daughter was a pupil at the same time as he was a teacher.

One thing I did not like was that there was no lunch break. School went on until 2pm with only one break, around 11am. The staff I can still remember are Mrs Greep and Miss Park, who taught maths, Miss Irvine (French), Miss Richardson (English), Miss Crockett (botany), Miss Peters (history), Miss Howell (PE), Miss Armstrong and Miss Lumb (music), Miss Fairbanks and Captain Douglas (Latin) and Miss Harris, who taught German, which was my favourite subject. I was the first German teacher in Limavady Grammar School.

'Her voice was soft, gentle and low, an excellent thing in a woman', was a verse framed and hanging in a corridor of Duncreggan. This to me epitomises the plus factor which Londonderry High School had. I have happy memories of my time there (1944–9) and am most grateful for all that it did for me.

Thelma Mehaffey (née Jackson)

before). So he took the bat and thought he would show them how to bat. When I bowled him out first ball he said 'that was very naughty'. He then called over another master and I was dispatched to play with the older boys.

Mr Craig taught history and English. In the leaving certificate I got a credit in English which greatly surprised Mr Connolly, as he had taken the top English students and I had better results than many of his class. For my last three years at Foyle, Mr Gillanders was my mathematics teacher, and he was superb. If not for these two teachers I would never have been accepted into the accountancy program in Scotland.

In those days there were no guidance counsellors, and it was the headmaster, Mr McConnell, who suggested that I consider a career in accountancy. He arranged for me to go to Glasgow and join the firm where his brother-in-law was a partner. It is also interesting to note that only one other pupil went across to Scotland that year – no one went to England. In my time at Foyle no sports teams went overseas and we never played in Eire or had a team visit us.

Every pupil played rugby in the winter and cricket in the summer unless they had a letter from their doctor stating they were unfit to participate. We changed clothes at the Upper School for rugby every Tuesday afternoon and on Saturday when we were playing for the school. It was a two-mile walk out to the playing fields at Springtown, where there was a small tin shed that we used when it was raining. We were usually muddy and wet on the way back to the Upper School, where there was a large bath (ten by ten feet square) which was filled about three or four feet deep with lukewarm water. We all jumped in and used the Lifebuoy soap if there was any available. You soon learned to rush back as the water became muddy and the only alternative was to wash in cold water at a hand basin.

In 1949 I played on the 1st XV rugby team under the direction of Mr Reid; this was his first year in charge. Stewart Connolly had been in charge of the 1st XV for many years. One Tuesday afternoon we walked out to Springtown in a light snow, and when Mr Reid called us out from the tin shed into heavier snow, we refused to go. The next day at assembly Mr Connolly called us out to the front and asked why we had not practised. He listened to the first two or three excuses and when it was my turn he said: 'You are all sheep', and would not allow us to play the following

Saturday against Coleraine Academical Institution. That decision was changed on Thursday and we all played on Saturday.

There was a cricket field at the Upper School which was only used for 1st XI matches. I played on the 1st XI cricket team for three years and the most memorable match was against Coleraine. In the Foyle innings seven batsmen failed to score, four scored nine runs between them and there were five extras: a grand total of 14 runs! The day was not all lost, as afterwards we watched the North West 200 lying on the grass near a bridge and breathed in the exhaust fumes as the bikes accelerated out of the turn.

Another memorable occasion was when the Medallion XV went to play Limavady 1st XV (it was the first year they played rugby at Limavady Grammar), and after the game we went along and bought Cokes. It was the first time any of us had ever had a Coca-Cola and we thought it tasted ghastly. In the years I represented the school at both rugby and cricket, it was usual that there would be only a handful of spectators. My father turned up only once, and that was the semi-final of the schools cup in 1950; my mother never saw a match. When I left Foyle in 1951, I returned my rugby jersey for £5. However Mr McConnell was there and took the money as my life membership subscription to the Old Boys Association.

After Mr Craig retired, I visited him at his home on Northland Road on several occasions when I was home from abroad. He was delightful, served tea and biscuits and wanted my opinion on many world issues (many of which I was not qualified to give). On one occasion my wife Eileen was assisting her brother Edgar Bigger at a school function, dressed in red, and Mr Craig approached Edgar and asked 'Who is that piece of goods in the red dress?' I never held that against him.

I have not commented on schoolwork up to now, and that's because we plodded along and got good results in our Leaving Certificate, which sent us on to the next stage of our careers. My wife attended the Londonderry High School at the same time I was at Foyle. She and I made many good friends at High School and often visit them on our trips to Ireland.

Alex W Roulston

REMINISCENCES OF NORTHLANDS SCHOOL OF HOUSEWIFERY, 1947

I enrolled at Northlands School of Housewifery in 1947 after completing high school. Northlands was situated at the top of Crawford Square – a lovely red brick building, with a tennis court in front and gardens at the back. We wore green dresses with white aprons and white caps and donned green overalls when we were cleaning.

I think the maximum number of girls would have been 20, mostly boarders, of whom a few came from the Republic of Ireland. We daygirls had to live-in for two weeks during the year. One week was spent cooking and then later on another week was for housekeeping. Miss Ritty was head of the school and was very strict. Miss May Glenn was the overall housekeeper. In 1947, with rationing in place, what a treat when a Donegal girl returned to school with fresh cream! There was a large range in the kitchen that had to be black-leaded every week. We had classes in dressmaking, knitting and first-aid, and joined ballroom dancing lessons down at Duncreggan. Dr Marshall Leslie came to examine us for our first-aid certificate but I don't think he ever failed anyone.

The boarders were allowed downtown once a week on Saturday afternoons. On one occasion a girl was later reprimanded by Miss Ritty for talking to a Foyle boy in Woolworths. On Sundays, the Presbyterian pupils went to Great James' Street Church and the Church of Ireland pupils went to Christ Church.

Morwenna Willoughby (née Thompson)

Northlands.

FOYLE DAYS

I entered Foyle College in September 1949, and left in June 1955 to proceed to Queen's University, Belfast. The headmaster during my six years was WAC McConnell (Archie), a Classics scholar and a laid-back administrator. When I started the deputy head was, I think, TR Norton (Tommy), a rather reclusive individual who taught physics and chemistry. He was succeeded in the early 1950s by WS Ferguson, who taught me Latin and Greek, and for whom I developed enormous respect and, dare I say it, some affection. The head of mathematics was George Gillanders, for whom I also developed some respect but absolutely zero affection! The head of English was Stuart Connolly, who tended to strike terror into pupils who misbehaved, even if ever so slightly, and who was headmaster during the period 1960–73.

Having little interest in the sports field or athletic track, my extra-curricular activities were concentrated in the annual production of a Gilbert and Sullivan operetta. The first was *HMS Pinafore*, presented in the Apprentice Boys' Memorial Hall just before Easter 1950, and the last (during my time) was *Ruddigore*, presented in the Guildhall in early December 1954. These were high-quality productions, requiring sustained effort and dedication from the supervising staff, and bringing considerable credit on the school.

The boarding school, located in the former Londonderry Academical Institution building on Academy Road, closed in June 1952 due to lack of numbers. I was not sorry at its passing! I was a boarder from November 1949; my account of some of the goings-on there appeared in the February 2006 issue of the Former Pupils' Association Magazine.

Robert Fleming

ENTHUSIASM

I entered Foyle in 1946. The headmaster, WAC McConnell, encouraged me in reading the Bible at assembly, confirming me in my calling for the sacred ministry. He also encouraged me to rehearse for *HMS Pinafore*. Later I was transformed from a humble schoolboy to the Mikado of Japan! It all led to a lifetime love of Gilbert and Sullivan operas. I was a member of the Intermediate relay team in 1949, which were Ulster School Champions. Our coach was RJ Macartney, a Cambridge blue, who introduced us to starting blocks, an innovation at that time. Another encourager! Encouragement goes a long way. I was also thrilled to be a member of the Medallion (1947–8) and 1st XV (1950–1) – both semi-finalists.

Dean Cecil Orr

BOARDERS, BELLS AND (FOYLE) BOYS
Derry, 1949. The clamour of the Guildhall clock, great stone walls with cannons at the ready, a sea of girls in blue-and-grey uniforms. Such was my first impression of the city where I was to spend the next five years of my life. My mother accompanied me and left me in

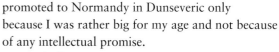

the very capable hands of Matron McClay. I started my boarding career in the dormitory known as Vanity Fair in Duncreggan House. On the wall in the corridor was a rather fine reproduction of part of the ceiling of the Sistine Chapel, which impressed me greatly and was probably the beginning of my lifelong interest in art. Soon I was promoted to Normandy in Dunseveric only because I was rather big for my age and not because of any intellectual promise.

The bells initiated each change of activity: we were wakened by a handbell rung by the duty prefect, summoned to breakfast by a cowbell, no doubt an unwanted souvenir of some long forgotten pre-war trip to Switzerland, and called to lessons by an electric bell. The last bell was the lights-out bell at 9.30pm. Of course we did not always go to sleep but talked and giggled until matron or the duty teacher came back and threatened us with taking away our weekend exeats.

After lessons, which mostly took place in rather cold and draughty Nissen huts, the boarders had to play games, hockey, netball, rounders or tennis, according to the season. Playing hockey five or six times a week in the freezing cold of the Derry winter considerably dampened my enthusiasm. As we learned to become young ladies(?) we were required to wash after games and change into afternoon dresses or twinsets and skirts. A famous tip from Miss McIlroy was: 'Gels, nevair wear gloves with a cardigan!' After tea – again summoned by bells – there was 'study', which ended at various times according to one's age. We then had about an hour for recreation. No television in those days, of course. The younger girls would play hopscotch and the older girls would read or gossip. At one time there was a fashion for playing cards, usually whist or gin rummy.

One evening we discovered a one-ring electric fire so for a while we had the luxury of making toast out of the bread provided for supper. There was no butter or margarine, (still rationed) but toast and jam tasted better than plain bread and jam! Before we burned the place to the ground a passing member of staff smelt the delicious smell of our toast and investigated.

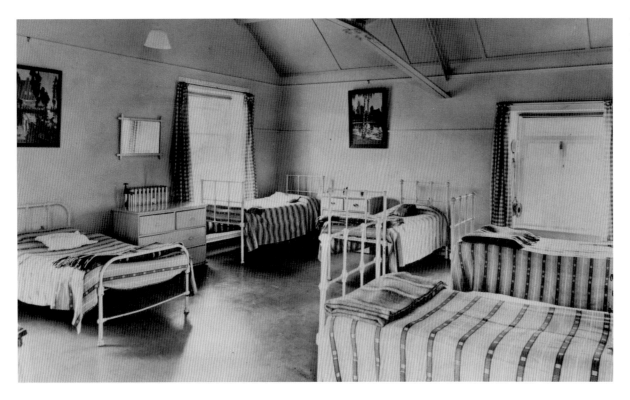

On Saturday evenings we had to do any mending required on the returned laundry. By sheer chance we learned that Matron McClay was a fan of the *Jalna* books which were popular at that time. When engaged in conversation about the latest book matron did not seem to notice the quality of the mending. We got away with many a cobbled darn and crooked patch due to the doings of the Whiteoaks family. After finishing mending we were allowed to get out the wind-up record player and practise ballroom dancing. The highlights of the year (when we reached fifth form) were the school dance and the Foyle dance!

But we managed to communicate with the Foyle boys at other times although it was strictly forbidden. Letters and glances could be exchanged at church. Sometimes we could persuade a daygirl to get her mum to write a letter inviting us to tea on Saturday and the afternoon would be spent with a boy in the seat of the Rialto cinema.

In the summer we could play tennis and sometimes the boys would come and hang about in the beech wood. On one occasion a teacher spotted them and phoned the police. The constable who arrived on his bike found that his son was one of the miscreants. Often there were mice in the boarding house and the year I was in St Lurach's there was an invasion of them. They ruined a box of chocolates someone

had hidden in the piano – we were not supposed to have food in the dorms – and ate a hole in Rosemary Lawson's Sunday coat.

About that time we played a wicked trick on a girl who was afraid of mice. Some All Bran, purloined from breakfast, was sprinkled on the girl's pillow. We then pulled the counterpane back over the pillow. When the girl went to get into bed she discovered these mysterious brown objects on her pillow. We all crowded round, shaking our heads and suggested that these were mouse droppings. Then the ringleader said, 'I know how we'll find out!' She then, picked several of the 'mouse droppings' and popped them into her mouth!

We were quite well behaved compared to the boarders in the 1960s. I only remember smoking once in the rhododendron bushes on the front lawn but I am told that a later generation actually smoked in the dormitory. Apparently the smell did not give them away because the matron of the day was a heavy smoker herself. I think Miss McCann, the housemistress, also smoked but perhaps I libel her.

On one occasion a girl called Marilyn was smoking in bed when matron's voice was heard in the corridor. Immediately the miscreant hid the cigarette, still alight, under the bedclothes. When matron appeared her friend said, 'Marilyn is not feeling

RIGHT: *LHS boarders group c.1950.*

RIGHT INSERT: *A plate from the LHS boarding school.*

BELOW: *Molly Kennedy.*

well, matron.' As she approached the bed Marilyn proceeded to stub out the cigarette but it broke off and burned her derriere. She claims to bear the scar to this day. The mattresses were made of horsehair and sometimes it penetrated the ticking and was exposed. One night we were disturbed by a scream. My friend had been dreaming that she was kissing a certain bearded Magee student and had awakened to find she was face down in the horsehair with some of it in her mouth!

There was an initiation ritual, called 'Convent Choir', for new girls. The new girl would be brought into a darkened room full of shadowy figures in dressing gowns with towels over their heads – an approximation of nuns' habits! The new girl would be invited to kneel down and be interviewed by 'Mother Superior'. The assembled company would then start to sing 'Abide with Me' but at the words, 'Fast falls the eventide', the rug would be pulled out from under her and she would fall flat on her face! This was not as unkind as it sounds because a pile of pillows was provided on which to fall.

We had certain words we used, of which I only remember two: the word for a hot water bottle was 'Paddy' and the word for lavatory was 'pell'. On another occasion most of the boarders went down with influenza and were confined to their beds. A couple of us did not succumb and regarded the others with envy as they were excused lessons. Ann Worrall and I devised a cunning plan. We went to matron and complained of feeling unwell so we were sent to bed. Later that day matron came to take our temperatures and we managed to put the thermometer into the hot water bottle. I shall never forget the look on her face as she looked at the thermometer! She did not say anything but came back a short time later with a large bottle of castor oil and a tablespoon! We were thoroughly dosed with the horrible stuff, pronounced cured and turned out into the cold.

When I joined the 'Old Girls' and met my fellow boarders it was like finding all the sisters I never knew I had. I remain deeply grateful to those dedicated members of staff who not only taught us, but, especially in the boarding department, gave us the benefit of their experience of life. The memories of the fun and friendships of those days will remain with me as long as I live.

Molly Kennedy (née Steele)
Boarder at Londonderry High School (1949–55)

BOARDING IN LONDONDERRY HIGH SCHOOL, 1969

The boarding house was closed in 1969. Two girls in their lower sixth year were allowed to finish their schooling in 1970 and for them the regime was very relaxed and informal.

A total of 40 girls aged between seven and 18 boarded in the late 1960s. The younger girls slept in Hunting Tower close to matron and Miss McCann the house mistress. The girls from forms one through five stayed in Normandy, St Jude's and St Lurach's, whilst the sixth form were in Vanity Fair in the main Duncreggan Buildings. Included in the 40 were four service families, one girl from India and another from Hong Kong.

Life was built around routine: breakfast in the dining rooms, which are now the offices and the staff room in Duncreggan. Miss Cowper, the principal, had all her meals with the senior boarders in the main dining room while the house mistresses, Miss McCann, Miss Christie and matron served tables in the junior dining room. The girls had their given seats and the staff moved tables on a weekly basis. The boarding house was looked after by Miss McNaul, the housekeeper and three staff, Annie, Georgie and Sally. Although they were all live in we had no contact with them.

Much of the day was routine breakfast: bed making, inspection, school, break and lunch in the

Above: *Isabel McNally CBE.*

Left: *Boarders fire drill evacuation.*

various churches. You had to have the appropriate gloves and shoes were polished. Church was not a boring time for the senior girls as it was a chance to meet and talk to the local boys. Silent movies would have had a lot to learn during those sermons. Many a story could be told.

Sunday afternoon was free for the senior girls to walk from 2pm–4.30pm, followed by tea and evening church. Whilst out of school the boarders always wore school uniform so on the Saturday and Sunday afternoon walks they were easily recognisable especially if you were travelling down Duncreggan Road on a motorbike or up in Bonner's for a wee smoke.

On one famous Saturday afternoon in the town the Civil Rights Movement and Ian Paisley had a rally. Two boarders strongly believed in the Civil Rights Movement and joined them on their protest. One protester told them: 'Look, luvs, you're in the wrong group you should be down there,' pointing to Paisley's group. They pleaded with them to leave. They assured them they were in the correct place. Boarders were not allowed in town except they had special permission so how this was not reported back or in the local press I'm not quite sure.

Life was routine. You bathed twice a week in three inches of water at a specific time. You washed your hair once a week. You had to have special permission to wash out your smalls as all washing went to the laundry. The vast majority of the girls were happy

boarding house plus our lunch hour (there was no mixing with the day girls). After school the junior boarders played games or walked in the grounds while the senior boarders were allowed a 40-minute walk unescorted. Back to freshen up and dress for tea, followed by study, supper and bed. Lights out between 9pm and 9.30pm. The juniors were in bed by 7.30pm.

Weekends were also routine. Saturday morning was study after room inspection as on Friday evening the minister came in for religious education. The guides also met on Friday evenings. Saturday afternoon from 2–4.30pm the senior boarders were allowed out unescorted. This lead to many exciting ventures. However not all girls availed of this time. The evening was free after tea, when we listened to records, taught each other to dance or played cards. There was no television.

Sunday morning was letter writing after breakfast followed by uniform inspection before walking to our

A FAMILY ACCOUNT

My brother Jim Hatrick attended Foyle, from the prep school. My sisters, Margaret, Dorothy, Anne and I attended Londonderry High School from kindergarten; we all enjoyed a very happy school life. Our mother (formerly Berta Morrow) was art mistress at Victoria High School (1921–2) and one of her star pupils was Jan Caldwell (later Jean McCandless), who taught us art many years later in Londonderry High School. One of my mother's colleagues was Miss MF McIlroy, who was later our headmistress at Londonderry High School.

Kathleen Stewart (née Hatrick)

SEVEN FORMATIVE YEARS: 1952–9

I entered Form I at Foyle in September 1952 with my new blazer, cap and regulation short trousers. Of those early years I have few recollections other than that maths, Latin and English classes were in the Hut, Art in the Technical College and PE and swimming at the Academy Road. However, my lasting recollections are of Form IV when I joined the army cadets, became a stagehand/scenery builder for the Gilbert and Sullivan operas and was first selected for the 1st XV. Later years as a prefect, house-captain of Springham and Victor Ludorum of the 1959 Sports hold equally cherished memories. I am forever grateful for the superb education I received at Foyle, and my greatest appreciation is of George Gillanders, whose superb teaching of pure and applied mathematics and 3D co-ordinate geometry instilled any understanding that has served me for a lifetime as a professional engineer.

Professor Emeritus Eric K Beatty OBE BSc PhD CEng FIAE FIEI FIMechE

A DISCIPLINED ENVIRONMENT

When I left Clooney School in 1956 to go to Foyle I was, like so many of my generation, a first-generation grammar-school boy. There I experienced a top-class education, which inspired me in so many ways:

- *teachers of high scholarship. (My teachers for A-level were Messrs Mullan, Gillanders and Bogle);*
- *the top-class leadership of Mr Connolly;*
- *a disciplined environment;*
- *a deep spirit of service, where teachers gave of their time freely for the pupils (Messrs Mowbray, Bogle and Wallace gave much to me). I owe the school an enormous debt and I wish it well.*

Billy Young (1956)

Joy Coskery.

except the girls who did not see parents or family except at Christmas or the summer holidays.

When the boarding house closed the boarders left for various schools in Northern Ireland, namely Princess Gardens or Coleraine, and others to England. Through the Old Girls' Association and special Boarders weekend friendships have been maintained.

Isabel McNally

MEMORIES OF LONDONDERRY HIGH SCHOOL

My sister and I arrived at Londonderry High School at the beginning of the summer term 1952, wearing the wrong uniform, as Miss McElroy insisted we were growing girls and should buy the grey blazer in September. Not a happy beginning wearing the maroon Dalriada colour and looking like hopeful Foyle boys.

First impressions were of Miss McCann teaching us the intercostal diaphragmatic method of breathing, Miss Christie and French phonetics, Eileen Taylor inspiring us to read and a very young Heather Parr, making music fun. Hockey was a religion, literally, and you could avoid Miss Christie's after-school Scripture by having team practice. Only on very wet days were we introduced to When I was in Damascus'. Our headmistress had a French husband, possibly the reason for a very generous lunch break, when you could fit in a tennis match, a choir practice and an obligatory run round the hockey pitch.

It was a liberal school, ahead of its time in shared learning. Thus the girls went to FCD for A-level science and maths. I went to Magee to learn Spanish, while in the sixth form. Later and definitely not in the plan I returned through marriage to teach under Miss McIlroy, Miss Cowper, Miss Christie and finally in the amalgamated school. I remember fondly colleagues and A-level students. I am grateful for the opportunities given to our four daughters.

Joy Coskery

TEACHING IN LONDONDERRY HIGH SCHOOL

My first teaching post was at Londonderry High School in 1967 and it was my happiest appointment by far. After my unpleasant teaching practice in Cowley, Oxford, it seemed like a haven of peace and gentility, a place where one could actually talk about Shakespeare, Milton and Chaucer to receptive minds. The girls were charming, intelligent, funny and mostly hardworking, and all were closely attached to the school.

Miss Cowper with her imperious English ways was a formidable presence, living in regal splendour in the lovely house. She was beautifully complemented by the more sympathetic and eccentric deputy, Miss Christie, keeper of goats, a woman whose glittering eye fixed upon you like that of the Ancient Mariner and compelled in you the same frozen attention; then unexpectedly would come her disarming warm smile. She was a woman of droll observation.

With the Civil Rights movement of the late 1960s I was aware of history in the making. The views of our staff varied, our political sympathies often widely expressed but always there was a cheerful camaraderie. I felt it was one of the strengths of the school not to be identified with one entrenched position and having a non-partisan head helped.

The next stage in my career was going to work for BAOR in Germany. When I left I knew that I should never find a school so suited to me again, nor pupils whom I would like better. LHS will always have that special place in my affection.

Connie McCarthy (née Parkes)

FIFTY YEARS OF FOYLE

On entering Foyle at Lawrence Hill in September 1962 little did I know that I would still be there in September 2012 as the longest-serving member of staff. Many changes occurred in that time but Foyle and its ethos remains constant. Of my seven years as a pupil, almost five of them were spent at Lawrence Hill and the remaining two years and a term were spent at Springtown. Long service and loyalty have always been a feature of the staff of the school. Lawrence Hill was a dark, foreboding place served by, what seemed to me, old men in black gowns, and run under the strictest of disciplinary regimes by Stewart Connolly and George Gillanders. There was one fulltime female member of staff, Miss W Armstrong, later Mrs Wallace, and we experienced the gentler approach of female staff for short periods with Mrs Connolly who taught science, Miss Florence Rankin who attempted to teach us music as we jostled around a piano in the corner of the assembly hall and Miss Mulhern, later Mrs Mary Hughes, who tried to awaken our artistic bent in the weekly art classes we attended in the technical college.

On graduating from Queen's University in geography with geology and archaeology as subsidiary studies, I took up a part-time post in Londonderry High School as a substitute teacher for Mrs W Gilroy, head of geography. Towards the end of that time a post in the geography department at Foyle was advertised and I was appointed to the position with the benefit of a glowing reference provided by Miss Christie, principal of Londonderry High School. Then Foyle and Londonderry High School amalgamated and became the coeducational Foyle and Londonderry College. The period spent in both Londonderry High School and Foyle gave me some insight into separate education for boys and girls and aware of the diversity of approaches in the between the two systems, I approached the amalgamation with some foreboding. Much credit must go to Hugh Gillespie, who oversaw

the whole process and overcame many difficulties during the early years. Many of the older members of the Londonderry High School and a few of the Foyle staff retired leaving the way clear for the appointment of younger teachers who were more adaptable to the coeducational system.

After 1976, things settled down and the new coeducational ethos carried over many of the finer traditions from the earlier schools. The curriculum changed: new subjects such as technology, geology, business studies and computing grew in popularity at the expense of Classics, which has now disappeared and modern languages, which are undertaken only by a select few. The means of delivering the curriculum has changed out of all recognition. Chalk and talk have been replaced by white boards, interactive screens and data projectors. Computers, unheard of when I started teaching, are now everywhere. We employ them to record attendance, produce reports, monitor pupil behaviour and communicate with fellow staff on a daily basis. Gone are the Banda and Gestetner machines with their messy spirits or ink – our only means of reproducing multiple copies of work – replaced by photocopiers and laser printers that reproduce perfect copies at the press of a button. Textbooks are supplemented or replaced by lecture notes, worksheets and DVDs and are directed towards success in the never-ending succession of state examinations. We spend more time preparing or taking examinations than we do actually teaching. There is less time to offer a wider viewpoint on the topics being studied, and much of the wider educational experience is lost.

June 2012 saw the retirement of many long-serving members of the academic and support staff. Many of them came in 1977 or 1978 after the last major exodus of staff and have given unflinching service over that time. With the exception of Norman Taylor, who joined the Foyle staff the year before me, I have seen all of them appointed and have enjoyed their camaraderie over the years. I wish them well in their retirement and also the headmaster, Jack Magill, who retired in June after 18 years in that post. His major preoccupation in that time has been to facilitate the planning, design and move to a new single site school in the Waterside. As a representative of the teaching staff on the Board of Governors since 1988, I have witnessed the unending challenges and frustrations

Uniform of Foyle College, 1960.

STEWART CONNOLLY: THE SCHOOL FLAGPOLE

'There is a magic in the memory of school boy friendship,' said Benjamin Disraeli.

In was on a sunny morning near the end of the exam season in 1960 that it was spotted. A piece of lady's undergarment was dangling where, on special occasions, the school flag would normally be seen. Soon after the sighting a note from the headmaster was circulated to all classes summoning the entire school to a special assembly at 11am. Ten minutes into his tirade the headmaster demanded that the guilty party step forward. Ten seconds later the entire upper-sixth shuffled forward! The rest of the school was discharged to their classrooms and the guilty parties, all 26 of us, given a detention for the afternoon. Shortly after, in a one-to-one with the head-boy, a more reflective head mused 'What should I do with them?' Both shared the observation that he would be liberated from all of us forever in a few days time. Later that day the headmaster issued a second note to the upper sixth, cancelling the detention.

Roy McClelland

faced by him and chairmen past and present. Mr Magill retired before the move but we are now confident that by 2017, the school will celebrate its 400th anniversary on its new site providing all the facilities to continue the tradition of a first-class education for generations to come.

William Lynn

ABOVE: *Stewart Connolly MA LLB. Headmaster, 1960–73.*

BELOW: *Professor Roy McClelland.*

WEARING THE BERET

Art Byrne told us we were breathing the same air that Saint Columcille breathed. I still find that thrilling whenever I visit Derry. That was during one of his quieter Irish history classes, one that didn't include girls shouting out that the Fenians had no business complaining about people getting shot because they'd started it all. Denzil Stewart stalked out of an English class in a rage when someone said something similar after he tried to use a discussion of a Lady Gregory play to bring up the Troubles. Miss Armstrong, the terrifying Lulu, drew the blinds and returned without a word to the equations on the blackboard when an army helicopter landed on the hockey field and fit young soldiers began to leap out onto the grass.

Bloody Sunday happened just down the road, yet it was never mentioned in any formal way in school. There was CS gas in the air, riots, checkpoints, barricades on the streets, bombs and bombscares and gun battles. But that was Derry. This was Londonderry High School, which still had 'for young ladies' on the painted sign inside its big house gates and might as well have put Protestant in there as well. There would be taunts as we walked down the town. 'Look, boys, the greyhounds are out exercising!'

The grey beret was our stiff upper lip, though eventually it was conceded that girls whose berets were routinely snatched from their heads on their way to and from school could stop wearing them on days when there was trouble. Mrs McCloskey lined us up in the gym to measure the gap between our knees and the hems of our blue pleated skirts. We hitched up our waistbands as we walked out on to Duncreggan Road.

The High School was snobbish. When she was headmistress, Miss Cowper, with her whispery polished accent, used to rebuke us for misdemeanours with 'This must not be, girls.' Miss Christie was a fiercer kettle of fish with a nasty tongue and a witchy look about her. 'When I was in Damascus,' was her favourite preface during morning assembly.

Assembly could be inspiring, when we sang Saint Patrick's 'Breastplate' and 'Ye Holy Angels Bright' and other wonderful hymns with the orchestra playing and Miss Storey's choir soaring through the harmonies. I played trombone (how I wish it had been a cello) and for a time soldiers from an army band rehearsed with us. Miss McConnell bravely drove us off to exotic places like Magherafelt and Dungiven to take part in inter-school debates, great for talent spotting. In class, she despaired over our inability to master 'smooth, creamy custard'.

My best friend was Mandy Burton. We were adventurers, and school was too small. We roamed the town. We went to *Last Tango in Paris* at the Rialto cinema. We took off to Donegal to hear Planxty, Christy Moore, the Chieftains and Horslips. At 16, Mandy was already a brilliant actress. Sean McMahon directed us in plays and encouraged us to have big horizons. She was Miss Hardcastle and I was Toby Lumpkin. She was Lady Macbeth and I was Lady Macduff. There were anxious priestly looks as we strode into St Columb's College for rehearsals.

We had brilliant English teachers, including the Sweeney sisters, Mrs Overend, Miss Parke – and Hazel Cathcart. She persuaded me to study for a scholarship to Trinity College, Dublin, generously giving up many hours to coach me through the course. It included poems from Yeats's 'The Tower', a powerful introduction to poetry as a means to understand war and society. When she got the news that I'd won the scholarship she ran through the corridors looking for me but I was hiding out in the little room at the back of the language lab, smoking. She died, tragically, in a car crash, in the late 1980s. I wish she'd known I became a writer. I don't think it was a surprise to anyone that I never became a lady.

Susan McKay

(Award-wining journalist and author of the acclaimed Northern Protestants – An Unsettled People *and* Bear in Mind These Dead)

THE LAST YEARS OF THE LONDONDERRY HIGH SCHOOL

'When I was in Damascus…' Such was the much-mimicked catchphrase of Miss Christie, the diminutive but formidable headmistress of Londonderry High School. The announcement was usually the preface to a fascinating tale of her time as a missionary in the Middle East in the 1930s and 1940s. I remember her as a tiny, bird-like creature standing in front of a chair emblazoned with the school coat of arms, holding court with her 'gels'.

I was a pupil during the last two years of Londonderry High School 1974–6. It was definitely Miss Christie's school. Before being given a place you had to have an interview. My mother took me and my first impressions were highly favourable. It was a peaceful, perfect oasis: tennis courts, a hockey pitch, rooms with names, girls in crisp blue and white gingham dresses. Here was Derry's answer to Mallory Towers and I could go home every night! Then I met Miss Christie.

We were shown into her office by Miss McCloskey, a kind gentle lady with grey wiry hair and a mildly shocked look about her. Behind a huge desk sat this twig of a woman with grey hair pulled back into a large wide bun. She wore Dame Edna-ish glasses, her tiny form swathed in a black robe (all the teachers had to wear gowns). It was believed that she had a glass eye, so I spent the entire 'interview' trying to work out which one was real. One painting on her wall was of Lower Magazine Street with a no-entry sign – perhaps an omen. While I stared out the window to the gardens and trees beyond my poor mother sat in a state of high anxiety. I let her do the talking and ignored Miss Christie's questions. I eventually told her I wanted to be a vet. 'Congratulations,' she said, 'You've been accepted.'

The excitement of the first day at school was serious. Uniform had been purchased at vast expense from Moores of Ferryquay Gate: hockey stick, boots, tennis rackets, gym clothes, *Ecce Romani* Latin books – all on the list, including the famous navy-blue cherub knickers! Enamoured with my new briefcase school bag I had opened and closed it so often that by the time I got to school the lock had snapped. I must have looked like Frank Spencer! I had been warned about the initiation of the beret but I got off lightly. When Miss Christie checked on my progress in physics and chemistry (veterinary subjects), she must have been very disappointed, because I found them sinfully boring and completely impossible. However that was more than compensated for by English with Audrey Sweeney, a wonderful teacher and whom we had for our first two years. She read us Seamus Heaney and the world of literature was opened up for us as he was alive and shared the same language and scenery as us – and he'd been to school in Derry!

Sean McMahon came in to help with our play, *The Boy and the Cart*. I remember him, passionately rehearsing with us in the school library. Miss Sweeney used to show us films about horse-riding, got us involved in the debating society and generally enriched our lives far beyond the bleakness of Derry in the 1970s. She had green shoes, groovy clothes and a Dalmatian called Flurry and we all thought she was marvellous. We also had a wonderful general studies teacher called Miss Riddell. She was frightfully English, with a shock of thick grey hair. She wore sensible corduroy zip-up pinafores, liberty shirts and sturdy shoes. She smoked and had a fabulous husky voice. Miss Riddell had been a land girl during the war and taught us history (Mesopotamia featured heavily), geography, biology and art. She lived in one of the little lodge houses at the back gate of the prep school. Once after hockey I announced that I was sweating. She gently corrected me: 'My dear dear Fiona, pigs sweat, men perspire but ladies glow; from now on you will glow.'

For maths we had Mrs Hutchinson, who threatened constantly to knock our blocks off. We had dear Mr Millen for Latin. He seemed very old but was an absolute gent with a slight hunchback and one leg missing on his glasses, no hair and few teeth. He lived in a little room at the top of Duncreggan House; only now do I realise how tough and lonely his life must have been. He used say we were angels, learned ones at that, but he did not know that we 'cogged' the answers

Susan McKay.

IMPRESSIONS OF AMALGAMATION

Suddenly there were boys – everywhere! Shouting, running, barging, thumping their burgundy blazers, blocking out the light. They made the school untidy – dragging huge sports bags around whereas we girls had refined essential baggage down to a slim document wallet and lip-gloss, where previously regulation 'indoor shoes' had been a priority in the discipline stakes. Attitudes towards uniform seemed to relax entirely and pupils appeared with hair hanging lankly to shoulder length and earrings – and the girls were as bad! Woolly tights and blazers worn indoors! Miss Christie would have been horrified! Gone were the days of kneeling in front of headmistresses to have your skirt-length checked, when my navy blue mascara was considered the absolute height of rebellion. What culture shock!

As classes were not integrated at first we had to suffer the invaders only in morning assembly and around the corridors. In the Prefects' Room a wary truce was introduced over the kettle – once the girls had established that everyone did their own washing up. In the High School days the disciplinary system was quite straightforward – if Miss Christie caught you – you were in big trouble. To us the Foyle Prefects' Council had echoes of the Spanish Inquisition. After a first few meetings the macho spirit was modified and reason prevailed. *Robocop* was dead – long live *Sense and Sensibility*!

Soon some of the more feeble-minded girls went 'over to the enemy'. Couples appeared, canoodling in corners, roosting on radiators, usually with the least desirable individuals imaginable. While peering down our noses at them the rest of us secretly wondered what they had that we didn't. With our superior intellect and unassailable wit we intimated them!

There were some positive aspects – the introduction of the tuck shop for example, and the infamous sailing club – whose dinghies rarely left the slipway as the few select members rarely left the clubhouse bar. Above all it was great crack ... we knew we would all be leaving in a few months so we why not enjoy it while we could? Much socialising was done; there was excitement and sexual chemistry – and the biology wasn't bad either! Though it pained us to admit it, we were probably better off with them than without. Long live Co-Ed!

Rosie Turner (head girl, 1977)

Prefects Council, Rosie Turner (head girl), 1976–7.

he wrote on the board for our prep each day before we handed it in. Hence we usually obtained full marks. All was revealed with the the Christmas exams: I got 23 per cent, about average. Miss Christie ordered a stewards' inquiry.

For the next two years we were treated to more than an education. Miss Christie staged amazing exhibitions, my favourite 'A Hundred and One Beautiful Things'. The hall was transformed: Bohemian Glass goblets on pure silk Italian damask, embroidered Kaleen rugs from Turkestan, 17th-century bath dishes from Aleppo, Meissen china, Bedouin jewellery, copper from Damascus, 18th-century Irish silver. The most interesting was a bowl and vase from her former home on Mount Zion in Jerusalem. She said of her possessions: 'There is not one that does not evoke a person, a place – sometimes a conversation or a smell'. She sent us to a Norah McGuiness exhibition and bought a painting for the school.

There was a huge sense of pride in being part of this community run by this enigmatic and powerful little lady who was so committed to educating young women. Duncreggan House was out of bounds as Miss Christie lived there and the very glamorous sixth form had a common-room there. I once got past the back door from the modern building and was given a piece of exquisite silk to make a bookmark for a fundraising stall; it felt like I had reached the moon.

We had gingham dresses to wear in the summer with our grey blazers with royal blue ribbon. In the winter it was blue serge tunics with a great big belt around it, grey gabardine and berets. While not able to compete with the white-gloved young ladies trotting around Crawford Square in my great-aunt's day, it felt really special to be part of such a great school. In third year we were shipped up to Foyle College on the windswept hill at Springtown. It poured with rain on the first day and I remember reporters and photographers snapping away. Despite the fine displays of historic school swords, cups, caps and its much glossier interior it felt like a smelly, inhospitable, noisy institution compared to the lush sheltered maturity of Duncreggan. No cubby holes, ancient trees, hidden sitting rooms, warm airing cupboards; things were never the same again.

Both Miss Sweeney and Miss Riddell left but I was lucky to have Mr Helliwell for A-level English. He enriched every class by bringing seemingly impossible passages of *Paradise Lost* to life and actually making us laugh at Beelzebub. Chaucer became fathomable and *Middlemarch* is still one of my favourite novels. He also had a deep understanding of young people and was never judgemental or critical.

Miss Christie's departure was as dramatic as one would expect; she never lost the allure of other-worldliness. After a very emotional final assembly, she had just learned that a father and governor of the school had been shot dead by the IRA, she swooped out in tears after choking out, 'Au revoir, mes enfants'. I never saw her again. That was the end of Londonderry High School.

Fiona Henderson

AN AMERICAN VIEW OF FOYLE, 1978–81

In May 2011, I was at the City of Derry Rugby Club watching the Heineken Cup final with seven of my American tourist friends after a humbling day of golf at Ballyliffin. In the festive crowd was a large mixture of Foyle teachers and boys, some of whom I hadn't seen in 30 years. After some small chat about our dismal golf games, kids and occupations, it was like old times, as if I had never even left.

I attended Foyle 1978–81. My first visit was in the summer of 1978. In several weeks I would become an official 'Foyle Boy' and an astute member of the Lawrence House. Initially none of this made much of an impression on me, having recently moved to the city from Richmond, Virginia, with my father's work at Du Pont. I was 16 at the time and the oldest of four Clarke boys. All four of us started at Foyle that fall, two at Duncreggan and two at Springtown. It was a very different school environment to what we were accustomed to and a huge adjustment for us all. In time we all found our way and became true American-Irish. The friendliness and hospitality of the other students and staff certainly made the transition much easier for us all.

Some of the biggest adjustments for us were the school uniforms, riding the city buses, prayer assembly, teachers in gowns, new sports and a different curriculum. We all participated in rugby and for me it was the start of a real passion and I continued playing upon my return to the US for many years.

Our time in Ireland afforded us many opportunities. We were fortunate to travel to some amazing places and meet so many friendly people on our journeys. We visited Greece, Italy and Germany on school tours

Doug Clarke (left) with, brothers Allan and Jimmy and father Rex on recent visit to Ireland.

organized by William Lynn, saw spectacular scenery in the west of Ireland on geology trips, went skiing to France and Bulgaria and toured with the rugby teams to various parts of England and Scotland. The hospitality and kindness we were shown certainly made a lasting impression on me. I met some wonderful people in my three years in Ireland, some of whom have become lifelong friends. Looking back to that fall of 1978 I don't think any of us realised how big an impact those years at Foyle were going to make on our lives.

Doug Clarke,
Richmond, Virginia

OPEN DOORS

One blustery Thursday afternoon, some 15 years after leaving school, I peered through a windowpane of Foyle Books in Derry's Craft Village. A familiar face peered out: Mr Thatcher, my junior school French teacher. And like Bastian in the opening scene of the *Never Ending Story*, I stepped inside to take shelter from the wind. While I wondered if he had been headbutting any blackboards recently, as he would when exasperated with us, mon prof told me about a book he was helping to compile concerning 400 years of Foyle College, a sort of *Never Ending Story* in its own right. 'It might be interesting to hear what you, Ella and Jamie are up to now and what you remember about school,' he said. 'Besides, if you write something in the book you'll be more likely to buy a copy'.

The first thing that sprang to mind, given our location on that day, within the walls, close to the spot where the Free School stood, was that the school has a genuinely compelling story. Whilst the school moved

MEMORIES FROM FOYLE SCHOOL

I look back on my time at Foyle with great memories, from school plays with Mr Keown to rugby trips abroad with Mr McCarter; there was so much the school did for me. It was school drama that pointed me towards an acting career. My first film appearance was as Gerard Peters 458 in *Song for a Raggy Boy* (2003), a story about an Irish reform school. In 2006, I acted opposite Cate Blanchett and Dame Judi Dench (both of whom were nominated for Academy Awards for their roles) in the film *Notes on a Scandal*, playing the pivotal role of Steven Connolly, the schoolboy whose affair with his art teacher, Sheba Hart (played by Cate Blanchett), leads to disaster. In 2012 I made the docudrama *Saving the Titanic* as electrician Albert Ervine, the youngest member of the engineering crew.

Recent work includes the lead in a five-part production of Charles Dickens's *Nicholas Nickleby* for the BBC. Among other congratulatory messages were words of encouragement from Mr Keown, Mr Menown and Mr McBride. A perfect example of how the people in Foyle make it the success it is today. Above all I believe that it is the people that made my time there so special. Ann in the office was everyone's second mother and its people like her that make places like Foyle unique.

My friends and I still keep in contact with some of the teachers, who are all genuinely keen to see us do well in post-school years.

Andrew Simpson

ABOVE: *Andrew Simpson.*

BELOW: *Tabea Weyrauch.*

out of the walls, it remained on the west bank of the river, which, I always thought, was a great thing in the last decades of the 20th century, because it improved the cultural mix, bringing hundreds of maroon-blazered Watersiders into the 'city side'. Or maybe I was biased, living five minutes from Duncreggan and not having to endure a daily bus ride all the way from an exotic-sounding, far-off place like Magheramason.

While standing in Mr Thatcher's bookshop I realised how significant books were during those years. Little first-years walked at obtuse angles to support the weight of hardback exercise books for 15 subjects. Today, in terms of what we do for a living, with music, dance and film respectively, Jamie, Ella and myself don't consider books to be tools of the trade. That's probably the same for most people. But jobs aside, I imagine everyone must feel quite overwhelmed by technology in 2012 and rarely read a book.

Right now I'm half-way through *Hard Times* and I'm sure Charles Dickens took less time to write it than it is taking me to read it: every page is mouse-eared. The gist of the book, I think, is in line with most people's experience of Foyle College:

that education should be less about teachers drilling facts and more about inspiring an interest in life, whether that's a science teacher making something explode, an English teacher making an afternoon disappear, an art teacher uncovering a hidden talent or a geology teacher uncovering a lovely piece of sedimentary rock.

I just wish I wasn't having such a hard time getting to the end of this novel, but take solace in the idea that we are, according to some commentators, in the early stages of an electronic revolution expected to outweigh the industrial revolution by a factor of ten. Today, it doesn't seem unusual to receive a message from an old friend sent by iPhone from his tractor.

Times have changed in only 15 years, yet strangely, the chilling dystopia presented by educationalist Thomas Gradgrind as far back as those 'Hard Times' feels just as relevant to these: 'Every inch of the existence of mankind, from birth to death, was to be a bargain across a counter. And if we didn't get to Heaven that way, it was not a politico-economical place, and we had no business there'. And so, if parts of Foyle College's long history serve to promote the idea of free education with open doors to all backgrounds and an ethos that interprets 'education' in as broad a sense as possible, then long may its story be never ending.

Guy King

A GREAT TIME

I had a great time as a Foyle student. I made close friends, who remain my closest friends. When I had the opportunity to participate in RTÉ's *The Model Scouts* I had nothing but brilliant support from the school, especially from my form teacher, Mrs Ó Somacháin. Without that the ongoing experience of my working and travelling as a model might not have happened. I picked up many all-round life skills in Foyle, especially through participating in the Duke of Edinburgh Award Scheme and going on many amazing school trips! This helped give me the ability and confidence to deal with the day-to-day challenges that I now meet in my adult life. I think back fondly of my time at Foyle and while I may not have turned into the physicist – yet anyway – that Foyle was grooming me to become, I am delighted with the way things turned out. I hope that future generations of Foyle students benefit from the experience as much as I have done.

Tabea Weyrauch

THE FUTURE OF FOYLE

In 2012 the final allocation of £19.6m to build the new Foyle College, on land already purchased and cleared for £15m, realised the desire of the governors, parents and staff for a state-of-the-art facility fit for 21st-century education, to be sited on the Springham campus.

What kind of building will be appropriate to the needs of the Foyle of the future? In this sense, quite explicitly, we must build on experience – our experience of the kind of education Foyle has always offered.

Education is more than the mere content of curriculum; it is also a social experience. The subjects taught in schools have changed constantly over the years and with the passing on of knowledge from one generation to another the role of the teacher is primarily a vocation. Even with the youngest child, there is the need to 'socialise' the individual into an acceptance of his or her role in the congregation of others. A school needs to allow the teachers to teach to the best of their abilities and it must create an environment in which learners can interact with those around them. This interaction allows not only the acquisition of knowledge but also experimentation in its deployment, judged by the responses of others. We discussed the design with our teachers and agreed a plan for a traditional mix of classrooms and communal spaces.

This blueprint will permit a continuous flow of designated areas for different ages, different gatherings, different disciplines and different users. The desire to provide a location for all our pupils, past and present, is reflected in the allocation of space to an archive and to social spaces. The need for neighbourliness is supplied by the physical proximity and links to the proposed Ebrington primary school on the campus.

What Foyle brings to the community is the tradition of excellence. The expertise of teachers capable of achieving the highest results and the aspirations of pupils has sent pupils from Londonderry all around the world and has enabled them to serve in the most eminent of roles. That larger learning community will in the future benefit through the collaboration and the expertise, which are part of our tradition. We believe in academic excellence, a spirit of competitiveness – and that the game must always be played according to its rules. Now the Springham campus opens up the horizons of future pupils and allows us to provide them with the very best sports facilities that we can.

With the development of St Columb's Park as a sporting centre of excellence, the school can benefit from the facilities available to the wider community: for example, the Waterside Theatre and the Ebrington site. Beyond that, the heart of the walled city beckons across the graceful span of the Millennium Bridge. Finally, for those of us in Foyle there remains a need to keep our connection with the eponymous river. The main building will be high enough to be 'a grove the Foyle commanding'.

Jack Magill

OPPOSITE ABOVE: *Nigel Dougherty (Principal Ebrington PS), Robin Young (Chair of Governors) and Jack Magill (Headmaster FC).*

OPPOSITE BELOW: *Artist's impression of new school.*

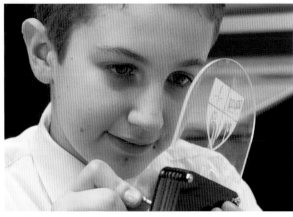

The announcement by the Minister for Education on Monday, 25 June 2012, approving the proposal to build the new Foyle College, was a culmination of many factors, including the constant and persistent lobbying by the college governors and the intervention of local councillors and MLAs from all political parties. The merit of our case was highlighted in an email from one of those MLAs:

It was always a case well made so whatever support I provided, it was to ensure the right decision was made. It is good news for Foyle and for Derry and a success we all have to build upon and deliver many more opportunities, especially for our young people.

The site has been cleared and the governors are working with the design team to finalise the plans. On-site construction will commence once all the statutory processes have been completed and it is envisaged that staff and pupils will be in residence well in advance of our quatercentenary in 2017.

However the allocated accommodation, based on a Department of Education handbook, is deemed insufficient to deliver the breadth and depth of curriculum expected by our pupils and their parents.

The governors have decided to supplement the accommodation by adding classrooms for specialist subjects, an additional laboratory, enhanced study space for senior pupils and social spaces for junior, middle and senior school. We will also provide an area for our vibrant Duke of Edinburgh Award Scheme and support the Combined Cadet Force by building a shooting range and drill hall.

There will be a Former Pupils suite sited on the top floor of the main building, giving panoramic views over the city, the river and the playing fields. Our vision is that the archives will have a permanent home and be available for all members of the 'Foyle Family' to peruse at their leisure.

The current estimate of this additional accommodation is almost one and a half million pounds. We have been heartened by the support of our parents and former pupils from across the globe. To bridge this funding gap your ongoing support for the work in Foyle will continue to be much appreciated.

With its future secured on the Springham campus, the proud traditions of Foyle College founded by the Merchant Taylor and member of The Honourable, The Irish Society, Matthias Springham will now be preserved for the generations to come and countless more will be able to say:

Be it latitude or longitude,
The poles or the equator,
You'll always find a man who boasts
That Foyle's their Alma Mater.

Robin Young
Chair of Governors

OPPOSITE, ABOVE AND RIGHT:
Today's Foyle at work and play.

Top: *Senior staff lead the procession on prize night.*

Above: *Staff assemble before procession on prize night.*

Left: *Staff on platform of Guildhall, prize night, 2011.*

APPENDICES

HEADMASTERS OF THE DIOCESAN FREE SCHOOL AND FOYLE

1617: Mathias Springham founds the Free School within the City walls.

1634: John Wood

1641: John Campion

1651: Theophilus Davis

1653: William Crofton

1656: William Finch

1657: John Shuter

1661: Peregrine Palmer MA

1664: Vincent Engham BA

1666: Knenet Rawlatt

1677: Andrew Henderson

1681: John Morris MA

1682: Ellis Walker BA

1694: David Jenkins BA LLD

1702: Roger Blackhall MA

1734: John Torrens MA DD

1734: Thomas Torrens BA

1773: Roger Blackhall BA

1780: Thomas Marshall BA

1790: George Vaughan Sampson BA

1794: James Knox BA

1834: William Smyth BA

1841: John Hamilton Miller MA

1848: Robert Henderson MA

1854: William Sweet Escott MA

1862: William Hunter Parret MA

1866: William Percy Robinson MA DD

1874: Benjamin Moffet MA

1877: Maurice Charles Hime MA LLD

1896: John Clarke Dick MA

[*Post Amalgamation of Foyle and the Londonderry Academical Institution*]

1911: Robert Foster Dill MA

1928: Arthur Edward Layng MA LLD

1933: Ernest Perceval Southby MA

1935: William Alexander Cuthbert McConnell MA

1960: James Stewart Connolly MA LLB

1973: Hugh Wishart Gillespie BA DIP ED DASE (from 1976 headmaster of Foyle and Londonderry College)

1994: William James Magill MA MA CERT ED

2012: Patrick Allen B SC PGCE PQH

HEADMISTRESSES OF LONDONDERRY HIGH SCHOOL

1920: Miss Margaret MacKillip MA

1927: Miss Rita McIlroy MA

1930: Miss Mary French McIlroy MA OBE

1962: Miss K Mary Cowper BSc

1973–6: Miss Mina Holmes Christie MA

Early Crest of Foyle College.

FOYLE COLLEGE OLD BOYS' ASSOCIATION

Foyle College Old Boys Association (FCOBA) was founded in 1928 following many appeals by headmasters of the school to set up such a body. In *Our School Times* February 1920, the editor suggests that with such a great number of former pupils now attending Trinity College, Dublin, with little organisation, an association could now be readily formed there. This is recognised as the source of FCOBA, with the expectation that branches would be formed in Derry, Belfast and Edinburgh. In 1879 a well-attended Old Boys' dinner was held in the Shelbourne Hotel and presided over by the Right Hon. The Lord Chief Justice of Ireland and Dr Hart, Vice-Provost of Trinity College. The eight toasts proposed on that occasion included 'The Queen and Royal Family', 'Foyle ', 'TCD', 'The Queen's University', 'The Army and Navy', 'The Learned Professions', 'The Headmasters of Ireland' and 'The Chairman'.

The association constituted in 1928 had as first president, The Right Hon. Sir John Ross, Bart, Lord Chief Justice for Ireland. A fine chain of office, bearing an enamel crest of the school, was commissioned and each incoming president is invested by his predecessor at the close of the annual dinner. The tradition of an annual dinner was established and held at first in the Northern Counties Hotel and later the City Hotel with an attendance of over 100 members and guests. Golf outings are a feature of the association with details of early competitions held at Castlerock and Greencastle published in the school magazines. A complete list of 220 members, drawn from former pupils and members of staff of the school was published in the 1929 magazine and details of reunion dinners and the content of speeches are recorded in the magazines. With a full dinner menu and many speeches the event would last five or six hours.

Today the association has about 700 members scattered across the world and although regional branches were never formally established, reunion functions are held from time to time in London and Belfast. Contact is kept through circulation of the *Former Pupils Association Magazine* and increasingly through the internet and its social networks. The annual dinner is held in the city each autumn and now less time is given over to formal proceedings to allow more time for past year groups to mingle before and after the dinner. The 'Song of Foyle' is sung with gusto, if not in tune, by the assembled company at the close of formal proceedings.

In 2011 representatives of the association met with representatives of the Londonderry High School Old Girls' Association (LHSOGA) empowered by a ballot of their members, to draw up a new constitution for a joint former pupils' association reflecting the coeducational ethos of the school since 1976. This new association will be termed Foyle Former Pupils' Association (FFPA) and will initially have both male and female presidents elected each year.

William Lynn

Rt Hon Sir John Ross, Bart, first president of OBA 1928–9.

PRESIDENT'S CHAIN OF OFFICE – FCOBA

FCOBA was founded in 1928 and a fine chain was commissioned, to be worn to dignify all official and social occasions. The chain consists of a single row of 28 silver shields on which the names of each president with the year of his office are engraved. Sir John Ross, Lord Chief Justice of Ireland, was the first president. When the first 28 shields were filled the back of each was used to continue the record until all had been used. In 1994 the headmaster, Hugh Gillespie, a talented silversmith, was commissioned to create an extension chain with 16 shields. The medallion which is fixed to the chain bears an enamelled crest of Foyle surrounded by silver lettering on blue enamel bearing the words 'Foyle Old Boys' Association' and above this in brown enamel the title 'President'.

When by 2000 the original box containing the chain became too worn for use the then president, Emil Hamilton, commissioned a new box to mark his year in office and to celebrate the new millennium.

William Lynn

Detail of pendant from OBA Chain of Office.

PAST PRESIDENTS OF FCOBA

1928–9: The Right Hon. Sir John Ross Bart
1929–30: Alfred Moore Munn BA
1930–1: His Honour Judge John Fitzpatrick Cooke KC DL
1931–2: Sir Samuel Thompson Irwin CBE BA MB CH FRCS DLMP
1932–3: Major James Sproule Myles MC TD
1933–4: Professor Charles Gibson Lowry MD FRCS FRCOG
1934–5: John Gallagher Michaels
1935–6: The Very Revd James Gilbert Paton MC MA DD
1936–7: Sir James McElmunn Wilton MC
1937–8: Thomas Carnwath DSO BA MB D SC DPH
1938–9: Isaac J Trew Colquhoun BA
1939–40: The Right Hon. Mr Justice William Lowry
1940–1: John Blakeney Gillies LDS
1941–2: Thomas Taggart LL D
1942–3: His Honour Judge Marcus Dill Begley QC
1943–4: The Very Revd William Corkey MA DD
1944–5: Sir William Athlestane Meredith Good KBE
1945–6: Robert Foster Dill MA
1946–7: Professor Frances James Brown MS D SC FRCS (ED) FRCOG
1947–8: Sir John Herbert McCutcheon Craig KCVO CB LL D
1948–9: Rupert William Jeffares
1949–50: Samual Milligan
1950–1: Samuel Russell Foster MC CROIX DE GUERRE MB
1951–2: John Foster Caldwell CB QC LL M JP
1952–3: The Very Revd Thomas McCurdy Barker MA DD
1953–4: The Right Hon. Sir David Callender Campbell PC KBE CMG MP
1954–5: William Cecil Glover MBE
1955–6: Henry Cooke Porter Cresswell
1956–7: Sir Robert Gransden CBE
1957–8: Charles Wilson BA
1958–9: Samuel Maxwell Alexander Lowry
1959–60: John Thomas Irwin AMIEE
1960–1: William Staveley Ferguson BA
1961–2: Major James Alexander Glen CBE ERD MA
1962–3: Joseph Boyd Irwin CSI CIE DSO MC BA
1963–4: Joseph Charles Eaton DL JP
1964–5: Professor Charles Horner Greer McAfee CBE D SC MB FRCS FRCIS FRCOG

1965–6: Samuel Douglas Irons
1966–7: The Right Hon. Sir Herbert McVeigh, Lord Justice of Appeal
1967–8: The Very Revd Austin A Fulton MA PH D DD
1968–9: Senator John C Drennan CBE HML JP
1969–70: The Very Revd Samuel James Park MA DD
1970–1: Armour Hamilton Matthews LDS RCS
1971–2: Colonel Oswald W Gilmour MA MAI C ENG FICE
1972–3: The Right Hon. Sir Robert Porter QC MP
1973–4: The Very Revd William Alexander Albert Park MA DD
1974–5: David Alan Eccles Roberts MA
1975–6: John Alexander Crockett
1976–7: James Stewart Connolly MA LLB
1977–8: Professor Emeritus ACP Campbell MB CHB FRC PATH FRCPE
1978–9: Professor JC Goligher MB CH M FRCSE FRCSE (Edin)
1979–80: JB Mullin BA H DIP ED
1980–1: Revd RK Greer MA BD
1981–2: RN Crawford CBE BCOMM SC FCA FRSA FBIM
1982–3: Real Admiral WJ McClune CB MSC MIEE
1983–4: J Piggot MB BCH FRCS
1984–5: AE Barbour BSC FBCO
1985–6: J Kincade CBE MA BLitt PhD
1986–7: DCG Craig BA
1987–8: SA Hunter BSC CENG FIEE
1988–9: HW Young OBE MA
1989–90: JC Lapsley BSC DLC DASE
1990–1: TH Armstrong BA DIP ED
1991–2: RJ Magowan BA DASE MSC
1992–3: Professor SG Carruthers MD FRCPC
1993–4: NJ Henderson BSC
1994–5: JHY Fergusson
1995–6: AG Kennedy BA
1996–7: Professor RJ McClelland MD PhD FRCPSYCH
1997–8: DR Craig BARCH ARIBA DIP TP MRTPI
1998–9: The Very Revd DC Orr MA
1999–2000: EW Hamilton
2000–1: JE Bigger MA DASE
2001–2: HW Gillespie BA DASE
2002–3: AW Roulston CA
2003–4: J Cowan BA DIP ED DASE

2004–5: IM Piggot
2005-6: JV Arthur BSC (EST MAN) FRICS IRRV
2006–7: ES Marshall BA FRSA MA LAGSM ALCM
2007–8: RS Tosh BSC BD PHD
2008–9: JAS Kelso BS MS PHD
2009–10: JAC McFarland BSC CENG FICE
2010–1: JSM Huey BA DIP ED
2011–2: RC Montgomery MB DMH DHMSA

Old Boys' blazer and tie.

LHS OLD GIRLS' ASSOCIATION

The Londonderry High School Old Girls' Association (LHSOGA) was founded in 1935 with the blessing of Miss Mary French McIlroy (Madame Loullier) who became the first president and served for the first ten years of the association's existence. Mme Loullier served again in the year 1964–5. Characteristic of the contemporary culture was the fact that in the early days women were happy to use their husbands' initials. The first magazine was published in 1935, a copy of which is in the archive.

Elizabeth Whiteside (president 1991–2) created the picture gallery of past presidents that hangs in the Duncreggan assembly hall. The chain of office records the names.

The Association is especially proud of its branches – Belfast, Coleraine, London, and most recently an informal group who meet once a year in Scotland. We have a rota of presidents from the parent association and branches which ensures diversity and interest beyond the city. Lunches and evening reunions are well supported and lively. Old Girls have been generous to the present day school and revisiting Duncreggan is in demand.

The future of the association is secure now that LHSOGA and FCOBA have combined to form the Foyle College Former Pupils' Association (FCFPA).

Joy Coskery, 2012

Stanley Huey and Pamela Jackson, Presidents OBA and OGA, 2011.

The LHSOGA President's Chain of Office

There was no symbol of the high office of president until the 1970s until Rosie Gordon (née Kyle), president (1947–8) and chair of the local branch (1954–71), sought permission from the committee to gift a pendant, which would hang on a royal blue ribbon and worn by the president of the association. A sub-committee under Jean McCandless, a former LHS art teacher and president (1983–4) was appointed to oversee the design, the work eventually carried out by Christopher Toogood of Belfast. The pendant is a replica of the LHS badge commissioned on 1956 by Miss McIlroy: argent on a cross, a triple-towered castle, the owl of the goddess Athene, (signifying wisdom) and two books representing learning and a reminder that LHS came from the amalgamation of Victoria and St Lurach's. The livery colours of blue, black and white /silver and the red cross from the city's arms indicated its location. The motto was engraved in the original Greek and translated as 'As ever in God's sight'. Of the two silver clips that attach the ribbon to the pendant one has the letters LHS and the other OGA.

Pearlie Taggart (née Wilson), president (1987–8) suggested that small silver plaques with the holder's name engraved on them should replace the blue ribbon and obtaining the committee's permission engaged Hugh Gillespie, then headmaster and a skilled silversmith to make the first four plaques. These were engraved with the names of Adelaide Park, teacher (1930–66) and president (1970–1), Jean McCandless, president (1983–4), Marion Berry, president (1978–9) and that of Pearlie herself, who made a gift of the reconstructed chain at the end of her year of office. Various adjustments were made in it since. It has become the privilege of each new president to supply the plaque that bears her name and some have rendered necessary refurbishment at her own expense.

The ribbon with its silver attachments is kept separately in a chain case, presented in 2000 by the Eaton family to the memory of Edith Eaton MBE, president (1960–1).

Dr Kanchan Chada MB B Ch BAO

Presidents LHSOGA

1935–45: Miss MF McIlroy
1946: Mrs HM Williams
1947: Mrs Killen MA
1948: Mrs ER Gordon
1949: Miss Osborne OBE JP
1950: Mrs H Robinson
1951: Mrs Doreen McConnell BA
1952: Miss MKM Aiken BA LLB
1953: Mrs John Watson MBE
1954: Mrs BH Lynn FRCS
1955: Mrs B Roe MBE
1956: Dr Elsie Johnston
1957: Mrs S Dowds
1958: Dr Violet Breakey
1959: Mrs N Young
1960: Mrs HJ Clarke
1961: Mrs JC Eaton
1962: Miss Grace Armstrong
1963: Mrs Jean L'Amie MA
1964: Marie Loullier OBE MA
1965: Mrs Olive McLaughlin BA
1966: Mrs RR Hunter
1967: Mrs GR Joscelyne
1968: Mrs JG Colhoun
1969: Miss Alice Rowan
1970: Miss EA Park BSC
1971: Mrs Mary Britton
1972: Miss MR Colhoun
1973: Mrs K Gillis
1974: Miss AE Stirling MA
1975: Miss MW Cunningham MA
1976: Miss M Anderson
1977: Mrs EWM Marr
1978: Mrs TR Berry
1979: Mrs MB Seaward
1980: Mrs MB Seaward
1981: Mrs R J Aiken
1982: Mrs J Moore
1983: Mrs J McCandless
1984: Mrs E Clay
1985: Mrs E Finlay
1986: Mrs M Welch
1987: Mrs JW Taggart
1988: Mrs D Stuart
1989: Mrs Gladys Black
1990: Mrs K Stewart

1991: Mrs E Whiteside
1992: Mrs Lorna Knox
1993: Mrs W Burns
1994: Miss Anne Wilson
1995: Mrs M Phillips
1996: Miss G Simpson
1997: Mrs R Ramsey
1998: Mrs B Hamilton
1999: Mrs Joy Coskery
2000: Mrs Helen Hilson
2001: Mrs C Corrigan
2002: Mrs J Milliken
2003: Mrs Thelma Arthur
2004: Mrs N Foss
2005: Mrs Molly Kennedy
2006: Mrs Elma McDevitt
2007: Mrs Isabel McNally
2008: Mrs Molly Sutton
2009: Mrs Phyllis Logan
2010: Mrs Ruth Hamilton
2011: Mrs Pamela Jackson
2012: Dr Kanchan Chada MB B Ch BAO

ABOVE: *LHS crest.*

RIGHT: *LHSOGA Chain of Office.*

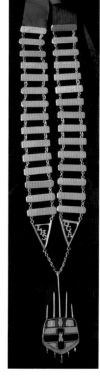

ABOVE: *Lawrence Medal recipients 1937–82 (Head boys).*

ABOVE RIGHT: *Head boys 1977–2011.*

ABOVE FAR RIGHT: *Head girls 1977–2011.*

RIGHT: *Headmasters of the School.*

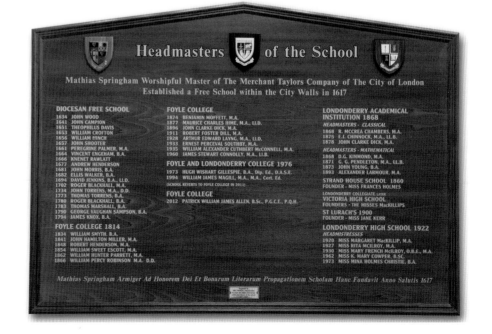

THE SONG OF FOYLE COLLEGE

The last version of the 'School Song', as it was known before amalgamation in 1976, encapsulates the history of Foyle College from its foundation in 1617 until its move to Springtown in 1967. It was sung at the close of the annual prize distributions in the Guildhall until amalgamation with the Londonderry High School. On those occasions all pupils at the school were required to attend, not just the prize winners and their parents as it is today. In preparation for the occasion, we were required to practise at assembly in the week leading up to prize night. It is still sung with vigour by the Old Boys and their guests at the close of their annual dinner.

A number of earlier versions existed and were published in school magazines. These included an early version written by a friend of Dr Hime.

William Lynn

When Scottish James in Ulster first
　　Established his Plantation
The sturdy planters for their sons
　　Soon craved an education:
And so in sixteen seventeen,
　　Our forebears' needs discerning,
Mathias Springham lent his aid
　　To light the torch of learning.

Chorus:　　Be't latitude or longitude,
　　　　　　　　The poles or the equator,
　　　　You'll always find a man who boasts
　　　　That Foyle's his Alma Mater.

That worthy Merchant Taylor came
　　From London town and builded
On Derry's hill a good Free School
　　That prospered as he willed it;
And there for nigh two hundred years,
　　Her fair repute maintaining,
The School stood fast through peace and war,
　　The Siege's scars sustaining.

Chorus:　　Be't latitude or longitude, etc

The year before Napoleon's fall,
　　Her size and fame expanding,
She left the walls and occupied
　　A grove the Foyle commanding;
And then in eighteen ninety-six
　　Her Academic rival
Uniting with the School produced
　　A vigorous revival.

Chorus:　　Be't latitude or longitude, etc

And nineteen sixty-seven when
　　Elizabeth was reigning
Saw Springham's School to Springtown come,
　　Her river view retaining.
Long may the Old School flourish, by
　　Her London patron favoured,
The Hon'rable Society
　　Whose help has never wavered.

Chorus:　　Be't latitude or longitude, etc

Now we, her children, sing with pride
　　The praises of our College
Who sends men forth through all the earth
　　Enriching it with knowledge.
Remember too our Founder's name
　　Renowned throughout creation:
Mathias Springham, Armiger,
　　Established this Foundation.

Chorus:　　Be't latitude or longitude, etc

SONG FOR THE FOYLE COLLEGE OLD BOYS.

Air—"Auld Lang Syne."

REMEMBER yet the Old School
　　That crowns the banks of Foyle;
Endeared by days of mirth and play,
　　And days of fruitful toil.
　　Chorus—The Old School, the Old School!
　　　　No deed of ours shall soil
　　The glory of the Old School
　　　　That crowns the banks of Foyle.

Though faint of heart we first approached
　　Its halls of ancient fame ;
We learned to love the Old School,
　　And triumph in its name.
　　The Old School, the Old School ! &c.

Oh ! boyhood's years, the lightsome years,
　　Full fast they sped away ;
And soon the world's loud clarion blew
　　Swift summons to the fray.
　　The Old School, the Old School ! &c.

And now stout hearts and steadfast eyes
　　We need in storm and strife ;
May each at duty's high behest
　　Still yield a loyal life.
　　The Old School, the Old School ! &c.

And may we still, as years increase,
　　Where'er our lot may fall ;
Though tossed like waifs on alien shores,
　　Our schoolboy days recall.
　　The Old School, the Old School ! &c.

And each to each stand leal and true,
　　Nor ever shame or soil
The honour of the School that crowns
　　The breezy banks of Foyle.
　　The Old School, the Old School ! &c.

HYMN FOR THE FOYLE COLLEGE BOYS.

[*Composed by the late Rev. ROBERT HENDERSON, M.A., who was Head-master of Foyle College from the year 1847 to 1853. Obit., October 1878.*]

C.M.

PRESERVE, O Lord, our youthful heart
　　From all pollution free,
From sinful thoughts and Satan's art,
　　To fix our trust on Thee.

Give us to feel Thy holy power,
　　When urged from Thee to stray ;
And may our minds each passing hour
　　Cling closer to Thy way.

In sportive hours all strife remove,
　　And angry words repress ;
So may we still Thy precept love,
　　Nor love each other less.

In study, too, Thy grace we claim,
　　A hallowed knowledge give ;
Help us aright our course to frame,
　　And usefully to live.

Exalt, refine, adorn each sense—
　　Each generous impulse fan ;
And let Thy holy providence
　　Mature us up to man.

General versions of the song of Foyle College.

LIST OF SUBSCRIBERS

This book has been made possible through the generosity of the following subscribers.

Derek R J Adair 1930–40
Albert Stuart Adams 1962–9
Ivan Aiken 1963–70
William Aiken 1936–41, Governor 1977–93
Geoff Alcorn 1959–66
Thomas Alford 1975–81
Professor James Moorehead Allen 1963–70
Peter D Allen 1952–7
Frances Anderson (*née* Dinsmore) 1967–74
Lorna Anderson (*née* Lynn) 1968–73
Nan Andrew
Henry A Armstrong 1947–52
Revd Wilfred J A Armstrong 1942–7
Eva Schenkel Arnott 1940–5
John V Arthur 1934–51, Governor 1977–2005
A C Austin 1948–53
Amy Austin 2007–
Clive Austin 2000– Staff
Matthew Austin 2011–
Alexander Baldrick 1950–2
Eric Barfoot 1951–3
Margaret Barker (*née* Williamson) 1950–6 LHS
D I Bartlett 1962–9
Professor Eric K Beatty OBE 1952–9
David Arthur Bell 1959–66
Harper J S Bell 1942–7
Dr Jim Bell 1948–54
Wesley C Bell 1951–8
Colonel D L D Bigger 1973–80
David Bigger 1942–7
Gladys Bigger 1942–7
J Edgar Bigger 1943–9, Staff 1954–91, Governor 1985–9
Robert D Bigger 1969–76
Doreen Black (*née* Lynn) 1965–72
Jason T J Black 1977–90
Joan Black (*née* McNally)
John A Black 1959–65, Governor 1989–
Karen E M Dalton (*née* Black) 1982–96
Michael J A Black 1978–93
Jack Bogle 1948–54, Staff 1958–2000
Noel J Bogle 1949–56
Thomas Bradley 1962–9
Professor J C Brihault 1965–8 Staff
Phyllis Brown (*née* Aiken) 1966–73
T R Brown 1936–43
E D A Browne (Anne Moody) 1954–9 LHS
H G Browne 1948–53
J K Browne 1946–51
M I A (Adele) Browne 1944–9 LHS
S A K Browne 1963–70
Jimmy Brownlow 1948–52
William John David Burns 1966–73
William Howard Burton 1935–41
Esther J M Byatt (*née* Gilchrist) 1979–85

Alan S W Campbell 1945–52
Craig F Campbell 1982–9
Dorothy E M Campbell (*née* Craig) 1952–8 LHS, Staff 1961–70, Governor 1994–2006
Gordon E Campbell 1985–92
Lisa Carlin 2002–4, Staff 2011
Billy Carruthers 1949–56
S George Carruthers 1957–63
Dr Patrick P Carson 1976–12 Staff (Vice-Principal 1999–2012)
Elizabeth Cathcart 1948–53
Gordon Chambers 1980–7
Kerry Chambers 1980–7
Doug Clarke 1978–81
Kyleen Clarke (*née* Colhoun) 1946–8
Roy Clements 1945–51, Staff 1955–6
David Cole-Baker 1967–72
Stephen Connolly 1956–70
Heather Corrie 1958–72
Dr Gail Coskery 1978–85
Joy Coskery (*née* Heenan) 1952–6, Staff 1967–2000, Governor 2001–
Siobhan Coskery 1980–7
Pamela Coughlin 1984– Staff
D O Coulter 1949–55
Derek Irwin Craig 1950–7
Dr Elizabeth Craig 1986–93
Henry Alwyn Craig 1951–8
Sylvia Craig 1959–65, Staff 1976–2011, Governor 1985–2001
W L Cunningham 1957–64
Alastair J Currie 1963–70
John Lithgow Currie 1960–7
Derek Curtis 1953–60, Governor 1989–2001
Albert F Danton 1942–5
Dr David William Davin 1929–41
Dr Haydn J H Deane 1962–9
Brian Deans 1980–7
David Deans 1981–8
Mrs M J Deans 1979–2012 Staff
Alison Delahaye 1994–6
George Allison Dinsmore 1936–42
Irene Dinsmore (*née* Barber) 1941–7 LHS
John Ferguson Dinsmore 1951–6
Carol Dixon (*née* McNeill) 1965–73
Connor B Doak 1994–2001
Jenny E Doak 1989–96
Jonathan Doak 1987–94
Carol Doherty (*née* Sproule) 1962–9
Edwin F Donaghy 1943–8
F R J Dougherty 1952–9
Melanie Dougherty 2003– Staff
Avril Douglas (*née* Bryans) 1960–73
David J J Douglas 1976–83
Charles Stewart Stanford Drought 1948–63

Terence Kenneth Drought 1952–66
Hazel Eakin 1994– Staff, Governor 2001–
Howard Eakin 1973–80
Ruth Louise Eakin 1970–83
Bob Elliott 1956–64
James R Ferguson 1958–65
William A Fisher
Dr Robert Fleming 1949–55
Robert J Fleming 1961–5
Charles Richard Forbes 1967–74
David Oliver Forbes 1971–7
Mary M S Ford 1940–50 LHS
Norah L Foss (*née* Kelly) 1934–40, 1943–4
Barbara Fowler 1967–74
J Douglas M Galbraith 1945–50
John Galbraith 1960–7
R Andrew Galbraith 1980–5
Jacob A Galbraith 2008–
Benjamin R Galbraith 2012–
William Galbraith 1962–9
Julie Galbraith 1990–7
Deborah Galbraith 1993–2000
Andrew Galbraith 1996–2003
Timothy Galbraith 1998–2005
Mark Galbraith 1999–2006
Adam Galbraith 2000–7
Simon Galbraith 2002–9
Hannah Galbraith 2003–10
Luke Galbraith 2006–
Alan Gallagher 1980–7
David Gallagher 1971–7
Kieran Gallagher 2001–8
Laura Gallagher 1997–2004
Mark Gallagher 2006–13
Timothy Gallagher 1993–2000
A T Gallick
Graham Gallick 1986–91
Keith Gallick 1980–7
Kenneth E Gamble 1950–7
Jeremy Gault 1980–7
Joan Gault 1985–9 Governor
Peter Gault 1980–4, Staff 1989–
Sylvia Gibson 1985–92
Robert K Gilchrist 1984–91
Donald Gillanders 1958–66
Tom G E Gillanders 1956–63
Alexander William Knox Gilliland 1995–2008
Caroline Patricia Gilliland 1996–2001, 2004–11
Catherine Christine Gilliland 2001– Governor
Conal Gilliland 2010–
David John James Gilliland 1994–2001, 2003–10
Hugh R Gilliland 1965–72
John William David Gilliland

Matthew Andrew George Gilliland 2000–
Rory Gilliland 2009–
John Gilmour 1946–51
Rachel Goldby (*née* Sinclair) 1991–8
James Sydney Goodman 1957–63, Staff 1977–2011
Paul Gosling
Dr Fergus Graham 1952–9
George Kenneth Graham 1955–60
Dr William Robert Gransden
Arthur Griffith 1961–8
Ian Hall 1969–76
Emil Hamilton 1944–50, Governor 1985–9
Alan Harrington 1998–2005
Derek Harrington 1995–2002
Jim Heasley 1986–2012 Staff
Colin Hegan 1968–75
Robert Jonathan Hegan (Jonny) 1958–65
W S Hegan 1952–9
Keith Hegarty 1974–83
Laura Hegarty (*née* Mowbray) 1974–83
Denis A Helliwell 1953–85 Staff
Brian James Henderson 1959–66
David Campbell Henderson 1948–52
Fiona Henderson 1974–81
John R W Henderson 1952–66
Richard Henderson 1958–72
Stewart Heney 1957–64
Sarah A Heney
David Hogg 1950–6
The Honourable The Irish Society
Michael Houston 1975–82
Jake Howie 2010–
Paul Howie 1989–96
J S M Huey 1952–9, Staff 1964–2003, Governor 1993–
Paul Huey 1947–54
Graham Hunter 1957–61
Jennifer Hunter 1959–70
Ronald Irwin 1947–53
Winston Irwin 1952–9
Pamela Jackson (*née* Nutt) 1964–72, Governor 1997–2005
Francis Joseph (Frank) Lyttle
Richard Kellett 1946–52
Professor Dr J A Scott Kelso 1958–65
Reggie Kelso 1940–4
Adrian George Kennedy 1944–50
Molly Kennedy (*née* Steele) 1949–55
E Fay Kincade (*née* Piggot) 1939–47 LHS
Dr James Kincade 1937–43
Revd Iain Knox 1958–64
Carol Kohler (*née* Aiken) 1957–9, 1959–66
William Samuel Edgar Laird 1957–63
W A Ken Lapsley 1952–7
Elizabeth Law
The Leira Kapell

Professor Claire M Leitch 1978–85
John and Phyllis Logan 1953–60
Robert Logue 1961–3
Brian Long 1977–84, Governor 2005–
Harry Long 2006–11
Rodger Long 2008–
David Loughery 1990–2012 Staff
Ann Loughery 1990–2012 Staff
Harriet Love 1966–73
Joanne Love 1996–2003
Michael Love 1993–2000
Dr Andrea Lynch 1988–96
Caroline Lynch (*née* Wright) 1971–8, Staff 2005–
Nadine Lynch 1990–7
Helen Lynn (*née* Coulter) 1939–43
David E Lynn 1963–8
Elma Lynn (*née* Hall) 1970–7
Susan Rachael Lynn 1995–2002
William Allan Lynn 1994–2001
William M Lynn 1962–9, Staff 1975–, Governor 1989–
Ian Maconachie 1974–81
Chris W Magee 1965–72
Katherine Magee 2006–13
Letitia Magee 2004–11
Matthew Magee 2010–
Richard Magee 2006–13
W J Magill 1994–2012 Staff (Headmaster)
David Manning 1969–76
Richard William Manning 1970–7, Governor 2001–
D H Martin 1985–9 Governor
James D Mason 1975–80
Catherine Mawhinney 1968–76
Elaine Mawhinney 1970–7
Robert Kenneth Mawhinney 1965–72
Dr Ken Maxwell 1955–62
James McBride 1963–70
Peter W F McBride 1977–84
Richard J McBride 1981–8
G R McCarter 1966–73, Staff 1977–2012
D Joy McCartney (*née* Kelly) 1934–45
Ruth McCaul 1980–2005 Governor
Jayne McCay (*née* Gault) 1962–9
Hilary Selfridge McClean 1942–8
John B McClean 1997–2004
John F C McClelland 1984–91
Roy McClelland 1954–61
Jennifer McClements 1974–81
Deirdre Gevers-McClure 1948–54
K J C McConnell 1945–51
Marc McCorkell 2002–9
Roger McCorkell 1966–73
Ken McCormack
Ian McCracken 1961–98 Staff

Dr Noel McCune 1963–70
Elisabeth McCurdy 1956–62
Ian McDade 1967–73
Rosemary McDowell (*née* Templeton) 1950–4
Alasdair McElhinney 1956–63
Bruce McElhinney 1963–70
Jack McFarland 1955–61, Governor 1993–
Captain John Barry McGrath 1958–64
Robin McGrath 1958–64
Stirling McGuinness 1952–7
S T McKean 1984–91
Norman C E McKinney 1950–4
Sinead McLaughlin 2000– Staff
David Henry McNally 1939–45
George McNally 1948–54
Isabel McNally CBE (*née* Mitchell) 1965–9, Governor 2005–
Basil McNamee 1950–6
Christopher McNee 1970–7
Janice McNeilly 1973–81
Sam McPherson 1962–9
Alex M McRitchie 1961–9
Malcolm A McSparron 1964–72
Sydney Alwyn McSparron 1962–9
Ray Menown 2002– Staff
Graeme Mercer 1976–83, Staff 1987–
Alison Mercer (*née* Smith) 1987– Staff
Reg Mercer 1960–5
Sarah Mercer 2001–3
Irene Millar (*née* Dinsmore) 1964–8
Ruby Millar (*née* Galbraith) 1950–6
Adrian S Millen 1970–7
Norman Miller 1982–9
William W Miller 1953–60
Brian Mitchell 1948–54
Brian Stewart Mitchell 1968–75
Jane Elizabeth Mitchell 2003–10
Peter Campbell Mitchell 1969–76
Samuel Patton Mitchell 1952–9 Staff
Mary Mokhebi 1968–76
Emma Monaghan 1993–2000
Rosemary Monaghan (*née* Moore) 1975–82
A L Montgomery 1952–9
Dr Robert Montgomery 1955–61
Alistair C Moorcroft 1992– Staff
Alan Moore 1973–80
Geoffrey Moore 1985–92
Lesley Morgan (*née* Cole) 1961–6, Staff 1991–2012
Norah Morrison (*née* Mitchell) 1943–7 LHS
William J Morrison (Billy) 1943–8
Very Revd Dr W Morton (Dean of Derry)
Conor Morton 2010–
Nicky Morton 2006–13
Patrick Morton 2003–10

Simon Mowbray 1987–94
Miriam Murray (*née* Hunter) 1955–64
Alan Neely 2000–7
Emma Neely 1999–2006
Joanne Neely 1977–84
Laura Neely 1983–90
Russell Neely 1982–9
Shauna Neely 1975–82
William A Neely 1947–52
Trevor Nutt 1985–92, Staff 1996–
Brenda Ó Somacháin 1999– Staff
H J L D S O'Neill 1958–62
Very Revd Cecil Orr 1946–51
Frank Orr 1973–80
Carol Parker (*née* Stringer) 1951–64
Joseph Patterson (Londonderry) 1947–50
Julie-Ann Patterson (*née* Black) 1979–93
Brian V Peoples 1966–73
T R Pickett 1966–73
I M Piggot 1940–4
Avril Pollock (*née* Miller) 1957–64
Rt Hon Sir Robert Wilson Porter QC 1938–42
Robert G Quigley 1954–8
Sam Quigley 1971–77
Dr Roy Ramsay 1960–7
Graham Alexander Rankin 1972–9
Ian Rankin 1962–9
B H E Roberts 1933–42
Anthea Roberton (*née* Keown) 1943–57
Alan S D Rosborough 1978–85
Kathryn Rough (*née* Huey) 1989–96
Lex Roulston 1946–51
Eileen Roulston 1951–2
Esther R Scobie 1952–9
May Scott 1948–53
David J Shannon 1955–61
S R Shannon 1952–8
Michele C Sheridan (*née* Young) 1973–80
Joan K R Simpson MBE 1947–51
R J B Singleton 1940–6
Blair Smith 1947–52
Revd Ivor Smith 1957–63
Deborah Steele 1998–2005
Elizabeth Steele 1980–5, Staff 1991–
Stephen Steele 1997–2004
Patricia E Stevens (*née* Baxter) 1940–6
Rachael Stevenson (*née* Galbraith) 1989–96
Ian V Stewart 1972–9
Kathleen Stewart (*née* Hatrick) 1933–45
Neil Stewart 1981–8, Staff 2005
Molly Sutton 1953–65
Mrs E F Swinson (*née* Thompson) 1949–55
John P Taylor 1960–7, (Headboy 1967)
Professor Kenneth T A Taylor 1962–9
Laura Taylor 1993–2000

Norman Taylor 1963–70, Staff 1974–2012
Paula Taylor (*née* Nicholl) 1963–70 LHS
Sylvia Taylor (*née* Davis) 1944–50 (Headboarder 1950)
Dr William J Taylor 1968–75
William J Temple 1950–5
Campbell Tennis 1961–9, Governor 1997–
Catherine Thatcher 2001–8
Emma Thatcher 1998–2005
Ken Thatcher 1960–7, Staff 1973–
Arthur E Thompson 1951–7
M E Thompson (*née* Browne) 1948–54
M Elisabeth M Thompson (*née* Young) 1963–70
William Hamilton Thompson JP 1947–53
David Thomson 1963–70
D W Todd 1946–51
Margaret Todd 1978–85
Jonathan Torrens 1996–2003
His Honour Judge David Turner QC 1965–72
Rosie Turner 1970–7 (Headgirl 1977)
Andrew Walker 1995 – 2002
Peter Walker 1990–7
R C G Walker 1954–60
Sir Gordon Ward OBE 1963–7 Staff
Ian Warnock 1961–8, Governor 1997–2009
Rosemary Warnock (*née* Dinsmore) 1965–72
Ann Watson 1967–74, Staff 1978–2007
Ian James Watson 1970–6
Sandra Margaret West Wang (*née* West) 1958–64
Michael Westgate 2000– Staff
Frances Wilkinson (*née* Clements) 1947–53
Malcolm H F Wilkinson 1946–9
William Williamson 1948–54
George Wilson 1946–51
J Brian Wilson 1953–60
Jillian Wilson 1991–8
John C Wilson 1949–57
Judith Wilson 1987–94
Mark Wilson 1984–91
Mrs R J Wilson 1953–60, Staff 1979–2006
Raymund Frank Henry Wolseley 1940–5
Dr Fred Wright 1940–5
Mrs H E Wright (*née* Crowe) 1962–7
Alan Wylie 1984–91
Isobel Wylie 1980–2012 Staff
Lynne Wylie 1982–9
Sandra Wylie 1980–7
June Young (*née* Martin) 1944–53
Lynn Young (*née* Graham) 1964–70
Robin Young 1962–9, Governor 1997–

INDEX

Italics denotes image / artist
Bold denotes contribution

ACKNOWLEDGEMENTS

We take this opportunity to thank the many people who have either by written contributions or other kindnesses helped in the realisation of *A View the Foyle Commanding*: Patrick Allen, Steen Anderson, Clive Austin, Norman Austin, Ian Bartlett, Eric Beatty, David Bigger, Jack Bogle, Doug Clarke, Kyleen Clarke, Joy Coskery, Alfie Danton, Mildred Deans, Mary Delargy, Kerry Eakin, Jenny Galbraith, Ken Gamble, Catherine Gilchrist, Hugh Gillespie, OW Gilmour, Jim Goodman, Ingrid Hannaway, Jim Heasley, Deirdre Heenan, Eva Hove, Stan Huey, Margaret Johnston, Molly Kennedy, Guy King, Jack Kyle, Brian Lacey, the library staff of TCD, Jack Magill, Kanchu McAllister, GR McCarter, Hilary McClean, Hilary McCloy, Roy McClelland, Rosemary McDowell, Martin McKeown, Isabel McNally, Joan Matthews, Dr James Mehaffey, Thelma Mehaffey, Alastair Moorcroft, Dean Cecil Orr, Margot Robertson, Alex Roulston, SR Shannon, Kathleen Stewart, Neil Stewart, Susan Thomas, Rosie Turner, Mike Westgate, Tabea Weyrauch, Morwenna Willoughby, Brian Wilson, Fred Wright, Billy Young and Robin Young.

PICTURE ACKNOWLEDGMENTS

Alamy 46, 54T, 171, 189T
Bridgeman 165T
British Museum 27
Country Life 54
Derry City Council Heritage & Museum Service 21, 35
Free Legal Advice Centres Ltd 186
Getty Images 12BR, 18, 167, 170R
HSBC group 164
Mary Evans 13BL, 16, 38
National Portrait Gallery 19, 23, 26, 157, 158, 162
PictureNation 32T

All other images Foyle College Archives
Special photography Martin McKeown

Every effort has been made to identify rights owners of the images in this book. Any queries or comments arising from image content should be sent to TMI Ltd, 2–5 Benjamin St, EC1M 5QL

A View the Foyle Commanding: A Portrait of Foyle College 2013 © Foyle College, Derry and Third Millennium Publishing Limited

First published in 2013 by Third Millennium Publishing Limited, a subsidiary of Third Millennium Information Limited.

2–5 Benjamin Street
London
United Kingdom
EC1M 5QL
www.tmiltd.com

ISBN: 978 1 906507 71 8

British Library Cataloguing in Publication Data
A CIP catalogue record for this book is available from the British Library.

General Editor	Sean McMahon
Design	Susan Pugsley
Production	Bonnie Murray
Reprographics	Studio Fasoli, Verona, Italy
Printing	Gorenjski Tisk, Slovenia

FREE SCHOOL 1617

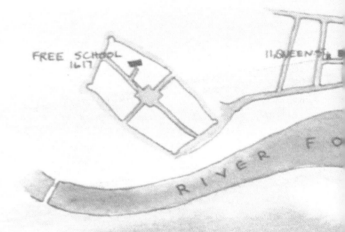

FREE SCHOOL 1617

RIVER FO

ACADE
INS

11 QUEENS

Matthias Springham Ar(miger)
Ad Honorem Dei et
Bonarum Litterarum Propagationem
Hanc Scholam Fundavit
Anno Salutis 1617

FOYLE COLLEGE 1814

FOYLE COLLEGE SPRINGTOWN 1967

The earliest school for girls was
Strand House School (1860-1915), for
most of its life in Asylum Road.
In 1877 the Misses MacKillip founded
Londonderry Ladies' Collegiate School
in 11, Queen Street, later moving
to Crawford Square
where it became known
as Victoria High School.
It was joined in 1922 by
St Lurach's School (founded 1900)
to become Londonderry High School
which extended in 1928 when
Duncreggan was bought.

ACADEMICAL INSTITUTION 1671

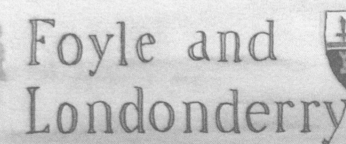

Foyle and
Londonderry